Praise for *How Women Mean Business*

'The book we have all been waiting for: a clear, visionary blueprint that moves the gender balance discussion into the realm of the practical and achievable.'

Mary van der Boon-Farmer, Director, Global Diversity and Inclusion, Philips

'*How Women Mean Business* is a must-read for any manager. Ms Wittenberg-Cox's book illustrates how gender balance in the workplace improves decision making, contributes to the customer experience and ultimately results in better business outcomes; something every business is interested in achieving.'

Emilio Umeoka, President, Microsoft Asia Pacific

'This is a welcome, practical guide to improving business performance.'

David Loughman, Managing Director, A/S Norske Shell

'I am delighted to see the focus on how to achieve better gender balance. As a firm believer that diverse teams make better business decisions, I applaud the focus on accountability that *How Women Mean Business* is driving.'

Frank Brown, Dean, INSEAD

'Avivah Wittenberg-Cox has articulated the business case for gender balance in a convincing and pragmatic way. Her inspiring guidance is a real enabler.'

Feike Sijbesma, CEO, Royal DSM

'*How Women Mean Business* is packed with real insights and actionable ideas; it is a resource that no organisation can afford to ignore.'

Jaspal Bindra, CEO Asia, Standard Chartered Bank

'This is a book that is desperately needed by all senior managers and their advisors. *How Women Mean Business* will go a long way to ensuring that all available talent is appropriately employed.'

Chris Thomas, Former Head of Global Board Practice, Egon Zehnder International

'Practical, intelligent and based on experience, this book offers solutions for executives determined to make a difference.'
Olivier Marchal, Managing Director EMEA, Bain & Co.

'This is a vital manual for 21st-century businesses who are serious about putting gender balance at the heart of corporate change. A must read – and more importantly, a must do!'
Cleo Thompson, Editor, TheGenderBlog.com

'At Cisco, this radically new approach has convinced me and my management team of the business opportunity that lies in effectively implementing gender balance – and *how* to do it. It has also made me progress on my journey to become "gender bilingual" for life!'
Laurent Blanchard, VP, CISCO Europe and General Manager, France

'Companies often unconsciously resist moving away from the *why* of gender balanced business into the realm of *how* to achieve it. Wittenberg-Cox has written the definitive work on the subject. This book categorically proves the bottom line reward is well worth the journey.'
Joanne Thomas Yaccato, author, *The 80% Minority* and *The Gender Intelligent Retailer*

'A call to action for savvy executives serious about shifting the focus of their companies from surviving to thriving.'
Lois P. Frankel, PhD, bestselling author of *Nice Girls Don't Get the Corner Office* and *See Jane Lead*

'*How Women Mean Business* offers a proven, step-by-step methodology to define and successfully deploy a strategy to build better gender balanced organisations. Only the companies who make a conscious effort to nurture gender balanced talent pipelines and master gender bilingual leadership styles will win in the marketplace of the 21st century.'
Rob ten Hoedt, President, Medtronic ECA

'This book provides new insights and great practical guidance on how to tap into the female talent pool and create results.'
Hilde Myrberg, Executive Vice President, Orkla ASA

'Finally! We all know that gender balance is good for business, but *How Women Mean Business* lays out a step-by-step plan to achieve it.'

Sally Helgesen, bestselling author of *The Female Advantage: Women's Ways of Leadership, The Web of Inclusion*

'Wittenberg Cox offers down-to-earth solutions about how to achieve what is now an acknowledged imperative: gender balance.'

Zia Mody, AZB & Partners, Mumbai, India

'This is the nuts and bolts of creating gender balanced leadership. It moves beyond rhetoric to action.'

Linda Tarr-Whelan, Demos distinguished senior fellow and author of *Women Lead the Way*

'Avivah Wittenberg-Cox provides systemic, hands-on guidelines on how to make things happen in practice.'

Richard Straub, President of the Peter Drucker Society, Europe

'Having led corporate transformation initiatives resulting in $4.4 billion in incremental spending from female customers, I believe this book is the best overview of the extraordinary business opportunity women represent. The business potential is limitless for those companies that authentically commit to winning with women, and bleak for those that do not.'

Julie Gilbert, Founder and CEO, Wolf

'We know now that the business case for gender balance is well-established. Gender balance is not just a social issue, but one that addresses two core challenges for all organizations: talent and market access. At Baxter, we focus on gender balance because it makes sense. *How Women Mean Business* is a very timely book which will make the journey to gender balance possible and realistic for all organizations.'

Gerald Lema, Corporate Vice President and President, Baxter International Inc. Asia-Pacific

HOW
Women Mean
Business

A Step by Step Guide to Profiting from
Gender Balanced Business

Avivah Wittenberg-Cox

A John Wiley and Sons, Ltd, Publication

CONTENTS

Contents

DEDICATION

To the men who care,
The women who dare,
And the companies (and countries) lighting the way.

FOREWORD

Companies have learnt the power of diversity. Many encourage people of diverse backgrounds to work on common challenges, share opinions, and bring creative solutions to issues – for instance, companies that have become more international benefit from people of varied nationalities working together. Diversity is today understood to be a real asset, constantly enriching a company.

Surprisingly, though, the most obvious diversity – gender diversity – struggles to progress at many companies.

Still, gender balance has become a leading topic in people strategies of private and public enterprises. In the war for Talent, companies simply cannot afford to deprive themselves of half of the population. Women represent the majority of graduates in the major countries of the world. Neglecting women in recruitment or promotion is neglecting half of the world's brain power.

Beyond this very basic motivation, I believe gender balance is a tremendous asset and a powerful differentiator for companies. First of all, it's a question of business and growth. Many customers and deciders are women, and people of their gender can understand far better their needs and purchasing criteria. No woman in your organisation could mean no sales to this powerful segment of the economy.

Also, gender balance is essential for stability and harmony in a company. Dual-gender teams work better and with a more balanced sensitivity to issues. Women leaders often bring to the table a more mature approach to their career ambition and create a different emotional bond with their teams and peers.

A gender balanced organisation aims at leveraging the complementary characteristics of men and women. We need both, expressing people's full personalities and differences for the good of our companies! Men and women must learn to work better together. Men, who are the dominating gender in the vast majority of companies today, should be more aware that managing a woman requires a different approach than managing a man. And women should not try to mimic men. Instead, they should cultivate their difference as an asset. The more managers are open to gender differences, the more inclusive business will be.

In the end, the question is not whether or not we should foster gender balance, but how it can be done.

In her first book, Avivah explained why women had become strategically important for companies, growing more powerful in the economy, in politics and in social influence. Avivah's second book takes the logical step to how to tackle the gender issue: not positioning it as a women's challenge but as a business one.

The value of gender balance seems so obvious, it should not need a book. The reality is that changing mentalities is always the most complicated thing in society. Every revolution needs a lot of change management. This is what this book is all about.

Jean-Pascal Tricoire
President and CEO
Schneider Electric

ACKNOWLEDGEMENTS

This book grew out of my parallel consultancy and publishing work helping companies become 21st century, gender bilingual organisations. These are exciting, groundbreaking times, and I would like to acknowledge the courage and conviction of the thought leaders who are reshaping their teams and their companies, and impacting the geographies in which they work. My thanks to the many managers who have argued through every point in this book through thousands of workshops, who have reacted to my speeches at conferences, and who have shared stories, anecdotes, and lessons that have endlessly taught me the depths and complexities of a topic I have been exploring with curiosity and pleasure for almost two decades. I am touched and encouraged by their enthusiasm and commitment, and thank them for having been so generous with their time, and for sharing their thoughts and experiences with me.

In particular, I would like to thank: Paul Bulcke, CEO, Nestlé; Jean-Pascal Tricoire, President and CEO, Schneider Electric; Feike Sijbesma, Chairman of the Managing Board, Royal DSM; Gerald Lema, Corporate VP and President, Asia Pacific, Baxter International; Michel Landel, CEO, Sodexo; Piyush Gupta, CEO, DBS Holdings Group; Bob Elton, former CEO, BC Hydro; Jaspal Bindra, CEO (Asia), Standard Chartered Bank; Damien O'Brien, CEO, and Chris Thomas, Partner, Egon Zehnder

International; David Loughman, MD A/S Norske Shell and VP Commercial Europe, Shell Upstream International; Giovanni Ciserani, President Western Europe MDO, Procter & Gamble; Jean-Marc Duvoisin, Deputy Executive Vice President, Human Resources and Centre Administration, Nestlé; Hallstein Moerk, Executive Vice-President, HR, Nokia; Augustin de Roubin, VP, HR, Air Liquide; Siân Herbert-Jones, Group Executive Vice President and Chief Financial Officer, Sodexo; Odiles Desforges, Executive Vice President, Engineering & Quality, Renault; Laurent Blanchard, VP, Cisco Europe and DG, Cisco France; Christopher Thomas, Parner, Egon Zehnder International; Joanna Fielding, CFO (China), Standard Chartered Bank; Saad Abdul-Latif, President, SAMEA (South East Asia, Middle East & Africa), PepsiCo; Ümran Beba, President, PepsiCo, Asia Pacific Region; Klaus Holse Andersen, Area Vice President, Microsoft, Western Europe & Microsoft Corporate VP; Olivier Marchal, MD, Bain (EMEA); Emilio Umeoka, President, Microsoft (APAC); Andrew Roscoe, Head of London Office, Egon Zehnder International; Adam Travis, Head, Diversity & Inclusion, Nokia; Laura Roberts, Co-Founder and CEO, Pantheon Enterprises; Daphne Mashile-Nkosi, Chairman, Kalagadi Manganese; Rachel Campbell, Global Head of People, Performance and Culture (PPC), KPMG; Marie-Thérèse Burkart-Arnoso, Corporate HR Manager, Nestlé; Claire Martin, Vice-President, Corporate Social Responsibility, Renault; Jean-Michel Monnot, VP, Diversity & Inclusion, Sodexo; Rohini Anand, Senior Vice President and Global Chief Diversity Officer, Sodexo; Stephanie Nash, Senior HR Director, Microsoft; Catherine Ladousse, Executive Director, Corporate Marketing & Communications (Europe, North America, Japan, and Australia), Lenovo; Elin Hurvenes, Founder and CEO, Professional Boards Forum; Collette Dunkley, Founder and

CEO, XandY Communications; Isla Ramos Cháves, Director of Strategy & Business Optimisation, Western Europe, Lenovo; Lisa Kepinski, Diversity & Inclusion International Director, Microsoft; Julie Gilbert, CEO and Founder, WOLF Means Business; Judy Feng, Director, Talent Management, Baxter Asia Pacific Region; Valérie Gauthier, Associate Dean of the MBA Programme, HEC; Mai-Lan Nguyen, HR Manager, Schneider Electric; and Kari Nelson, Head, Diversity & Inclusion, Standard Chartered Bank.

I would also like to thank the exceptional colleagues who brought some gender balance to this book, Morice Mendoza and Robert Youngblood. The superior quality of their research, interviewing, and editing skills is a pleasure to behold. Their invaluable assistance has proven the basic premise of this book: that gender balance produces superior results. It also made this venture a lot more fun.

To the rest of the 20-first team, especially my COO, Jennifer Flock and my PA, Joelle Couthouis, goes deep gratitude. They have supported me every step of the way, helping me find some balance between the books and the business.

I would also like to extend my thanks and gratitude to the wonderfully supportive team at Wiley. Several years ago, when I first approached them with an idea of a two-volume series on the WHY and the HOW of gender balance, it seemed a distant dream. Ellen Hallsworth, Nick Mannion, Caroline Baines, and Michaela Fay have all lent their enthusiasm and talents to the success of this project, now fully realized. They have helped make it a pleasurable and professional journey.

And finally, and as always, to Karl, without whom not one word would ever have been written. And to Adam and Alexie, for whom they are all written.

INTRODUCTION

'Women's economic empowerment is arguably the biggest social change of our times.'

The Economist, 2010

'It's extraordinary', Sir John Bond said recently, in reference to the fact that women still account for only 12% of FTSE directors in the UK. Sir John, who rose to the top of HSBC, one of the world's largest banks, is currently chairman of Vodafone. 'When you think that over half the clients of Vodafone are women and so many of the big choices in life are made by women ... apart from being unjust, it's bad for business.'[1]

For decades, ever more competent and ambitious women have been pouring into the workforce, acquiring professional skills and qualifications, and becoming the majority of today's Talent. *The Economist* recently noted the extent of this revolution: '... more women are working than ever before. Coping with this change will be one of the great challenges of the coming decades.'[2] In addition to Talent, the power of the purse has also soared to new levels: women today control $20 trillion of consumer spending globally per year.[3]

Still, few companies can say that they truly understand the women who have become the majority of today's Talent pool or the women who influence so many purchasing decisions of their products and services.

In four words, Sir John encapsulated why this failure to respond to the strategic challenge of managing female Talent and marketing to women customers matters: 'It's bad for business.' Businesses that don't 'get' women are unlikely to see lasting corporate success in the 21st century.

Why business needs balance

Companies must secure the best leaders available and must bring together a complementary set of skills into leadership teams. Women are conspicuously missing from those teams. Over and over again, studies have shown significant improvements in decision making quality in more gender balanced leadership teams (usually at least one third each from both genders). Women clearly bring new perspectives and skills to the table.

Old fashioned (male) bosses might see women as problematic because of their obvious biological differences and the likelihood that they will require more time to spend with their families. Sharper, more modern leaders will see the Talent entering the marketplace and be keen to shape business cultures and working practices so that the majority of that Talent pool can thrive. And not just women: many men now are more involved in their families and will eagerly embrace a smarter way of working, one that enables them to give their best to their employers as well as manage their outside commitments.

This is not about the advancement of women: gender balance – a relevant mix of both men and women – is simply better for business. Companies benefit from having gender balanced workforces from top to bottom. So if a management team is dominated by women (as happens in some Asian countries), it should look at the reasons why more men are not coming in. We need to achieve a healthy and creative mix of skills and views, not one or the other.

In addition, companies need to think deeply about the way they market to their customers and end users. For too long the implicit view has been that men are buying everything. Companies need to challenge the old ways of thinking underlying their processes, systems, and cultures to ensure that they are reaching the women who influence directly or indirectly the majority of purchasing decisions in today's markets. Any company that fails to reach women consumers and end users effectively, whether it sells computers, cars, or fashion clothing, risks the loss of business on a large scale. Can companies ever afford to be so cavalier, let alone in a period in which the world has been rocked arguably by one of the biggest recessions in the past century?

Finally, investors are increasingly aware of the proof that gender balance improves the bottom line. Companies that fail to develop and advance women to the top risk attracting the ire of shareholders who will judge that they are not realising a satisfactory return on their investment in that most valuable resource: Talent.

Many companies simply don't realise how badly they are marketing to or managing women. I have been a consultant on the issue of gender balance for almost two decades. I've found that most men are well-meaning *and* progressive. The problem is that they have not generally perceived gender balance as a top business priority that requires their attention, focus, and constant vigilance. I am convinced that this is why change has been so glacial.

I prefer to see businesses developing their own systems, processes, and cultures to become fully gender balanced. This is much healthier than having the change imposed on them by government quotas, as happened in Norway recently. Companies listed on the Oslo Stock Exchange had to comply with a tough new regulation that both genders had to be represented by 40% of the board. Far better that companies manage the process themselves and develop better methods to foster gender balanced leadership pipelines and bring more women through to the top executive levels, a much more meaningful measure of balance. This will help to create the gender balanced organisation, in which the whole culture is more attuned to men and women, with leaders who understand the nuances and differences between the sexes, sharpening their ability to manage women and men in the workplace and sell to both of them in the marketplace. Managers who achieve this fluency are what I call gender bilingual.

I have written this book because I believe it is imperative that entire companies become gender bilingual. It will enable them to utilise the full Talent base, bringing to the top a whole new set of female leaders with new skills (many of which may be ideally suited to manage in the hyper-fast, connected global economy). This will lead to optimised Talent and marketing strategies and more sustained business success.

From understanding the *why* to implementing the *how*

Knowing it needs to be done, however, is a very different matter from doing it. Too many failed initiatives have jaded people's expectations in this area. There is a simple and straightforward approach to creating the gender bilingual organisation. But certain key steps need to be taken on the way and certain cul de sacs avoided.

The most crucial ingredient of all is that the most senior leaders are convinced of the need to make this a business priority and are committed to change. They will have to counter scepticism and lethargy. But if they can follow some basic rules, use simple but effective indicators, and sustain the commitment to change, they can create much more effective businesses through gender balance.

Judy Feng, the Talent Management Director at Baxter Asia Pacific, part of healthcare company Baxter International, points to an example of how more gender balanced leadership has improved the company's bottom line: 'We have a woman Business Unit director in our China business (previously she was a sales representative), who has introduced a great motivating and coaching style to the team. And the business in her Business unit has increased at a much higher rate than the market growth in the last five years.'[4]

At Microsoft, Emilio Umeoka, the company's Asia Pacific head, can see the benefits of increasing the proportion of women in senior roles. He has seven women and six men in his leadership team and four of his Country Managers are women out of a total of ten in the region. He believes that women bring many important qualities to teams such as sales acumen and sensitivity in regard to the market and consumers. On being asked whether the region has benefited from greater gender balance his reply is clear: 'Yes, I think APAC has benefited. The region has performed well. We have achieved the highest employee satisfaction rates in the whole of Microsoft in the last two years – including retention performance. We have improved customer satisfaction levels – the level of customer focus within (measured by our "customercentricity index") and the level of satisfaction of customers and partners. We have received Best Employer of Choice in some of our countries. It's very hard to measure but I'm convinced it has impacted [performance].'[5]

These are just some of the examples of the benefits that have started to emerge. Much more evidence will accrue once gender balance starts to become the norm.

From smashing glass ceilings to removing gender asbestos

To get there, we need to take a fresh look at an old subject. Gender is not new. The benefits of getting it right have never been greater. But the way that the issue has been framed and managed until now has not been effective. Part of the problem is the analysis of what is actually going on. Metaphors like the 'glass ceiling' illustrate this. In most managers' minds, and in much of the media coverage, women are joining and moving up in companies in record numbers. Then they are suddenly blocked (at a very senior level) from the upper reaches of the firms – the C-suite or partner status.

This interpretation has led to decades of research and reports on what women are doing or not doing and what they should change, strengthen, or repackage in order to reach the heights of the existing corporate pyramids. The underlying question is 'what is wrong with women that they are not making it to the top?' The corporate response has been to develop a wide range of initiatives to fix the women, by 'helping' them. This question, now that 60% of university graduates in countries around the world are women, seems obsolete.

The reality is that there is no glass ceiling. The truth is a lot more sobering and the problem more endemic. It is in the very walls and cultures of companies. I call it gender asbestos. In every company, the number of women relative to men drops at almost every management layer – almost from the very first one. In every sector, in every country. The question for *this* century is not what is wrong with women. It is what is wrong with companies that fail to attract, retain, and promote the majority of today's educated Talent pool – or to connect with a majority of the market.

This shift in perspective will characterise the modern meritocracy. The work now to be done is to understand the nature of the asbestos, and rid the company of its harmful toxins, wall by wall. Because gender asbestos affects everyone and everything – corporate performance, consumer understanding, shareholder relations, Talent management, product development, R&D, etc. It is a completely transversal and global issue. Eliminating gender asbestos will require the combined efforts of both men and women, in a shared understanding that this will be better for business.

From imbalance to balance in four steps

Most companies want more gender balance. They are increasingly convinced of its benefits, but they still struggle with how to actually implement it successfully. This book is designed to help companies manage the journey from imbalance to balance. It is organised across four simple stages: Audit, Awareness, Align, and Sustain.

Audit

Companies around the world are rolling out gender initiatives under the multiple pressures of Talent issues, mirroring their markets more accurately, and responding to a diversity of stakeholder pressures. When managers start these programmes, they are often tempted to jump straight into an action plan. Too often, that results in approaches that do not actually resolve the issues. Companies should instead take time to step back and analyse the starting point.

The first section of this book outlines the three pillars of a thorough gender Audit, devoting a chapter to each pillar:

1. **What's the balance?** Chapter 1 sets the stage for a complete analysis of a company's current situation, both qualitatively

and quantitatively, concerning every aspect of the gender issue, as well as the legacy of any past efforts.

2. **What do others do?** Chapter 2 considers the pros and cons of benchmarking what other companies have done and how to build on best practice and avoid ineffective approaches.

3. **What do we say?** Chapter 3 looks at the questions of image and reputation, including what has been and is being communicated publicly on the issue and the implications of the current programme.

By the end of the Audit Phase, a company will be in a strong position to frame the gender issue in business terms and bring the data to the leadership team for debate and action planning.

Awareness

In the Awareness Phase, the results of the Audit Phase go to the Executive Committee for debate and decisions and then to the rest of the organisation. First, the top team must build its own awareness of the gender balance issue. The leaders can review the facts and data from the Audit, analyse it in light of the company's future strategic directions, and define how urgent and relevant the issue is for the business.

The Awareness Phase is probably the most important and yet the most neglected part of any gender initiative. Like any change programme, a gender initiative is doomed if the leaders involved fail to grasp the full strategic importance of the issue. So this section explains how to get this subject where it belongs – onto the agenda of the Executive Committee or the local leadership team. It will show the reader how to take it there, how to frame it, how to use it to facilitate debate and get buy-in, and then to end up with an aligned team, capable of defining an appropriate and sustainable action plan. From there, the process moves downward in the organisation.

1. **Why should business care?** Chapter 4 lines up the results of the Audit against a company's business strategy. In comparing the two, it invites the most senior executives to analyse whether gender can be a lever for their business and if yes, why and how. The result of this chapter is that the leadership team will have built a gender business case relevant to the company and context.

2. **Leading gender bilingual:** Chapter 5 shows how to start rolling out a similar level of awareness to the rest of the company's leadership. How do you deliver a gender initiative to a variety of markets, businesses, and cultures around the globe? And how can gender initiatives serve to role model the kind of leadership the top leaders are encouraging their colleagues to aspire to?

3. **Working gender bilingual:** Chapter 6 illustrates how to cascade gender bilingualism across all managers, and whether specific efforts are useful for female managers. It introduces ten tips for bilingual managers, guidelines for managing in the 21st century.

4. **The action plan:** By the end of the Awareness Phase, leaders and managers will have become fluent in the differences and opportunities of gender bilingualism. This means that they are ready to craft an action plan for their individual company; one that will be relevant, fact-based, and designed by the very leaders and managers who will be

responsible for its implementation, and accountable for its outcomes.

The Awareness phase creates leadership teams that are both convinced and convincing about the business case for gender balance in their own organisation. And they will have developed an action plan based on an in-depth understanding of the issues and opportunities involved.

Align

The Alignment Phase aims to anchor the shifts in management mindset and awareness about gender into the processes and systems of the company, including all the established procedures and strategies. This requires a thorough review of both the Talent management side run by HR and the customer-facing functions run by Sales & Marketing. Systems need to be updated and adapted to the shifting gender realities of Talent and Markets. The three chapters of the Alignment Phase explain how.

1. **Training:** Chapter 8 reviews how specifically targeted and adapted gender training can help different functions maximise gender balance benefits in their areas. Managers, HR, and Sales & Marketing all have a role to play that will be facilitated by a better understanding of the issue and how they can contribute to balance.
2. **Talent:** Chapter 9 focuses on the key HR responsibilities that affect the gender balance internal to companies. This covers the overall policy framework and then looks more closely at recruitment, retention, and developing more gender balanced teams.

3. **Markets:** Chapter 10 looks at the external Markets issues. It addresses customer analyses and segmentation, the actual product issues themselves, marketing and communication questions, and where enhanced gender bilingualism from Sales & Marketing staffs can drive sales and customer satisfaction.

The Alignment Phase ends with an organisation whose systems and policies effectively support the gender balancing objectives defined.

Sustain

It takes a cultural shift to move a business towards gender balance. The time required depends on the strategic urgency and relevance of the change. Indra Nooyi, Chairman and CEO of PepsiCo, estimated it would take her organisation one to two decades to complete the change.[6] Gerald Lema at Baxter, Asia, achieved gender balance in four years, Bob Elton at BC Hydro in Canada in six. Whatever the goals and timing you have set, ensure that everything is in place to maintain the momentum built up in the previous phases and keep the programme on track. This phase is all about how to sustain the initiative every day across the whole organisation, leading to improvements every year.

1. **Communicating**: Chapter 11 provides a guide to the key issue of communicating the aims and goals of gender balance to internal and external audiences.
2. **Measuring**: Chapter 12 deals with the need to define, measure, and track success, highlight challenges, communicate

regularly, and keep the pressure on for change in order to sustain it.

3. **Rewarding**: Chapter 13 concludes the 'how to' for a gender initiative with the important issue of rewarding leaders, managers, and employees who successfully communicate and lead on the issue of balance.

The Sustain Phase delivers an ongoing mechanism to ensure the continuity of the efforts and evolutions required to create and then maintain balance over time.

This book's four phases are designed to provide senior managers with a clear understanding of how to approach the challenging process of shifting an old corporate culture into the modern age. Readers who follow the general guidelines and suggestions will be able to set up and sustain their own successful gender balance programme. They can develop their specific methods of carrying this out, based on their starting point, goals, and timing. Some will focus on Talent management issues such as retention. Others will look to changing their Markets approach. Some will change many factors across the board.

This book is a broad manual, building on the economic opportunity of women revealed in my first book, *Why Women Mean Business* (written with Alison Maitland). At my consultancy, 20-first, I have developed a range of online tools and resources to help companies further when they are looking for more detailed practical information to profit from the fundamental advantages gender balance offers companies, internally and externally.[7] Leaders can instigate gender programmes according to their needs and shaped to fit their cultures.

I hope this book will help businesses to avoid costly mistakes and enable them to build strong foundations to successfully manoeuvre through this major change. The result will be vibrant, creative organisations that fully capture the promise of 21st century Talent and Markets around the world.

Part I

AUDIT

Where are we?
What is going on?
What have we
done?

Chapter 1

WHAT'S THE BALANCE?

'How wrong we were, and how far we have come.'

Douglas McCracken, former CEO, Deloitte Consulting

The first step in a gender balance programme is to get a thorough picture of where the company stands on all dimensions of the gender issue. This includes understanding how much gender balance affects each different part of the business. It involves collecting all the relevant data on Talent, customers, end users, and competitors. It involves understanding the culture and mindsets of the organisation to evaluate how ready its managers – men and women – are for any change initiative.

The objective of this phase of the Audit is to provide a complete, fact-based overview of the gender balance opportunities and challenges facing the company.

There are three points to include:

- **What a company needs to know** – collecting the relevant metrics, internal and external, as well as the qualitative data necessary to evaluate the scope and priority of the gender issue to the company as well as the readiness of the culture to evolve.

- **What has been done** – looking at what the company has done about gender in the past and what legacy those initiatives have left.
- **What matters most** – analysing the metrics to identify where the main gender issues are – Markets, Talent, Leaders, or all three.

What a company needs to know

Collecting the relevant metrics does not have to be a mammoth exercise. Not all companies have ready access to all their employee and customer data by gender, and much of what they do have tends to be relatively recent, without a great deal of historic context.

While many consulting companies propose huge surveys to collect vast amounts of data, what's more important when going through this phase is to focus on a few key metrics that will highlight the major issues, such as the balance of men and women in the top tiers of management, promotion trends (Fig. 1.1) or the ratio of men and women saying they are most satisfied with the company's service or products. Focus on representative data to facilitate a meaningful debate on the question: Is there a business case for gender balance and, if so, what is it based on?

The best way to get that information is to conduct the Audit in two parts: a quantitative survey and a qualitative one. Do this as simply as possible, gathering the key facts and opinions

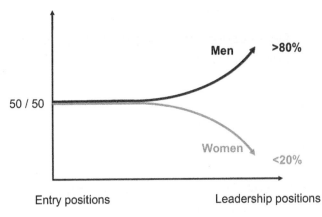

Fig. 1.1 Promotion trends

you need to make good judgement about the way forward. I list below a good approach to both parts of the Audit. The two equally important dimensions of the Audit are the internal Talent-related aspects alongside the external Markets-related ones. The sections below cover the quantitative and qualitative surveys for these two perspectives.

Building the big picture: the quantitative survey

All gender balance Audits should start with a quantitative survey, bringing together the data that will help the company to understand its starting point better. It will also need these numbers when it starts interviews with managers and executives in the qualitative follow-up stage. The quantitative data should gather the key elements that contribute to a strong but simple review of a company's starting point.

Key questions for the quantitative survey – Talent (internal)

The Audit must first assess the company's gender balance, in percentages and absolute terms, and adapted to its terms, categories, and segmentations, by:

1. **Grade level**: This might find sudden shifts in the gender balance at a particular level.
2. **Age**: This might reveal retention issues at particular ages or career phases, and whether they differ by gender.
3. **Division, country, and business unit**: This shows if some areas of the business or the world are more or less balanced than others.
4. **Recruitment**: New employees, by level.
5. **Retention**: Turnover, including by level and age.
6. **Talent identification**: High potential groups.
7. **Development**: Training, including participation in recent leadership and management development programmes.
8. **Promotion**: Promotions by grade and average time spent in each grade.
9. **Key position holders**: For example, top 50, 250, 1000, the top jobs that lead to the Executive Committee.

There are some key trends to look at for the Talent Audit at this stage: evolution, recruitment, retention, and promotion.

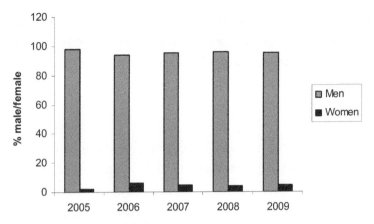

Fig. 1.2 Key positions 2005–9

Evolution

Try to get a snapshot of how the gender balance has changed over the previous few years, if the numbers exist. This tells the company whether or not there has been recent evolution in the balance. Managers, for whatever reason, often believe that things are improving organically. Data can help challenge or validate such assumptions. In companies that have not had a proactive approach to gender, there is usually a flat trend higher up the management chain, with the ratio of men and women remaining the same despite changes in personnel. It can be an important eye opener to see how a trend has remained constant over the years, leaving little room for doubt about the existence of a systemic issue (Fig. 1.2).

Recruitment

Comparative statistics on recruitment may reveal that the organisation is not attracting Talent in a gender balanced way. Many companies in traditionally male dominated sectors find that they have a very small percentage of women at entry level.

Companies in retail, cosmetics, and luxury sectors are beginning to find that they have too few men at entry level. Get a
specific measure of the gender balance at the entry level to the
Talent pipeline, and check if it is evolving at all.

Retention

Retention is a major gender issue for many companies (Fig. 1.3).
The leadership needs to understand the degree – and cost – of
turnover and at what grade levels and age groups talented men
and women have been leaving the company. The data will show
at which points in the career pipeline women start to leave
in greater numbers than men, and whether the change gets
worse at higher job grades or older age groups, or is limited to a
specific life phase. Most companies find that more women than
men exit in their 30s.

Develop metrics like those shown in the graph (Fig. 1.3), which
indicate for each of the past years the relative gender balance in
hiring compared with departures. Focus further if you can on

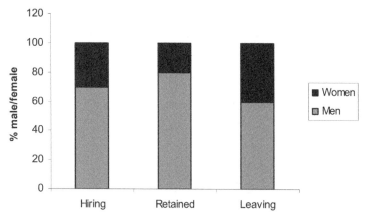

Fig. 1.3 Retention

unwanted departures. This graph will give you an idea whether the efforts many companies are making to recruit more women are being lost by similar numbers of women leaving.

While companies often assume that women are leaving for family reasons, surveys show that women leave for a variety of reasons, ranging from a lack of role models, with very few women in senior roles, to seeing male colleagues getting most of the promotions and development opportunities. Lack of flexibility is also a key issue, and if companies have not adapted to the reality of dual career couples and the pressures those couples experience as parents, they will find that retention is likely to be an ongoing problem, and not just for women.

 Three Talent questions to answer

- What is the gender mix in the high potential Talent pool?
- Are women recognised as having potential in the same proportion as their male colleagues?
- What is the gender balance in management development programmes, in key assignments, in mobility programmes or international job scopes?

Promotion

After checking the figures for recruitment and retention, companies should review how effectively they are developing and promoting some form of gender balance in their leadership teams. Evaluate, in the sort of chart presented here, whether there is a sudden drop in the gender mix at a particular grade level. In my

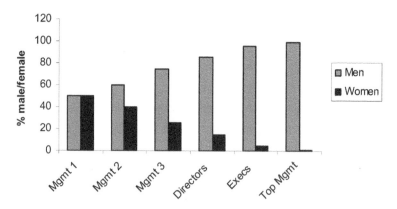

Fig. 1.4 Gender balance by grade

hypothetical chart (Fig. 1.4), the percentage of women managers plummets from around 40% to 20% as Talent gets promoted to Management Level 3 (Mgmt 3) from the level immediately below. Most companies would like to see the trend lines of these charts flatten out so the entry level gender mix for managers stays fairly constant over time. The sort of chart presented here suggests some form of systemic bias that can then be monitored.

Other variables that should be assessed by gender include:

- The lengths of time male and female managers spend at each grade level.
- The gender balance in developmental positions, and in key positions.
- Operational versus staff positions.
- Leadership development programmes.

Generating the data to answer all the Talent questions listed above will point to particular sets of issues and explanations for gender imbalances. Identifying the problems is the essential starting point for designing effective solutions. For instance, I have seen a host of companies aggressively recruit women in an effort to improve their gender balance, without having first examined their retention problem. As a result, they expended a lot of money and effort only to lose the women a few years later.

 Talent is the issue[i]

Klaus Holse Andersen, Area Vice-President of Microsoft Western Europe and Microsoft Corporate VP, ties his commitment to the issue around the need for the best Talent in the world. 'It's not about numbers and quotas. What it is about is getting the best Talent possible in a global economy – that's what it all boils down to. I'm convinced that at least half of the best Talent in the world is female.'

Hallstein Moerk, Executive Vice-President, HR, at mobile phone company Nokia agrees with this view: 'Gender balance must be one of the most important elements of diversity. Women are 50% of the population and therefore half of the Talent base. Gender balance must have a great impact on issues relating to innovation, Markets, and consumers.'

External – measuring the market balance

The issue of Markets rarely gets the attention it deserves in gender balancing programmes, particularly in Europe and Asia. Women are making the majority of the purchasing decisions in many sectors globally, including more than 80% of those decisions in many consumer goods areas.[2] But many companies have not updated their marketing, customer systems, and thinking accordingly. Gender initiatives, often run by HR, tend to focus primarily on internal Talent issues. This may turn out to be the right priority for some companies, but an effective Audit needs as wide a snapshot of the gender balance issue and its implications as possible. This part of the quantitative Audit provides a picture of how well an organisation is reaching female and male customers, clients, and end users, and evaluates if there are significant differences and opportunities that lie in any of the gaps.

 ## Key questions for the quantitative survey – Markets (external)

The first part in understanding whether a company has significant gaps in its external gender approach is to assess where it has been and where it is now.

Consumer analysis

- Break down consumers by gender across segments, businesses, and countries.
- Who buys the company's major products or services? How does the gender balance compare with the sector wide data?
- How does the gender ratio vary between different products (Fig. 1.5) and different markets for the company, and how does that compare with competitors or among different regions?

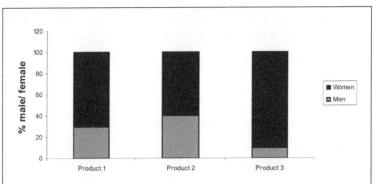

Fig. 1.5 Consumers by gender and product.

Gender bilingualism[4] analysis

- How is the brand perceived by men and women?
- What is the gender balance in the marketing department and, externally, in the company's advertising agencies?
- How do men and women rate the shopping experience, or the contact with service personnel or call centre operators?

Research, products, and services

- Does R&D and product development track gender differences in their research and focus group studies? If yes, what are the major gender differences?
- Do research approaches and agencies differentiate between genders?
- What is the gender balance in the R&D, product development, or customer service departments?

One example of how this might look is in the computer games industry. 'More women in the 18- to 35-years age bracket play console games than men,' says Belinda Parmar, professor and founder of the Lady Geek consultancy, which helps technology companies understand and sell to women. 'The average woman spends three times as much on technology – from MP3 and HDTV to mobile phones and laptops – than she does on cosmetics or pampering. This amounts to a market worth £15bn in the UK.'[3] But how many companies in this sector have gender balanced executive teams or gender balanced marketing and product development teams? How many have considered the impact of women as consumers and whether they're communicating to them well in terms of both their user and retail experiences?

Attitudes and mindsets: the qualitative data

The most impactful part of the Audit Phase is often the qualitative work. These investigations into what male and female managers really think about gender as a business issue reveal how ready the organisation is for this sort of initiative and why similar efforts may not have succeeded in the past. It is, therefore, a crucial complement to the statistics of the quantitative survey. This section describes one approach for the qualitative work.

At Nestlé corporate headquarters, Marie-Thérèse Burkart-Arnoso, the HR manager responsible for Talent and organisational development, said that what really surprised the Executive Committee when they received the Audit report was the qualitative feedback. The leaders were fairly familiar with the quantitative data and the lack of women at senior levels, as they had seen the numbers before. What really shook them was 'what people were saying, the feedback from their peers. There was, for example, a high level of disenchantment from the women in the company. This even applied to those women who had made it.'

The Audit Phase should include a high level review of a wide variety of examples of the company's corporate culture and communication style. This can include everything from print and web media, to the language of leaders in speeches and presentations, to the visual design of offices and recruitment advertising. (See Chapter 3 for more on this.)

In the Audit, many companies unthinkingly collect and present data only on or about female employees. Such an approach risks limiting the analysis to a female only perspective, and neglects the role that managers play in achieving gender balance. It can also lead to the impression that the company is concerned exclusively with the situation of women in the organisation. For example, it might focus on the fact that women are not advancing to top management levels in sufficient numbers. This makes the issue about the lack of progress of women. The company needs to correctly frame the questions if it wants to get a sustainable gender balance throughout the organisation in areas relating to both internal Talent development and external Markets issues.

It makes sense to pre-empt the common misperception that gender initiatives are just about women by collecting and comparing data about both men and women. Differences or gaps between the two populations will quickly stand out. It takes only a small shift to make sure that all the data present both genders in every statistical presentation, but it will fundamentally alter the conversation. Visually, in many companies today, it will underline not only the lack of women at certain levels, but also the overwhelming presence of men. Equally, these data will show companies where they have too few men, as is often the case in certain functional departments such as HR and Communications.

The qualitative work gives businesses a sense of the corporate culture and the individual motivation and readiness of leaders and key influencers to push for proactive change. It also shows how much work will be required in getting mindsets to evolve.

Ideally, companies should use an external gender consultant to carry out the interviews for this part of the Audit. It is important that the anonymity of interviews be guaranteed and that each interviewee has the chance (and protection) to speak freely about the subject. This is the only way of getting a real sense of all the attitudes that exist in the company. The qualitative step aims to provide the organisation with a snapshot of what management and women in different countries and at different levels perceive to be the key issues, so it should feature interviews with managers across geographies and functions.

While these surveys do not aim to be statistically representative, they are extremely useful in measuring the culture and readiness of an organisation relating to the issue of gender balance. In addition to auditing local realities, these interviews also prove a first opportunity for interviewees to become more aware of the issue. The results must include people with a variety of different views on the topic of gender balance (those who are open to the issue, as well as those who are more sceptical or even hostile to the idea). All opinions must be represented.

Suggested interviewee profiles to consider include the following.

- **Top management:** It is helpful to interview every member of the Executive Committee, as this group will be critical in leading and implementing the initiative. Measure the alignment of this group around an understanding of the business case for gender balance. The top executives probably have never discussed the gender issue in this way and the results can go far in revealing each individual's perspective on the issue. It is the obvious starting point in the discussions.

 Well meaning but wrong

At Deloitte Consulting, the senior partners were unaware of the problem – yet other firms were poaching talented women Deloitte had invested in. The then CEO, Douglas McCracken, recalls: 'To be frank, many of the firm's senior partners, including myself, didn't actually see the exodus of the women as a problem, or at least, it wasn't our problem. We assumed they were leaving to have children and stay home.' The partners felt that they were doing everything they could to retain the women and prided themselves on the firm's 'open, collegial, performance based work environment'.[5]

- **Broad cross-section of managers:** As the real issue in gender balance is often harnessing the buy-in of the company's managers, the majority of whom are usually men, it is important to interview a broad and representative sample of managers, especially line managers with the responsibility and power to carry out the necessary changes. This is the population companies are trying to impact. Interviewees should be managers from different countries and functions, including representatives from both the Talent and Markets areas. It is crucial to understand managers' thinking on the issue. Are they sceptical or doubtful? Do they think it is yet another management fad? Are they convinced of the business case?

- **Women:** The focus cannot and should not be solely on the women in the company, but the interviews must include women from across the company and its divisions. While their operation or level may well be covered by another interviewee, it is important to understand how the women feel about the organisation and the idea of a gender balance programme. Women often feel uncomfortable about the issue, in that it could be construed as positive discrimination. They may be sceptical that it will make any difference. It is helpful to interview women of different ages and seniority levels to get as broad a picture as possible.

Generally, the most senior women are wary of any initiative that might make others suspect that they have risen to where they are because they are female, rather than because of their competence. They are tired of being dragged out every time there is a need to position the company publicly on this issue and they don't much appreciate the repetitive questions they get asked about their gender. The younger

Dominique Senequier, CEO, AXA Private Equity

The Financial Times journalist Richard Milne interviewed Dominique Senequier, Chief Executive, AXA Private Equity, in September 2009 for the newspaper's online video series, *View from the Top*. Telling her she was the first woman CEO he had interviewed in the 18 months of the series, Milne proceeded to ask for her views on the persistently low number of women in senior positions in business. She avoided going into any detail on her views on the issue, seeming to accept it as a fact of business life. She said she had worked hard (seven days a week) and travelled a great deal for her work. In other words, she had made sacrifices to rise to her position.[6]

women think that the entire issue is obsolete and do not see any problem at all. They do not appreciate having it raised. Handled strategically, positioned as a business issue, and run inclusively as a gender balance issue rather than a 'women's' issue, women quickly – and enthusiastically – come on board. Until that has been demonstrated, many women will fall in what I call the 'Patient' segment, although few will be outright resistors. (See below for definitions of the different segments: Progressive, Patient, and Plodding.)

- **Younger staff**: Include some young people in the interviewing to monitor for significant differences in perception because of generational differences. Gen Y (those born from 1979 to 1994) may have very different attitudes to work and organisational life. They tend to tell surveys that they are motivated by meaningful work, the ability to work flexibly, and having the chance to network.[7]

While many people assume that gender issues are disappearing and will become obsolete as a younger generation moves in, this is not what I have found in my experience with companies. On the contrary, the senior leaders are often far more open to these topics than are their younger (male) colleagues, who will be facing for the first time the full brunt of the competition from a massive wave of female Talent. However, with younger generations expressing much more interest in lifestyle and flexibility issues, as well as in family roles, that trend may help align the objectives of both male and female managers to some degree.

- **Former employees:** Include the results of exit interviews for male and female managers that the company is sorry to have seen go. Those interviews, if they don't already, should find out why the men and women left, the level of their job satisfaction earlier and upon departure, the advantages and disadvantages of the job, their view of the company's career planning and, crucially, the conditions for their return. Look for similarities and differences between the men and women.

Table 1.1 is a representative sampling of some of the analyses by men and women in response to the question of whether gender balance is a business issue for their companies. These responses come from different organisations and different sectors, but reflect some of the feedback that you can collect. Interestingly, I find that the men are often far more convinced

Table 1.1 What managers say

Men	Women
'It makes business sense. People to whom we market are mostly females. All the data shows that women are making the purchasing decisions. And women are likely to have a better understanding of women.'	'Women bring a different, more cooperative outlook. Men are like countries, always competing. Gender balance is like sustainable development, women think more about the future, and about children.'
'We've heard about this for 10 years, and nothing happens. Just incoherence.'	'It has been a lot of effort over the years with very little to show for it.'
'It's not a business issue. It's an opportunity. Half the world is female. We would have people who better understand our consumers and we would bring in people with softer skills, and get a better blend.'	'We are in an industry where there is no excuse not to have women in leadership.'
'The most urgent issue [in regard to gender] is window dressing to improve the external image of the company.'	'Our consumers are evolving into a more holistic society. Gender balance is a very important policy to respond to this trend. It's a real business priority.'
	'It's like embracing shareholder value or corporate governance. ... We need to get into the 21st century.'

(Continued.)

Table 1.1 (*Continued.*)

Men	Women
'Evolution in management requires increasingly feminine attributes such as intuition, consensus, emotional intelligence managing the grey zone, being less hierarchical, and being a skilled multitasker.' 'Women don't need to show they know everything. Men have to show off and prove their worth to their leaders. Women bring other styles of leadership.' 'We'll miss out on competitiveness if we miss out on women.' 'More women in senior roles leads to more objective, professional behaviour for everyone. It takes the boy's club away from the boys.'	'This isn't a problem about women or a women's problem. It is a problem that affects the efficiency of the company and stops it being all it can be.' 'Women think differently from men – gender balance is very beneficial.' 'Purchasing decision makers are women. We should reflect this in balanced management teams. Not having half the population represented is a key issue. It affects our understanding of market analyses. The fact-based way men argue doesn't relate to consumers as people.' 'We recruit 50/50. Very few of the women I've recruited are still with the company – they left for excellent opportunities elsewhere and felt they were not moving here.'

of the business case for gender than many people might give them credit for. This is all the more reason to involve them in gender balancing initiatives from the very beginning.

Mapping managers, from progressive to plodder

To get a fast and easy insight into where different managers stand on the gender issue, I recommend using a simple mapping tool that places interviewees into one of three categories: Progressive, Patient, and Plodding (Fig. 1.6). Progressives have a clear sense of the need for change in gender and are probably searching for the best way to tackle the issue. People who are in the Patient group may be receptive to the idea of gender balance but do not feel any sense of urgency to make change. The third group, Plodders, contains the out and out sceptics as well as those who are completely unaware of the issue.

This mapping tool provides a sense of the task ahead. In most organisations I have surveyed, the results have been remarkably similar. Usually, the men are distributed roughly equally across the three categories, while the women tend to be mostly Progressive or Patient – but rarely Plodders.

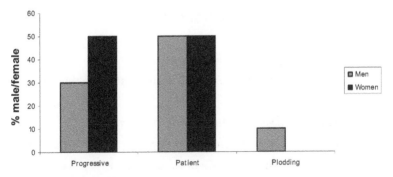

Fig. 1.6 Manager segmentation.

Example of a qualitative gender survey (internal)

Introduction

Objective and use of survey
- Rules of confidentiality
- Who is the interviewee: role, age, length of time with company, previous companies, etc.

General comments about the issue of gender balance
- What does gender balance mean to you?
- Do you think that gender balance is a strategic business issue for business today? Why or why not?
- Are there business opportunities in addressing gender balance issues?

More specifically, at the company
- Are employees gender balanced at different levels?
- What is the gender balance among your clients? How about the end users?
- How would you describe a typical leader in the company?
- Have you observed any evolution in the company regarding this topic over the past few years?
- Is there any internal or external communication on this topic?

For your own division, department, or team
- What is the situation (statistics) regarding gender balance in your area and on your team of direct reports?

- Do you have any specific issues regarding this topic?
- What are, for you, the main obstacles (if any) to women's advancement?
- Is there any need for proactive action internally or externally?
- If yes, what are, for you, the key success factors of a gender balance programme?
- Do you see any obstacles to implementing such a programme in the company?
- What perception do you think male managers have of gender issues in the company? In your division or department?
- What perception do you think female managers have?
- Do you think you have a particular role to play in such a project?
- What actions might be implemented to attract more women into the company?

Additional questions on individual career evolution

- Why did you choose to join this company?
- Could you describe your career path?
- What have been your main success factors?
- Did you encounter any obstacles or difficulties?
- What are your ambitions today?
- Why have you stayed and what keeps you at this company?

Personal (if possible in your country/legal framework)

- Does your own spouse/partner work? Full time, part time, career?
- Do you have children? How many?
- Any other comments/suggestions you would like to make?

The results from the qualitative interviews often surprise companies by not falling into the gender patterns most managers expected. Men may complain about lack of flexibility and women may be upset at any sign of positive discrimination.

In one example, a global multinational company conducted exit interviews for male and female managers and discovered that the men particularly disliked the lack of transparency and honesty (possibly related to a frustrated career), whereas the women especially disliked a mix of things related to the organisation and its culture, including politics, size, the gender issue, and lack of transparency. Asked about the company's approach towards men and women, some of the men replied that they had never seen a company where so many women were employed as managers.

 What women (still) say

Here are some comments from women's exit interviews at a global multinational company, to indicate that what many people think has largely disappeared from corporate life is still quite present in some companies, countries, and cultures across the globe. This is not as uncommon as many think, and in such a context, gender balance initiatives are likely to take more time and effort.

Sex, seduction, sexism
- 'As a woman you have to walk a fine line between letting the flirting happen in order not to become an outcast and not

leading the men on. At off-sites, often as the only woman, you need to have armour to defend yourself against a constant barrage of seduction. As a woman in this organisation you need to find a way to deal with this.'

- 'The women in this organisation know all the guys they need to stay away from at conferences, because they will harass you. Yet these guys get promoted.'

Corporate culture

- 'You are expected to spend a lot of time outside work with your team, to show loyalty. For a woman, if you have a family to take care of, it is difficult to spend enough time on this. I don't think the top guys get to see their families a lot. It is difficult to make a career here if you are single or do not have a spouse who takes care of things at home.'

- 'A lot of the political effort and networking revolves around drinking after hours, which I just wasn't interested in. Most women weren't. And when you're not in, drinking with the group, you're just not in.'

- 'It's all about who can fly more miles, how many weekends spent away from home. It doesn't promote an environment where people can work flexible hours.'

This thorough review of the data will have provided an overview of many of the issues that the company may be facing on the Talent side. Now, it is time to take a look at what is going on externally, on the Markets side.

Qualitative – external

The Markets side of the equation concerns key external stake-holder groups such as clients, customers, end users, suppliers, shareholders, communities, and the media. Above all, it is critical to survey representatives of your customer base – male and female. This will give an idea of the possible gaps between the marketing and sales strategies and women customers. Many companies fail to analyse their female customers, often because they simply assume they have the same attitudes and shopping patterns as their male customers or because they have failed to fully integrate the modern reality that women are the majority of consumers into their processes, systems, and thinking.

There is more on the analysis of customers in Chapter 10, but in the Audit Phase, a handful of focus groups will round out the Audit analysis and pinpoint key issues. Use an external gender analyst to query customers and stakeholders in very women-friendly environments. Focus on key future markets or key product segments in very open ended dialogues that cover a wide range of topics and elicit new ideas and input, rather than specific responses to closed questionnaires. In the same way that the internal review buttresses quantitative analysis by interviewing a representative sampling of managers and leaders, record what customers actually say. Quotes should be included (although not in the sense of an exhaustive market review) to give some indications of gaps or opportunities that can be highlighted.

What has been done?

Gender is not new. It's good to summarise what the company has already done in the past on the topic of gender, if anything. Many companies have years, if not decades, of history on the gender issue, and it is good to list all the things that have been tried in order to get some accountability on the efforts, investments, and return to date.

Sometimes it is easier to start a gender initiative with a clean slate, without the legacy of past approaches. This is particularly true in Latin America, Europe, and Asia, where companies do not have the same history on gender as North American companies. Many companies now launching gender initiatives worry that they are a bit late on the topic, but they have the advantage of being able to bypass approaches that did not work out too well (see Chapter 2 for a list of what has been done elsewhere).

Has it worked?

Ask if past programmes have inadvertently been doing one of the following:

- **'Fixing the women'**: One of the reasons why gender initiatives sometimes fail is because organisations think they can improve the gender balance simply by focusing on women. 'Fix the women' programmes are usually led by women, often on a voluntary basis in addition to their regular job responsibilities.

- **Giving the wrong message**: Women's networks could send the wrong message to the rest of the organisation. Such networks can seem to suggest that women are mainly to blame for the low number of females in senior positions in the company. Of course, women must take responsibility for their own careers, just like men. But, as I will show in future chapters, there may need to be some systemic and cultural shifts first to level the playing field.

- **Being ineffective in isolation**: None of these initiatives are wrong in themselves, but they are proven to be ineffective if they are done without any parallel efforts to work on all managers and on wider issues.

- **Using the wrong or no metrics**: Some companies don't discuss the key indicators for a gender balance programme, something that is needed from the start. Metrics are essential in measuring whether these sorts of efforts actually deliver, and against what objectives. Companies need to design the metrics before starting, so that they can measure the progress being made and then introduce scorecards to track progress over time.

Legacy

Do not underestimate the imprint made by past company efforts. These will emerge from qualitative surveys and should be captured as a context for the current mood. Many women will have seen initiatives come and go – most of them failing to deliver on their promises – and will be understandably sceptical. Many of them will want to distance themselves from any new programme. Men, typically, will think the issue has little to do with them. Send them a memo with the word 'women' in the headline and they are likely to pass it on to a female colleague. Most companies need to address their past record on gender balance before adopting a new initiative. They need to demonstrate why things will be different this time round.

At one company, the leadership had tried to appoint women recruited externally directly to the Executive Committee several times. For one reason or another, none of them worked out. When the leadership introduced a different initiative, it had to deal with a great deal of scepticism. There was also a widespread perception that the women hired earlier were failures and had been appointed only because of their gender. This type of negative perception lasts years, and it harms all women who are subsequently appointed.

What matters most?

Your company is now ready to produce a complete overview of where it stands on gender balance, both quantitatively and qualitatively, with some historical context and with the combined perspectives of internal and external stakeholders.

This is usually a mass of information that can be used to analyse where the biggest challenges and opportunities lie. What, in all that data, best presents the business case and clearly and simply summarises it? Determine whether the central issue for your company is a Leadership, Talent or Markets issue.

Leadership

Studies show that companies with a significant number of women in leadership positions perform better than others with fewer women at the top. Boards that have a good gender balance are also more likely to be better at governance. Shareholder pressure for gender balance is increasing, and new investment funds are being created to invest in more balanced companies.

The Audit will provide an opportunity to see how well or how badly an organisation does in terms of the gender balance of its leadership teams – both at corporate level and globally throughout the business. It shows how open the leadership team is to the benefits of more balanced leadership teams. Highlight the readiness of the top team, as revealed by the qualitative survey, because it will define how much of Phase 2 Awareness work will be required.

Talent

Sixty percent of university graduates in Europe and North America are women. Girls are also outperforming boys in school, and in academic research around the globe. Companies are increasingly hard pressed to explain why their supposedly meritocratic systems end up promoting a majority of men to the top.

The Audit should underline how well the company is performing on each part of the Talent management cycle and if there are any significant gaps between men and women. You will be able to highlight whether the company has a recruiting, retention, or development issue, or whether there are challenges at each of these stages.

Markets

A recent article stated that women worldwide control about $20 trillion in consumer spending each year, a figure that might grow by 40% in the next five years.[8] With that kind of purchasing power, it is incumbent on companies to understand how well they are set up to connect with and sell to women.

The external Audit should give the company indicators (a set of key measures) on whether they are reaching male and female consumers, clients, or end users with comparable levels of success. Underline all the gaps in perception and consumption patterns between genders, as these will be the major business opportunities that the company may want to consider focusing on in the future.

There are a couple of further steps to the Audit Phase. Now that the company has a complete overview of its own situation, it is time to take a look at what other companies have done and what they have been saying to the world.

Checklist

- [ ] *Have you organised your Audit into two distinct phases – qualitative and quantitative?*
- [ ] *Have you organised this into the two issues of Talent (internal) and Markets (external)?*
- [ ] *Have you identified the key data you need to measure in the quantitative audit?*
- [ ] *Have you selected the key groups that will take part in the qualitative stage?*
- [ ] *Are you aware of the company's legacy on gender?*
- [ ] *Can you identify which aspects of gender matter most to your business – Talent, Markets, Leadership?*
- [ ] *Has the top leadership team agreed to set aside time to discuss responses to the Audit?*

Chapter 2

WHAT DO OTHERS DO?

'At the end of the day, it is not about creating processes to change women; it is about creating processes to change the company.'

Piyush Gupta, former CEO (South East Asia Pacific),
Citigroup

Most global businesses have felt the need to do something about gender for years, some for decades. Equal opportunity legislation, corporate social responsibility, shifting consumer, and market realities, and the view that diversity improves performance have all played a part in this. So as we enter the second decade of the new century, plenty of companies have gender balanced leadership teams, right?

Wrong. My overview of the world's top companies, presented below, shows that in most of the world women are still not present at top executive levels. A number of research studies have indicated that progress on moving women into leadership has slowed to a crawl in the past decade.

Still, when they launch gender initiatives, most companies look at what other firms are doing and then craft 'action plans' to do very similar things, with little regard as to how (in)effective those efforts have been.

Worse, ratings agencies and various accreditation or award bodies evaluate initiatives based on criteria they like to call 'best practices'. Company departments like HR need the awards and rankings these organisations offer, so they adopt the very practices that have failed elsewhere.

In the past decade in North America, and now rolling around the world in an American-led wave, you can see the results. Company after company and almost all the professional services firms are creating networks, mentoring programmes, and coaching and leadership training, all for women. These are fine programmes, and the delight of consulting firms like mine. They are popular with most women, happy to have some developmental focus. Having run many of these for a number of years myself, I know just how empowering and energising they can be.

The only problem is that they usually don't work – at least not in isolation. The focus on women in companies leads to a host of unintended consequences. And the results don't lead to more women in leadership positions, which is the intended consequence.

What those programmes do end up doing, though, is deflecting attention from where it really belongs and instead reinforcing misunderstandings. These 'fix the women' strategies encourage women to conform more closely to the dominant masculine norm and culture. Women are very ready to agree that they don't do enough networking, self-marketing, making themselves more visible, and so on. And the senior men who are invited to introduce these sessions as 'supporters' and 'champions' usually acknowledge that women need a little extra help in order to be truly ready (in some distant future) for leadership. That way, organisations discover, everyone seems to be happy. The women are 'happy': they have a sense that they are overcoming handicaps. The men are 'happy': the programmes 'prove' that women have handicaps.

Instead of following others, business leaders should ask themselves:

- Does it make sense to encourage half your workforce to spend time learning and adopting the communication styles and career behaviours preferred by men and giving up many of the natural advantages they bring to the company?
- Do your customers want you to reprogramme the women in your company? Have you carried out customer satisfaction surveys to see how appreciated your brand, corporate image, and products are among men and women?
- Are you looking to the future and promoting what your employees and clients consider your top performers? Or are you simply advancing those managers preferred by today's leaders for their availability, expressed ambition, and reassuringly familiar perspectives?

Before we transform the new, still different culture of female Talent into pseudo male behaviours, let's understand the consequences. Companies are desperate for new leadership competencies, new collaborative cultures, and newly innovative minds to prosper in this new century. If they fail to make these ideals their norm, they will not only become obsolete but in the process will lose the Talent of the half of the population that is naturally aligned with these new perquisites: women looking for just such workplaces.

Global benchmarks

In 2009, I launched an annual survey called WOMENOMICS 101 to highlight the fact that there is one core metric of a company's success or otherwise in gender balance. This is the balance of men and women on the Executive Committee. There has been plenty of focus on the proportion of women on the board, which I was personally involved in as President of the European Professional Women's Network (it pioneered an annual survey of the proportion of women in the boardroom). However, boards are oversight bodies, whereas the top executive team is responsible for running the company and meeting strategic objectives.

Companies that have developed gender balanced leadership pipelines will have a healthy balance at the top executive level. This is rare, as the survey shows that only a handful of the top global companies have achieved that balance. The rest are disproportionately represented by men. So, when companies show off their gender balancing credentials or rest on the laurels of having set up a glitzy women's forum, the question to ask is: What's the gender balance on the Executive Committee?

The WOMENOMICS 101 measure also makes it clear to most managers in a company just how serious their leaders are about gender. They will know that the company means business if it makes sure that the company's business is run by a balanced team.

From outside the company, it can be hard to measure a company's commitment using our yardstick. Many companies are making it more difficult to identify who is on the Executive Committee, camouflaging on their websites and in annual reports the gender of the corporate leaders. They increasingly use various techniques, like removing all photos, reducing first names to an initial, or adding large numbers of people to something called 'the Leadership Team' which in some companies numbers up to 60 people. But the very use of those techniques says a lot, and probably more than just about gender balance.

The core metric of gender balance
Tokenism vs critical mass

If companies have only a single woman at the Executive Committee level, they are usually in the early phases of their efforts – or are practising tokenism. Having one woman in a group of men usually results in her adapting to the dominant norm of the group. Thus, the company squanders the benefits it could gain from the differences that women's perspectives can bring.

Only a handful of companies in the world have achieved the 'critical mass' of at least 30% women on the executive team, the threshold where research[1] has proved that women's presence and perspectives start to pay real dividends for a company.

Executive Committees are often considered to have reached critical mass when they have three women. Or, as one manager laconically said, 'One woman is a token, two is a conspiracy, and three becomes part of the team.'

Fifteen percent of the companies in our WOMENOMICS 101 list of the top 101 Fortune Companies in the US still have only one woman on the Executive Committee (Table 2.1). It is silly to expect a single person to adequately represent any large group, let alone have one woman represent more than half of the human race.

Justice Ruth Bader Ginsburg was recently asked how she felt about having Judge Sonia Sotomayor join her on the US Supreme Court, after three years as the only woman alongside

Table 2.1 Companies with 'critical mass' (WOMENOMICS 101 Survey, 2009)

Executive committee gender balance	% Women
Archer Daniel Midlands	43
Hartford Financial Services	43
Pfizer	40
Johnson & Johnson	38
Kraft Foods	36
Wellpoint	33
Allstate	33
Metlife	33
Prudential Financial	33
Lockheed Martin	33
Macy's	31
J Sainsbury	31

eight men. She replied, 'I feel great that I don't have to be the lone woman around this place.' She added, 'It's almost like being back in law school in 1956, when there were nine of us in a class of over 500, so that meant most sections had just two women, and you felt that every eye was on you. Every time you went to answer a question, you were answering for your entire sex. It may not have been true, but certainly you felt that way. You were different and the object of curiosity.'[2]

A study of top UK companies, published in the British newspaper *The Observer*, in August 2009, revealed that only 3.5% of the corporate executive officers sitting on the boards of FTSE 350 companies were women.[3]

Line or staff roles
One of the key criteria to explore when benchmarking is whether the women on the Executive Committees or in senior positions are in operational or staff roles. By operational roles, I mean someone with profit and loss responsibility, while staff roles are functional or support positions (most typically HR, Communications, legal, and finance).

Why this emphasis? Only a few staff roles are represented at Executive Committee level. Most of the people running companies are actually running parts of the business. Companies that promote women into leadership only through staff roles demonstrate that they have not yet learnt how to gender balance their leadership development systems and Talent pipelines. Women there are limited to a small number of specific roles and opportunities, and have not developed into the full breadth of functions and responsibilities. If a company wants to benefit

20-first's WOMENOMICS 101 Survey

In 2009, 20-first launched the first of its annual WOMENOMICS 101 Surveys, which reports on the number of women in senior executive positions in the top 101 companies in the US, Europe, and Asia as ranked by *Fortune* magazine (303 in total). The key findings (based on those companies where information was available) were:

US leads: The United States was far ahead of the pack, with 89% of companies having at least one woman on their Executive Committees. Only American companies had more than three women on their top executive teams – Kraft Foods, WellPoint, Macy's, Allstate, Pfizer, and Wells Fargo – with the one exception of UK supermarket chain, J Sainsbury.

Europe and Asia trail: Europe and Asia had barely embarked on the gender journey; 82% of companies in Asia and 68% of companies in Europe had not a single woman on their Executive Committees. Both regions were inching towards at least tokenism, with 21% of companies in Europe and 17% of companies in Asia having a single woman at this level, usually in a staff role.

Women promote women: Only 12 companies out of 303 had achieved a critical mass of women on their Executive Committees, at 30% or more. They were mostly US-based, and three of them were run by women CEOs: WellPoint, Kraft Foods, and Archer Daniels Midland.

Lack of women in operational roles: The majority of women promoted to the Executive Committees of the surveyed companies were in support roles (76% in the US).

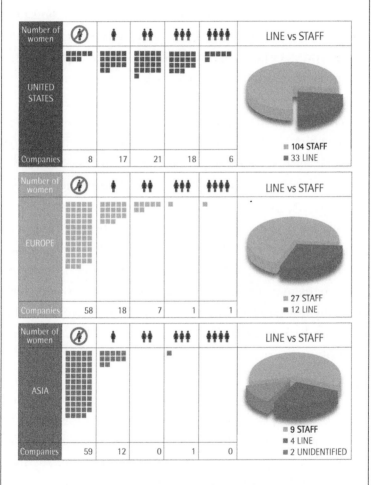

Fig. 2.1 WOMENOMICS 101 data for 2009.

57

from the effects of gender balance and the complementary skills that men and women bring to the table, it must spread balance throughout the organisation.

Truly successful gender balancing initiatives produce senior levels of men and women across the board, including non-traditional roles and areas. That creates the role models and breadth of experience for both men and women that guarantee the future sustainability of gender balancing approaches.

Personal choice versus systemic adaptation

Many companies and leaders are still convinced that lack of gender balance is mostly a question of personal choice – meaning that women choose to prioritise family over their careers. Until they adapt their systems and mindsets to enable the conciliation of these two issues, gender balance will remain an elusive goal. Until now, it has not been a problem for most men to have both a career and a family. It is easy for them, therefore, to claim that women must choose between the two. Men have generally not had to make that choice. They have been able to throw themselves into their careers 100% while their wives have taken care of the family at home.

The error now is that too many businesses assume that this is still the norm. In today's world of dual career couples, men as well as the women are increasingly searching for more family-friendly organisations that enable them to pursue their ambitions to the full without having to turn their backs on having a family as well.

Jack Welch, the former CEO of General Electric, articulated this widespread view when he said at a business conference in June 2009 that there was no such thing as work–life balance. In his typically blunt style, he said, 'There are work–life choices, and you make them, and they have consequences.' Welch added that those who took time off for family could be passed over for promotions if 'you're not in the clutch'. He said he would love to see more women moving up faster but 'they've got to make the tough choices and know the consequences of each one'.[4]

Most of the top corporate men in America are married and have children. What they call imbalance is a relative term. They may not have much time for their children, but they have some. At another conference that featured Welch with his wife, a young South Korean woman asked Suzy Welch for some advice on how to make it as a woman in one of the most gender unbalanced professional workforces in the world. Suzy replied that she should 'stop thinking of her sex as an issue'. What Suzy Welch failed to appreciate was that most of the men around this woman will continue to see this woman's gender as a major issue, expecting her to leave the workforce as soon as she has children.

Many managers echo this version of reality with its strong emphasis on fixing the women, or ignoring the fact that they are women. If women want to rise up the corporate ladder, this view implies, they must compromise on family, a decision men rarely have to make. A recent US study underlined that most senior executive men are married, but almost half of senior women in the US are not. The research[5] found in the sample that only 57% of the high achieving women over 40 in corporate jobs were married compared with 83% of male achievers. Overall, high achieving women either marry early or not at all. Just 10% of the women surveyed got married for the first time after age 30, and 1% after age 35. The survey also found that 49% of women over 40 earning more than $100,000 a year were childless compared with 19% of men in the same category. Only 14% of the women in the study said they had not wanted children.

Advancement has required conforming to a masculine norm of long hours, endless travel, and office politics. Many women, without the advantage of a full time wife at home, have clearly had to make sacrifices not usually required of men. Women who instead choose to halt careers for their family deplete the Talent pool from which companies can draw. Does it have to be that way?

Current thinking does not allow for the possibility that there are other ways of working and organising corporate life that might enable more women (and men) to balance life and work. Such accommodation would go against the kind of thinking expressed out loud by Jack Welch – the man who launched a major gender initiative at GE in the 1990s. Today, the gender balance on GE's corporate executive team is 80% men and 20% women.[6]

Benchmark out of the box
Most companies conduct benchmarking exercises against their major competitors. While this may make sense in terms of specific products, it makes little sense in gender terms. They are not necessarily competing for Talent only with companies

in their sector. Smart young women graduates, like their male counterparts, will be looking for employers who will allow them to reach their fullest potential, no matter what their sector. Women are working in companies across the spectrum today, but are looking increasingly closely at the gender balance at the top to gauge how open these companies are to female Talent. Businesses must be careful before they benchmark against the gender imbalance achieved by their key competition. On gender, they should be benchmarking against what the most gender balanced companies in the world – no matter what sector they are in – are doing to attract and retain Talent and to respond to the Markets opportunities of selling to both men and women. Women will go to companies that want them and know how to develop them, right to the top. Businesses may have to look beyond the limits of their industry to find 'best practice' in this area.

Marginalising women or involving men?

An insistence on solving everything by fixing the women is one of the main reasons why companies have failed to benefit from better gender balance over the last few decades. The problem with this approach is that it excludes men. Men are running most organisations today. They are usually at least 70% and often 100% of the leadership. The idea that you can effect lasting change without their involvement is laughable. Companies don't try to create a new customer-centric culture by asking a few people in the sales department to form a network and get better at service. A major improvement requires the whole organisation to shift its culture and attitudes in the right direction.

The current approach also ignores the big changes taking place in the modern workplace, where the reality of dual career couples is becoming the norm. In this light, both men and women need to find better ways of balancing life and work during their careers. Men have just as much interest in seeing new management models being crafted that enable both sexes to work to their best without putting intolerable strains on their capacity to meet their external commitments.

Barbara Annis has provided a useful list of five common approaches to gender balance and why they don't work if done alone.[7]

1. **Filling the pipeline**: Twenty years of the 'revolving door' phenomenon – with women thinning out as the pipeline moves up – have discredited this approach. Simply hiring more women won't lead to gender balance; in fact, as few women advance out of ever larger pools, it can make the problem worse by encouraging scepticism about the company's commitment to balance.

2. **Reducing turnover**: Companies assume that retention strategies will combat the 'revolving door' syndrome. But companies fail to address the real reasons why women leave. Managers tend to assume that women halt their careers for family reasons, which can be true to some degree, but most of those women have no desire to sacrifice their ambitions. Plus, women take career gaps for many other reasons, which can sometimes surprise their managers. Even then, retention without hope of advancement and fulfilment is doomed to failure for competent and ambitious workers, men and women alike.

3. **Building women's networks**: These are useful if they are part of a wider gender programme and if they channel the women to productive and serious ends. The trouble is that they can become talking shops, sometimes known as 'wine and whine clubs'. They also tend to exclude men, isolating women from the mainstream. In one company, the network launched with a fashion show, giving the wrong impression to the rest of the organisation. It made it look as if the women were not serious about the business.

4. **Providing mentoring**: Men mentoring women should be effective. But men can have trouble with the different ways men and women handle advice. Many fear offending the women they are mentoring and being accused of sexism. Often, they end up soft pedalling instead of giving tough but effective feedback.

5. **Responding to the reasons women leave**: Companies often misdiagnose why women leave. For example, they often assume exits are related to difficulties balancing work and life. But this is a problem that affects more and more men, so it is not exclusive to women. Companies need to get the diagnosis right before they can really curb the exodus of women.

Small, incremental changes to the corporate culture can be useful. Sometimes this happens when male managers mentor high potential women and get to understand their challenges. One senior male manager at Sodexo, a services company that provides 'Quality of Daily Life solutions', realised that his female mentee's input was being routinely relegated to the end of meetings. He decided to make sure that her issues, and those of other women, were put closer to the top of the agenda.

Bigger cultural shifts are also starting, which may create more women-friendly organisations.[8]

The challenge is to make the gender issue a strategic business opportunity that focuses on shifting the systems and mindsets of organisations, and thus involves men as well as women.

Senior leaders at global financial services company Citigroup learnt this lesson after ten years driving a women's leadership programme. In the 1990s, the bank started with the 'usual things', Piyush Gupta, then the CEO (South East Asia Pacific), recalled, 'such as women's councils and women's groups'. A decade later, he could see that the effort had failed to make changes. He concluded, 'At the end of the day, it is not about creating processes to change women; it is about creating processes to change the company.'[9]

The best performing companies and leaders have learned how to sustainably attract, retain, and promote both men and women in a gender bilingual way. Most others have not yet achieved anything like satisfying results. Many have not even started any real process of change. A recent FTSE 350 survey published by *The Observer* revealed that only a quarter of the companies listed said that they offered flexible work. Trish Lawrence of the group Opportunity Now said: 'The majority of workplaces are designed around a mid-20th century lifestyle, with an outdated approach to where, when, and how work happens. Flexibility … should be a business imperative.'[10]

There are many reasons for today's continued lack of gender balance, and increasingly we know what has failed. Let's move beyond history and out into the 'blue ocean' of opportunity that awaits companies that truly harness the benefits of better gender balance.

Measuring if it works

Too often, gender balance initiatives are not accompanied by the kind of basic metrics and accountability that accompany other corporate programmes of the same scale and ambition. I suggest some of these in Chapter 12, but it is interesting to note how little companies have applied them to their gender policies until recently.

A Gender Balance Benchmarking study produced by Bain & Co. in 2008 suggested that the sorts of gender initiatives run by most companies were ineffective – and often weren't even measured for results. The study found that that while most companies have a solid grasp of the gender mix at different levels in the organisation, 'the majority do not track differences across key stages of the Talent pipeline, including recruitment, attrition, or time-to-promotion.' In addition, four of five did not have 'quantitative goals established for these key Talent management measures'.[11]

The Bain study confirms the prevalence of tick-the-box approaches to gender. They are the legacy of a compliance-based approach to balance that aimed to avoid lawsuits. Unfortunately this approach is spreading. For instance, in France, the Label Egalité accredits companies that simply carry out a list of actions focused on women and equality issues.

Auditing Renault

In 2009, Claire Martin, Vice-President, Corporate Social Responsibility, Renault, took over responsibility for gender balance from the HR department. She describes the key metrics that the automaker faced at that time. '16% of all employees at Renault are women. You can take into account we have a male dominated culture common in the auto industry not only because of the product but also because of the nature of the industry. And we used to be 18%, and now we are at 16%.'[12]

The department's first step in gender balance and diversity in general was a major audit of the whole company to get as full a picture as possible. It began in November 2009 and was projected to last about eight months: 'This was never done before because there was always someone who said: "We are okay. What is the problem?" We consider we need an objective picture to start with to really know if there aren't any problems.'

The methodology of the audit uses a 360 degree approach to compare the professed intentions of the company regarding diversity against the reality. It incorporates data, statistics, facts, and figures at corporate level, country businesses, different sites, as well as the opinions of a wide range of staff including Managing Directors, trade union officials, employees, and HR. 'It will assess the reality – what the Japanese call the "Gamba" – on the ground floor, in the plants, in sales, in engineering centres.'

This approach does not frame the issue as a business imperative. Instead, in a well meaning way, it distracts companies from the opportunities and gains of gender balance by forcing them into generation after generation of compliance and 'fix the women' programmes.

The results are clearly depicted in a recent survey of more than 5000 people carried out by IPSOS and a network of alumnae from France's 'Ivy League' type universities. It found that, despite all the efforts and talk, there just isn't any progress. While most companies had gender initiatives, 80% of the men interviewed still believed that women and men were treated differently in management. While 86% of the managers agreed that gender balance was a business imperative endorsed by their company, only 7% of the women said that they had ever seen any benefit from the efforts. And 77% of respondents said it would take more than 20 years to get anywhere close to parity.[13]

The strategic advantage and imperative of gender balance is now so obvious that the compliance approach, based on respecting regulatory minimums or conducting tick-the-box activities, seems obsolete. It gives managers the impression that they can simply run a few events, rather than actually be held responsible for delivering improved balance.

Tick-the-box gets more awards than results

Defining and measuring results requires that the objectives are defined. So in evaluating the results of other companies' efforts, evaluate whether objectives were specified and if they have been achieved. And if not, why not?

Some awards and rankings have a range of criteria, not all related to hard numbers (see 'How they are judged' below) and not necessarily aimed at changing company culture. As companies become increasingly interested in being recognised for their gender balancing credentials, they often end up developing programmes to fit the criteria set out by major awards, such as those run by Catalyst in the US, or the Women-Friendly Companies rankings in many other countries. Companies should be wary of benchmarking their own approaches based on plaudits for programmes that aren't backed up with hard numbers, especially the gender balance of the top leadership team. Simplify measures to the bare minimum, to get a clearer idea of whom to benchmark against.

Most of the measures provide enough room for companies to get points for doing a lot of things without necessarily getting a gender balanced result in the end. In the US, huge efforts go into promoting women to the top to win companies awards and rankings, but most of those senior women are in staff roles.

If you look behind the statistics of many companies, many have simply inflated their leadership teams so they can add their top women, who are usually heading up HR, communications, and community affairs. This is an effective PR tool, at least in the short-term, but it does not build real and beneficial gender balance.

How they are judged

Various awards and rankings celebrate companies for their gender balancing successes. Most of these awards come from the Anglo-Saxon countries, whose companies have been the first to focus on these issues. Yet while a few US companies are leaders in terms of gender balance, the US and UK are not recognised leaders in international studies on gender balance in business.[14] So have these plaudits really changed the gender balance in business in a sustainable way?

20-first's WOMENOMICS 101 Survey

This is the only annual survey to focus on the key metric of the gender balance on the Executive Committee of top global companies. It also tracks the proportion of women executives who are in staff versus line positions.

Catalyst awards

This US research organisation gives annual awards for companies that have done well across a number of criteria:[15]

1. **Business rationale**: Company explicitly connects the initiative to the business strategy.
2. **Senior leadership support**: Top management demonstrates commitment to the initiative.
3. **Accountability**: Formal monitoring mechanisms measure the initiative's impact, holding individuals accountable for results.
4. **Communication**: Employees are well informed of the initiative and its business rationale.
5. **Replicability**: Other organisations can implement all or parts of the initiative.
6. **Originality**: The initiative must have innovative elements and generate knowledge for the business community.

7. **Measurable results**: Data must show the initiative's degree of impact and improvement.

FTSE 350 ranking

In 2009, *The Observer* newspaper in the UK and the Co-operative Asset Management research team launched the 'Good Companies Guide' of the FTSE 350 Companies. They ranked companies according to three criteria: the gender balance in their management (to board level) and the workforce; the availability of flexible working opportunities; and the level of equal opportunity policies.[16]

The Female FTSE index and report

Since 1999, Cranfield Management School in the UK has produced an annual Female FTSE benchmarking report measuring the number of women directors on the boards of the UK's top 100 companies. In 2009, the school initiated a similar study of companies listed in Hong Kong.[17]

NAFE top 50

The NAFE (National Association for Female Executives) Top Companies for Executive Women recognises US corporations that have moved women into top executive positions and created a culture that identifies, promotes, and nurtures successful women. This explicitly looks at the gender balance results at senior levels, including the issue of the number of women in line positions versus staff ones. Unfortunately, it is not the best known or most used of the rankings.[18]

1. **Representation of women**: Including higher management levels, top earners, and profit and loss responsibility.

2. **Advancement**: Policies and programmes to advance women (availability and utilisation).

3. **Work/life support programmes**: Availability of programmes to help professionals balance work and family.

Some of these excellent and well meaning surveys give companies the opportunity to win recognition without having sustainably improved the gender balance at all levels in their organisation. Perhaps they put too much emphasis on yesterday's need for good change efforts. It may be time to start focusing more on the results. It's not just companies that need to adapt to the new realities. Women's organisations may also want to up the ante.

Forget benchmarking, innovate

Consistently, the key success criterion common to organisations that have balanced their teams is leadership commitment. This is hard to measure but is quite clear in hindsight. The leaders that I interviewed for this book are on different parts of the gender journey. Some have already achieved balance, some are just starting out. But all are extremely aware that it takes their personal commitment and leadership to drive change around the gender issue.

One type of leader who deserves appreciation for commitment is the much maligned female. For all those who wonder if women promote other women as much as their male peers, it should be noted that in 2009, some of the most gender balanced leadership teams in the world were those headed by women. The Fortune 500 boasts only 15 female CEOs, and they have promoted more gender balance than a group of progressive male peers who came out publicly in support of more gender balance (Table 2.2).

Progressive male CEOs on record

In 2008, 17 CEOs and Chairmen of Boards wrote to the *Daily Telegraph*, the UK newspaper, to express their strong support for promoting women to senior positions in business.[19] The 17 included such big names as Roger Carr, Chair of Cadbury and Centrica, and Sir John Parker,[20] Chair of the National Grid Group (see Chapter 4 for more on this). They represent a larger group of 33 leaders of UK business and public organisations who have committed their time to working with senior women in FTSE 100 companies through the Cross-Company Mentoring Programme, sponsored by executive coaching company Praesta Partners.

The chiefs are to be congratulated for supporting the advancement of women and giving their time to mentoring, one of the practical ways to make a real difference. At least 52 women have been mentored so far, according to an October 2008 article in the *Financial Times*. Of those 52 women, eight have joined the main boards of FTSE 100 companies and four have taken up non-executive directorships with other FTSE companies. Two have become non-executive directors of non-profit bodies, one a trustee of a government organisation, and five have been promoted in their companies.

Table 2.2 compares a dozen companies headed by some of the male signatories of the letter to the *Daily Telegraph* with 12 companies run by women. Three of the 12 male-run

Table 2.2 Comparison of 12 male-run and 12 female-run companies

Companies run by progressive men	Number of women on board	Number of women on Executive Committee	Companies run by female CEOs	Number of women on board	Number of women on Executive Committee
Cadbury	1	0	Wellpoint	6	4
Centrica	2	2	Archer Daniels Midland	3	3
Telefonica	1	0	Sunoco	3	4
United Utilities	1	2	PepsiCo	3	1
Tate & Lyle	1	0	Kraft Foods	4	4
Thomson Reuters	1	1	TJX Companies	3	3
J Sainsbury	3	3	Rite Aid	1	2
Sodexo	4	2	Xerox	4	8
BP	2	1	Sara Lee	3	1
National Grid	3	0	Avon Products	5	4
BAE Systems	0	1	Reynolds American	3	4
Shell (Global)	1	0	Western Union Holdings	3	6

Source: 20-first.com, 2009

companies we selected – services solutions company Sodexo, utility company National Grid, and UK supermarket chain J Sainsbury – have reached the magic figure of three women on their Boards, the critical mass that has been shown to begin to change the character and nature of debate at the top table.

Sodexo, which features elsewhere in this book for its progressive policies on gender balance, has recruited four women to its Board (Patricia Bellinger, Astrid Bellon, Nathalie Szabo, and Sophie Clamens) and advanced two women to its Executive Committee (Siân Herbert-Jones, Group Executive Vice President and Chief Financial Officer, and Elisabeth Carpentier, Group Executive Vice President and Chief HR Officer). J Sainsbury has three women on its top executive team (Gwynn Burr, Customer Director, Imelda Walsh, HR Director, and Dido Harding, Convenience Director). But eight of the 12 organisations run by men have either a token woman executive or none at all.

When women lead

Eleven of the 12 women-headed companies listed have at least three women on the board and many of them have more, including six directors at health benefits company WellPoint. Only Rite Aid falls short, with one woman member. Two of the companies have just one woman on the Executive Committees – PepsiCo and Sara Lee. The remaining ten companies run by women have two to eight women on their Executive Committees. The company with the highest number of women executives is Xerox, with eight women on the top team. This is a company that has a female Chairman, Anne M. Mulcahy, and a female CEO, Ursula M. Burns. Mulcahy made history in 2009 when she became the first woman CEO of a leading US company to pass the succession on to another woman.[21]

What can we conclude from this comparison? As the male heads are aware, the process of change is painfully slow. Some, like J Sainsbury and Sodexo, are making a public commitment to change things and proving it with the gender balance they have accomplished. But most of these established organisations find it hard to change their cultures to drive women through the pipeline quickly enough to make rapid change at the top.

Most of the women CEOs we have highlighted seem not to have that problem. This suggests at the very least that they make a personal effort to find women for their boards and Executive Committees, supporting the view that the more women we have running companies, the faster change will happen.

So, the fastest way to gender balance may be to appoint a female CEO. In the meantime, all benchmarking exercises should focus on results before imitating the actions of other organisations that are unproven in the gender balance field.

Gender has a long history. We are now in a position to learn from the lessons of the past. Beware of benchmarking and awards that recognise effort more than results. Conviction and commitment work better than box ticking. Companies that lastingly gender balance their organisations will have a huge competitive advantage over their competitors, one that takes years to build – and years to catch up with.

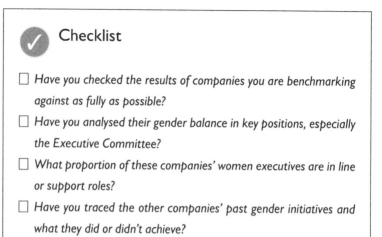

Checklist

☐ *Have you checked the results of companies you are benchmarking against as fully as possible?*

☐ *Have you analysed their gender balance in key positions, especially the Executive Committee?*

☐ *What proportion of these companies' women executives are in line or support roles?*

☐ *Have you traced the other companies' past gender initiatives and what they did or didn't achieve?*

☐ *How are these companies perceived on the issue?*

Chapter 3

WHAT DO WE SAY?

'Naissance Capital believes that we can earn higher returns, and fulfil an important social objective, by investing in companies demonstrating "best practices" with regard to Gender Diversity.'

Naissance Capital, 2009

Communication is a most delicate and important aspect of a gender balance initiative, as in any change management programme. What the company has said and how it says it can affect the implementation of even the best designed plan.

A company cannot hope to succeed in any gender initiative if it doesn't constantly focus on what people, internal and external, female and male, are hearing and are thinking. Has the company been telling managers, other employees, even clients, customers, and potential recruits that it is truly and solidly developing a gender balance? Is the company gender bilingual, in that it can truly speak the corporate language of women as well as men?

Often the message must climb a wall of management scepticism. Jaded by previous initiatives that seemed to achieve little, managers wonder whether their senior leaders are serious about the issue. For many, both male and female, the effort can look like another politically correct initiative, somewhat faddish, and unlikely to last.

Looking at what other companies have said and done can offer clear points of comparison – and lessons for avoiding miscommunication. Looking at your own company, ask: What reputation has the company and its leaders built around the topic of gender, if any? And how will that affect the credibility and perception of any future actions?

Mean what you say

Some gender programmes lack the personal commitment of the CEO. Never underestimate the impact that this lack of leadership belief can have on the fate of a change initiative of this type.

In other instances, the executive team lacks a shared, coherent view. Some are for, some are against, and others just don't know. This lack of alignment needs to be dealt with to have any hope of success later on. I was recently at a large bank that had run gender initiatives for many years with little success. The Executive Committee was entirely composed of men – and always had been. At a top management conference, the CEO surprised his managers with a new determination to press forwards on gender balance. The financial crisis and its fallout seemed to have made him personally committed to fundamental culture change, and he saw gender balance as a lever in supporting the shift. But even though the CEO made it look like the policy would be driven seriously 'now', the managers still expected that if he was serious, he would send the clearest signal by changing the composition of his own team. But he didn't, and still hadn't at the time of writing. In every company, the Executive Committee sets an example to the rest of the organisation. Practise what you preach.

Though important, CEO belief may not be enough in itself to drive change in this area. Some may see the CEO's commitment as a slightly incomprehensible personal belief or passion. The challenge for progressive leaders is that they often assume that their colleagues share their understanding and perspectives on the benefits of better gender balance. There are few leaders who are both comfortable and competent in presenting the topic in a compelling way to their own colleagues.

Leadership – the critical factor

Leadership is the Number One predictor of success in gender balancing initiatives, and it involves two dimensions: being convinced, and being convincing. This was the key success factor, for example, at healthcare company Baxter International, where Gerald Lema, Corporate VP and President of the company's regional business in Asia, led a successful gender balance programme from 2005 to 2008. A Catalyst Award winner in 2009, Baxter in Asia Pacific achieved its target of close to 50/50 parity for management-level and critical positions two years ahead of plan. 'One of the reasons for the programme's success in persuading and convincing our managers was the commitment coming from our top leaders. Gerald Lema, our President, strongly believes gender balance can make a big difference to our business,' says Judy Feng, Director, Talent Management, Baxter Asia Pacific Region.[1] (See Chapter 12 for more on Baxter.)

In the Audit Phase, a company needs to evaluate both those dimensions (commitment and communication).

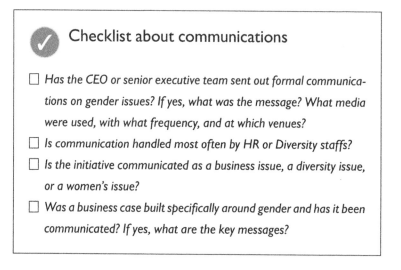

✓ Checklist about communications

☐ *Has the CEO or senior executive team sent out formal communications on gender issues? If yes, what was the message? What media were used, with what frequency, and at which venues?*

☐ *Is communication handled most often by HR or Diversity staffs?*

☐ *Is the initiative communicated as a business issue, a diversity issue, or a women's issue?*

☐ *Was a business case built specifically around gender and has it been communicated? If yes, what are the key messages?*

Language, consistency, and leadership

After looking into what the leadership has said and done about gender, it is time to examine what people outside think. What is the company's image and track record on the topic externally?

I recently asked the Dean of a major European business school whether he believed that his institution was attractive to women students and in what way. He did not understand the question. He focused on the notion of the quality of teaching and learning as factors that attract the best students. The Dean's attitude showed how leaders are often not used to thinking about how their brands and their organisations appear to women.

Business school websites offer a rapid education in gender bilingual communications. The schools with the greatest balance communicate a very different message from the schools without. Especially given the research on how men and women look for different things when selecting a business school (Table 3.1).

Table 3.1 Factors in selecting a business school

Women	Men
Cost	Prestige
Curriculum	Quality and reputation of faculty
Personal fit	Rankings
Location	Reputation of alumni
Diversity	

GMAC Registrants Research, 2004.

Comparing the website languages and descriptions of their respective programmes is helpful shorthand for companies to compare language and culture. What you say, in gender terms, is what you get. Table 3.2 gives a few examples.

Table 3.2 Examples of business school websites' descriptions of their programmes

Gender rank (*Financial Times*, 2009)	School	MBA student gender balance female/male	What business schools say
MOST GENDER BALANCED			
1	Boston School of Mgmt.	45/55	'The Art of Business' 'Contemporary business leaders must have an ability to think beyond the data analyses, to probe potential outcomes not predicted by the numbers. They need to "think horizontally" across an organisation, anticipating consequences and using informed intuition in combination with rigorous quantitative analysis. They must have a "feel" for a business, well-honed interpersonal skills, and an ability to envision possibilities – all part of the "art" of business integrated in all our curricula.'
4	Stern Business School, US	41/59	'Our Mission': • To deliver the highest quality management education to the brightest business students in a dynamic environment of mutual learning, teamwork, and support. • To advance the frontiers of business knowledge by fostering creative, cutting-edge research. • To leverage to the maximum extent our vital connection to New York City – our home, campus, classroom, and laboratory.'

LEAST GENDER BALANCED

94	IMD, Switzerland	22/78	'Every year, thousands of business leaders from around the world come to IMD's global meeting place in Lausanne, Switzerland to learn and network. Expert Faculty offer cutting-edge knowledge based on relevant, innovative, and rigorous research. IMD's unique "Real World. Real Learning" approach allows executives to immediately apply new insights to their business challenges.'
99	Marriott School, BYU, US	21/79	'Character, Attitude, and Drive' 'The ultimate success of the business my parents founded was due to their character, attitude, and drive. Their parents and teachers ingrained these qualities in them from the time they were small. These qualities are why BYU graduates are sought after by corporations throughout the world and one of the reasons my family is so honoured to have our name associated with this great school.'
100	Australian School of Business	21/79	'Australia's leading business school.' • Over 11,000 undergraduate, postgraduate, and research students. • Nine schools, nine research centres, and four affiliated research centres. • 220 full-time academics and researchers who are global leaders in their fields. 'Our reputation is built on our outstanding staff, students, and alumni and a cultural diversity which ensures an international focus.'

Improving the balance at HEC

At the French business school HEC, the proportion of women MBAs has increased recently to around 30%, says Valérie Gauthier, Associate Dean of the MBA Programme. While this is not poor compared with other top business schools, HEC wants a better gender balance. Its own research has shown that gender balance improves the atmosphere for the students.

'Groups that didn't have women felt something was missing and demanded a feminine point of view in their group; comparatively, those groups that had two to three women in attendance were perceived to perform better with a better quality of life. This was one of the motivations for us to recruit more women into the programme.'

One change was to reduce the age requirement so that women could get an MBA before starting a family. 'One push approach is to target slightly younger women, say 26- to 27-year-olds, rather than the usual profile of 30-year-olds. Women are said to be more mature than men, so the younger age profile might be workable.'

The school also started a part time modular MBA aimed at 25- to 35-year-olds with about six years of work experience. 'This is particularly suitable for women,' says Gauthier, 'because it is modular – meaning that they can have a child and still complete the course.'[2]

The most gender balanced schools adapted their communications approach to include the themes most likely to interest women, focusing more on atmosphere, community, and collaboration. The others communicate, almost stereotypically, about performance, competitiveness, and positioning, and so miss out on a critical applicant pool.

The oil business and women

There is often a discrepancy between what companies say and what they have done. And all too often, between what they say and what they are still doing. This kind of disconnect creates a reputational risk for a company on gender balance, and more, among key stakeholders.

The oil industry is an example. For years, companies in this sector announced gender balancing policies and approaches. They communicated far and wide on these initiatives, both internally and externally.

Exxon Mobil

Exxon Mobil states on its corporate website that it is 'committed to promoting leadership opportunities for women globally and improving the gender balance in our company'. It offers data: 'currently, women comprise about 25 percent of our worldwide workforce, excluding company operated retail stores. Approximately 12 percent of executive employees are women, compared to 9 percent in 2000.'[3]

If prospective candidates, attracted by the rhetoric, clicked through to see the Executive Committee, they would have

BP – walking the talk?

'A commitment to diversity and inclusion is firmly established at all levels throughout our organisation – we believe that by engaging our workforce in the support of policies and initiatives in this area we can create a culture where Talent thrives and discrimination is not accepted.'[4] So says global petroleum giant BP on its website. A glance at its Executive Committee tells a different story. At the time of writing, only one woman sat alongside eight men. The ratio indicated to the outside world – fairly or unfairly – an unproven commitment. This metric also proves to internal employees that the commitment from the top is more in words than in deeds. But BP's situation is more complicated than Exxon Mobil's or that of many other oil giants.

Senior women rush for the door

In fact, BP used to have a significant number of senior women, but they left. In June 2009, Vivienne Cox stepped down as head of BP's Alternative Energy business after 28 years with the company. In the two years before Cox's departure, six other senior women had left. In an earlier wave of departures, the Group Vice-President for marketing, one of the key players in the development of the company's Beyond Petroleum 'helios' branding, left in 2000. A year later, a marketing and innovation Vice-President resigned.

Leadership (in)consistency

The later exits may be linked to changes that followed Lord Browne's sudden resignation as CEO in 2006. In a public address

> at Stanford University, his successor, Tony Hayward, said that BP had too many people 'trying to save the world' – a reference to the Beyond Petroleum green vision developed in the Browne era. They had forgotten, he said, that the company's 'primary purpose was to create value for our shareholders.'
>
> Hayward's strategic focus on the old parts of the business – oil exploration and production – risked alienating many of the BP's top women, costing it the broader perspective that gender balance brings. The company may also have strengthened nascent competitors, with some of the women moving into leadership positions in the alternative energy sector.

found a row of five male faces. How would an ambitious woman view this lack of consistency in Exxon Mobil's message? While it talked of developing women's careers, it had not yet managed to appoint a single woman to its top executive team in the first decade of the 21st century.

In some cases, changes of leadership abruptly shift the focus from gender balance. Yet the communications history does not change. It stays as an external contradiction that must be managed into any new initiative.

Shell
In 2009, Linda Cook, a top executive, left Shell after successfully running its gas and power business for several years. After three decades at the company she was regarded as a serious contender for the CEO position. When the (male) CFO was

picked, Cook resigned. A year earlier, Lynn Elsenhans resigned from her position running Shell's refinery business to take her chances elsewhere. Elsenhans is now the CEO of Sunoco, the first woman to lead a large oil company.

It is already hard to attract and retain talented women in the oil and gas industry, despite the fact that they are a significant source of Talent for oil firms. In 2006–2007, 45.4% of UK postgraduates in science related fields were women.[5] But after a decade of communications, efforts, crises, and departures, women (and their male colleagues) have good reason to be sceptical about their chances of long-term success in the sector's unbalanced companies.

When stakeholders become judges

From financial investors to consumers, external stakeholders are increasingly interested in companies' gender balance. Outside groups compare companies' rhetoric and actual accomplishments, surveys like my WOMENOMICS 101 index chart balance, and women, who control most spending, expect companies to acknowledge and address their needs and wants.

Wider scrutiny

As the link between balance and corporate performance is ever more documented, funds and financial institutions are using sources to monitor numbers and track records to see how credible companies are on the topic.

Nicole Schwab, co-founder of the Gender Equality Project, for example, has called for companies to report regularly on their gender balance. The Co-operative Asset Management Group in the UK has focused on the link between corporate gender balance and investment, publishing its Good Companies Guide with *The Observer* newspaper in the UK. This report ranks the FTSE 350 companies by their approach to gender diversity and their ability to promote women to senior management and board positions. In 2009, it found that women occupied only 242 out of 2742 seats on the boards of FTSE 350 companies and that they held only 34 executive board seats out of a possible 970. The newspaper reported, 'As a result of this work, Co-operative intends in future to consider gender and diversity when it is assessing companies from an ethical, social and governance perspective.'[6]

Investor interest

Swiss-based fund management firm Naissance Capital started a Women's Investment Fund in 2009. It says that: 'Naissance Capital believes that we can earn higher returns, and fulfil an important social objective, by investing in companies demonstrating "best practices" with regard to Gender Diversity.'[7] The fund also plans to take minority interests in companies with no gender balance to 'use its ownership to encourage change'. The fund's board includes Kim Campbell, the former prime minister of Canada; Cherie Blair, a lawyer and the wife of Tony Blair, the former British prime minister; and Jenny Shipley, the former prime minister of New Zealand (as well as, full disclosure, the author).

An earlier vehicle, Swiss-based Amazone Euro, invests in companies with female board directors.

The customer is always right

Consumers are also paying more attention to how companies treat gender issues. Besides concerns about balance within the organisation, any company with a retail presence must monitor its public image, including (and perhaps especially) its advertising, to avoid sending the wrong signals as well as to push the right ones. Smart, validating, honest messages can win respect and loyalty from customers. One woman I interviewed now only uses Dove soap and products because she was so enthusiastic about the 'real beauty' advertising campaign executed by its manufacturer, Unilever (see 'How Dove Made the Business Case for Its New Approach to Marketing', Chapter 10).

Beyond the message

While a number of companies have become adept in recent years at appearing gender balanced, or at least women-friendly, stakeholders are catching up, looking beneath the surface to see whether an organisation has just developed savvier communications strategies. Get a sense of who are the company's key stakeholders, then check if and how gender issues have been integrated into the communication and relationships in those areas (Table 3.3).

What you say shows what you think

How companies talk to or about women (or don't), whether through institutional communications, websites, recruitment, or product advertising, reveals an enormous amount about

Table 3.3 Evaluating the message by stakeholder group

Stakeholder group	What to review
Investors, financial groups	Annual Reports Website Gender balance on board and leadership
Potential recruits	Employer branding Website Recruitment advertising
Consumers	Products Advertising Customer communications Customer Relationship Management programmes
Media, general press	Media relations on gender Press briefings/appearances by CEO

their internal attitudes. A recent *Harvard Business Review* article underlines the outdated approaches that characterise so many companies and sectors, even those that target a majority of female consumers. 'Women feel vastly underserved. Despite the remarkable strides in market power and social position that they have made in the past century, they still appear to be undervalued in the marketplace and underestimated in the workplace,' wrote two authors from the Boston Consulting Group in the article. They noted that companies still communicate to women as if they don't make the majority of purchasing decisions, coming across as patronising or insulting. 'Look at the automotive industry. Cars are designed for speed – not utility, which is what really matters to women. No SUV is built to accommodate a mother who needs to load two small children into it. Or consider a recent ad for Bounty paper towels, in which a husband and son stand by watching a spill cross the room, until Mom comes along and cheerfully cleans up the mess.'[8]

When reviewing all of the communications above, keep these questions in mind:

- Does the number of women and men who appear in your corporate communications reflect the real gender balance in your company at all levels?
- Do the images, vocabulary, and metaphors in your internal and external communications speak to both men and women?
- Do the images of women that you present, especially in consumer advertising, feature a variety of working women, of different ages, reflecting the reality of most women's lives?
- Do the images of men that you present, especially in consumer advertising, include a variety of roles for men, including fatherhood, sonhood, and husbandhood?

Also, do your corporate communications and internal management speeches tend to be sprinkled with metaphors inspired by sports and war, performance and pinnacles? Many of the stereotypes that companies are publicly committed to overcoming live on in what they say. This Audit aims to make this contradiction visible and understood by both men and women.

Measuring the value of credibility
Besides highlighting missteps in communication, the Audit will help companies to evaluate how credible they are in terms of gender diversity internally and externally. There is a huge

amount of potential value in having a strong and credible position on gender balance – both in terms of connecting with Markets and in accessing large segments of global Talent. The corollary is that there are substantial costs to *not* being strong in gender bilingualism. Being hidden from the balance sheet might lead some managers to assume that gender balance and credibility are not important. But too many stakeholders today, including investors, are watching the issue, knowing that it can lead to performance improvements.

No matter how many initiatives a company runs, perceptions of performance may vary widely and be based on criteria not fully integrated into a company's plan. Generally, running a few focus groups will yield a wealth of information, as will the qualitative survey.

Communicating well on the issue of gender is a critical component of success. The CEO has a major role in making this work, and leaders literally 'make or break' these initiatives, in part by what they do, in part by what they say. This is why it is so important to check at the start what has been said up until now, what was heard, and what impact it has had.

Understanding the different stakeholder groups affected by past communications will set the stage for future efforts and outreach and develop a full, all round perspective on how the company comes across.

The Audit is the base on which the rest of the gender initiative will be built. Its facts and data tell whether the company is on firm ground or something a bit trickier. It determines whether you need a few extra levels of concrete to strengthen the terrain, or whether you can start erecting the flagstaffs.

Altogether, the Audit Phase holds up a giant mirror with a particular gender reflecting lens. The data, the perspectives of employees, customers, and stakeholders, as well as a summary of what was officially said and communicated, paint a potent and often eye opening portrait of a company – one that many of its leaders may not have been at all aware of.

That is the content of the next phase: To make leaders and managers more aware of how they got to where they are, and what they need to do to lead the company to a more gender balanced future.

✓ Checklist

☐ *Have you reviewed how the CEO or senior executive team has sent out formal communications on gender issues?*

☐ *Can you describe the message that has gone out, in what media, how often, and to whom?*

☐ *Has the gender issue been communicated as a business imperative, a diversity issue, or a women's issue?*

☐ *What are the external communications on the topic? Who has been reached, when, and how?*

☐ *Is there disconnect between what you are saying and what you are doing?*

☐ *Is your company credibly committed to gender balance or will the new initiative have to overcome some historical context?*

Part II

AWARENESS

Where do we want to go?
How do we ensure buy-in?

Chapter 4

WHY SHOULD BUSINESS CARE?

'Women are 50% of the population and therefore half of the Talent base. Gender balance must have a great impact on issues relating to innovation, Markets, and consumers.'

Hallstein Moerk, Executive Vice-President, HR, Nokia

Most company executives are convinced that they – and their colleagues – understand the 'business case' for gender balance. Time and again, I am told, there is no need to spend much time or effort here, because they have heard it all before, and are convinced of the reasons for gender balance (the *Why*). They would like to move to the implementation stage immediately (the *How*). This desire for action is typical, but can be danger-ously rash in this type of initiative, which requires plenty of discussion and planning first. Less haste, more speed should be the mantra at this stage.

In my experience, top managers rarely understand the issue well enough at this point. Most executives have a hazy under-standing of gender balance, the 21st century realities behind it, and the impact and opportunities that it represents for their businesses. As well, the top team is usually not aligned on any of these subjects and therefore needs some open discussion to tease out differences before a more concerted view can be framed.

As a result, many companies try to kick-start their efforts, often leaping too quickly to set targets and create an action plan from the moment they have decided to focus on gender. This does not deliver the shifts in gender balance that they were after. There are usually two results of these sorts of policies, depending on the culture of the organisation:

- **The good soldier:** In organisations where managers are relatively obedient to corporate instructions, they start trying to meet the targets. They promote all the women they can find, whether or not the women are entirely ready, and then discover that they have 'used up their pipeline', to quote one manager at a large oil company. Some of these appointments don't work out too well, everyone mutters that women are promoted only because they are women, and after a couple of years, everyone who could have been promoted has been, and there is no way to sustain the effort.

- **Flavour of the month:** In other companies, managers simply avoid the issue, and the CEO discovers a year or two after having set the targets that the numbers have not shifted at all. He looks around at his team and wonders what has gone wrong. Probably, they did not really understand the need for such an initiative, and had no idea how to actually implement it. At this point, everyone is pretty tired of the topic, and starting it up again carries the legacy of repetition and *déjà vu*.

Pushing managers to be open to "risk" at Microsoft

Emilio Umeoka has encouraged his colleagues to promote more women since he became President of Microsoft (APAC) in 2006, overseeing Southeast Asia, Korea, Australia, New Zealand, Bangladesh, Brunei, Sri Lanka, and other parts of Asia-Pacific. But he steered clear of quotas and targets. 'It is really about pushing managers to be more open to risk in terms of encouraging more women to take up new challenges,' Umeoka says of his managers.

Microsoft APAC has picked out its next generation of leaders – about 57 out of 2200. 'I know them well,' Umeoka says, 'and connect with them through meetings, phone meetings, and roundtable discussions. And I say that they need to take up a bet and encourage women high-potentials. And it really creates momentum when they see some of the results of their peers.'[1]

Where most leaders do tend to agree is that their companies should practise fairness and equality towards men and women in the workforce. But in describing the issue this way, they miss the real and more compelling business case whereby a true blend of men and women on teams generates significant improvements in performance, from innovation to market success. Even if some executives are convinced about the case for gender balance, they will need hard facts and figures to win the argument with their colleagues.

Getting gender on the Executive Committee's agenda

Companies make effective progress on gender balance when they have built a business case that convinces the majority of leaders and managers. This case will differ across industries, sectors, and companies, but whatever its particular focus and character, the business case is going to be the fundamental building block of any change management initiative. The business case for gender balance has two dimensions: internal and external.

The internal case is that companies must draw from the whole Talent pool to create world class workforces and management teams. Companies increasingly realise that they need a wider mix of Talent with different perspectives and opinions to help them drive new ideas and innovation, as well as to better understand the outside world. And they cannot afford to lose significant numbers of the women they have invested in as the women climb the career ladder.

Externally, business could harness huge opportunities by adapting sales and marketing approaches to the women who have become a huge influence in all markets spanning the globe.

If a woman meets a rude or patronising salesperson in a car dealership, hardware store, or electronics outlet, the company does not just lose a sale. It risks losing the lifetime's custom of that woman. Further, she is likely to spread the word to others. Women spend trillions of dollars today, so this is a very significant moment for businesses.

Changing a company's marketing outlook requires having teams of male and female decision makers in the organisation, balanced teams that can drive new ideas and have a broader and more intuitive understanding of all customer groups.

The first big test of any gender initiative is to ensure that the Executive Committee takes the time to debate and design the case for the company. Given how busy they are, and how crowded their meeting agenda is, sometimes simply getting the executives to agree to give up time to discuss the issue properly is one of the key objectives – and early successes – of the Awareness Phase. A full day, ideally facilitated by an external gender expert, is the best way to accomplish the multiple objectives of an effective discussion at the top executive level. Companies should aim for an open and honest discussion that includes debate about:

- *the reasons for a gender initiative,*
- *its business relevance,*
- *the results of the Audit and its implications,*
- *the key underlying gender issues to take into account, and*
- *what to include in a strategic and impactful action plan.*

Who should make the case?

Why do I argue that gender has to be dealt with at the top from the start? It is because other, more common approaches are less than effective.

Most organisations automatically hand the task of defining the business case on gender to the HR department, the head of Diversity, or a senior women's network. This sets the whole initiative up in precisely the wrong way, limiting its scope and potential benefits.

HR will tend to look at gender in the context of Talent issues, and is unlikely to widen its vision to include Markets strategies, product sales, and customer relationships. It will usually define a business case entirely based on internal, Talent issues. Yet the greatest business opportunities for many companies lie in the external, Market opportunities. A complete business case on gender is transversal, and needs to take into account other parts of the organisation, principally product development, market research, marketing, sales, and customer service.

So, automatically turning to HR can limit the initiative to Talent management.

The head of Diversity will look externally, but usually from a Talent point of view. He or she will discuss the benefits in terms of perception and public relations, potentially drawing new Talent as well as kudos as an employer. However, the Diversity chief will not always be familiar with how better gender balance inside the company can generate improved products and sales approaches, nor how to present these ideas to the sales and marketing teams.

As for a women's network, it is often assumed that women understand the gender issue better than men. This is not necessarily true. And it implicitly suggests that somehow the issue of

Nokia connects gender balance and future success

Nokia, the largest mobile device company in the world, competes in one of the fastest moving sectors in history. IT changes so fast that products can be outdated in weeks not years. 'Our market is extremely rapid – players come and go. They can be successful or not so successful in a matter of weeks and months,' says Hallstein Moerk, Executive Vice-President for HR at Nokia. The threat is not only from the speed of technological change. It also comes from companies like Apple, which introduce compelling new business models around products that inspire users and create solutions for them, leading to loyal and ongoing customers.

Hallstein recognises that gender balance and other forms of diversity are essential to the company's future success. 'We need diversity to drive new thinking and new innovation. This also will drive the creation of new systems and processes that might help drive innovation.'

Building an organisation that attracts and retains men and women equally is a key goal for Nokia. Moerk hopes that having a more gender bilingual culture will enable women to bring their complementary differences and perspectives to work, releasing new ideas. Individuals who no longer feel they need to conform to fit in 'will think more authentically and bring new thinking to the company that is potentially important for innovation and strategy', he says.[2]

gender balance is the responsibility of women. Yet it is not a women's issue. It is a massive 21st century business opportunity. Nokia has started on a new gender balance journey precisely because it sees it this way (see 'Nokia connects gender balance and future success'). But only those companies that start by framing the issue as a business case have any hope of extracting the full range of opportunities from gender balance.

It is the responsibility of the leadership team to analyse the issue from a company perspective and decide whether gender balance is important to the business. The leaders should also be accountable for the objectives that they then set.

So keep the issue in the hands of the top team, which maintains a helicopter view of the organisation. Let it prioritise where the greatest opportunities lie. Usually, once they have been been through this Awareness Phase, the top executives will embrace the fact that gender balance is a corporate culture change issue that requires direct leadership by the CEO. Getting this right is a critical success factor that will determine what commitment the initiative will command and the ultimate business benefits it will yield.

Building the business case

Until the Awareness Phase, most Executive Committees are neither convinced nor aligned around a business case. They are largely unaware of the impressive statistics on women's economic power. How many of them realise that women are the majority of Talent and consumers across the world? Knowing the full scale of the actual and potential impact of female Talent and consumers on economic and business growth can be very persuasive but it must be seen as a whole. Much of this was covered in my earlier book, *Why Women Mean Business*,[5] but I list some key data toward the end of this chapter. These (usually mostly male) Executive Committee members rarely have been asked to debate or analyse the issue, and unless there is some form of experiential buy-in at this level, little progress will be made.

The CEO should be involved in the discussions and he or she should challenge group members to air their views honestly. Political correctness can be the death of the gender dialogue. The facilitator should present the macroeconomic statistics and explain to the leadership team how gender balance can drive improved performance and sustainability at the company through, for example, breakthroughs in Markets, Talent, or innovation. A summary of the results from the qualitative and quantitative surveys run during the Audit Phase should also be presented, preferably by the executive who was responsible for gathering the data.

In most cases, the executives will then chew through the numbers, relate this information to their internal and external situation, and debate the issue and its strategic relevance. They should get expert input into gender differences and how to manage them. Then they can craft the action plan specific to their company, complete with defined objectives, timetables, and accountability – and commit to it.

If they don't have the time, or decide it is not a priority, they might as well not bother. Non-strategic gender initiatives do

Gender balance in 6 years at BC Hydro[3]

Bob Elton, former President and CEO of Canadian power company BC Hydro (an energy company and electricity utility that is owned by the Province of British Columbia, and that supplies electricity to 95% of its population), proved that, with commitment from the top, companies can move fast on gender balance. He moved to BC Hydro in 2001, then as CFO. Two years later he was appointed CEO. There were few women in senior leadership positions at that time. In November 2009, BC Hydro announced that Elton would step down as CEO on January 1, 2010 but would remain a special advisor to the Board as well as Executive Chairman of Powertech, the company's clean energy subsidiary.[4]

During his tenure as CEO, Elton managed to gender balance the company's leadership teams. By the end of 2009, Elton's top executive team was made up of five women and four men. Two of the women were in operational roles and three in support roles. 'By 2009, half of the management team is female and pretty well every team is gender balanced. It is really hard [to achieve], but it can be done,' Elton said. Was it worth it? Definitely. Women brought a new richness to the company, Elton believes. 'For me personally, I've had the pleasure of working with some truly outstanding women leaders. I've been enriched by their ability to manage many things and by their ability to bring all of themselves to work, connected to what they are passionate about. If we get this right, women's ability to connect work, communities, and families will enrich all of our lives, men and women.'

BC Hydro's executive management team, 2009

- Bob Elton, President & Chief Executive Officer (through end of year)
- Teresa Conway, President & CEO Powerex
- Debbie Nagle, Chief Human Resources Officer
- Chris O'Riley, Senior Vice-President, Engineering, Aboriginal Relations and Generation
- Charles Reid, Executive Vice-President, Finance and Chief Financial Officer
- Leigh Ann Shoji-Lee, Senior Vice-President, Field Operations
- Ray Stewart, Chief Safety, Health and Environment Officer
- Bev Van Ruyven, Executive Vice-President, Customer Care and Conservation
- Susan Yurkovich, Senior Vice-President, Corporate Affairs

---

as much harm as good, sometimes more. Leadership teams may include men and women, but are usually dominated by men. Gender mix brings added depth to the debate but is not essential to reach the key objective: to get today's leaders to understand the gender balance issue and to define how significant a priority it is for their business.

It helps to focus the discussion on the key drivers and get the Executive Committee to decide on what, if any, are the more pertinent gender balance issues for the business and sector. I outline below the main arguments for gender balance that leading multinationals have identified.

Key gender drivers

The key benefits of gender balance initiatives today are fairly consistent across companies, sectors, and countries. Benchmarking the reasons why other companies have pushed this subject is a good introduction; then each company needs to prioritise and understand the opportunities for its own business. Below are the top line messages that can be presented and debated in the light of each company's own reality. Most executives have never looked at the whole 21st century macroeconomic view of gender balance on a range of topics, from leadership styles to consumer evolutions to Talent demographics to innovation research. The data, once summarised and powerfully packaged, often prove extremely convincing, even a bit overwhelming. The more detailed 'proof' and research around each of these issues are summarised later in this chapter for easy reference. Figure 4.1 illustrates the key gender drivers: Leadership, Talent, Markets.

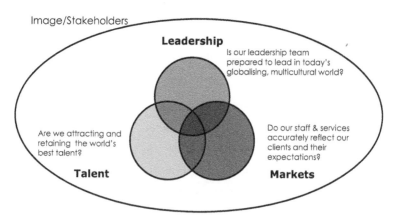

Fig. 4.1 Key gender drivers: Leadership, Talent, Markets.

Leadership

Gender balanced leadership teams are shown by studies to deliver better bottom line corporate performance, owing to the different and complementary skills women bring to the table. A Catalyst study showed, for example, that companies with a higher proportion of women on their leadership teams achieved 112%-plus greater return on invested capital than companies with the lowest number of women.[6] McKinsey research[7] in Europe showed similar results, as did a number of other studies listed at the end of this chapter.

> 'Today, I definitely see gender balance as a strategic issue. I am in my management position to deliver performance, not to be a nice guy! Currently, my job is about reducing operating costs, improving revenues, and differentiating the company. Now, how do I do this? What are the leadership skills I need from my top people? I believe the situation requires different leadership skills from people who can change the way we are driving companies. [Women] would utilise a more team-based, collaborative way of thinking; not a top down approach. … My key driver is to improve performance. And to do so, we need to have more women.'[8]

Laurent Blanchard, VP, CISCO Europe, DG, CISCO France

Organisations should ask some tough questions of themselves. For example, is it appropriate and relevant to have an entirely male dominated leadership team in a context where companies seek to reinvent themselves into more solutions oriented, customer focused, and global entities? Is this the best reflection of the new thinking needed in the post crisis era? Is it a proper reflection of the reality of 21st century Talent and Markets?

Most companies have become aware enough of the incompatibility of their leadership teams' profiles to their various stakeholders, and some have sought to remove any public trace of the gender makeup of these groups. While this may not be terribly useful in gender balancing, it does show that awareness of the issue has spread among business leaders. Doing something about it will, hopefully, be the next step.

Markets

The majority of key consumer goods purchasing decisions in the US and other Western markets are made by women. Everything from product development to marketing to sales to customer service and advertising must be rooted in a sophisticated appreciation and understanding of this critical reality. Many businesses still act as if men were the primary consumers. Most women can recall having been patronised by salesmen when buying a computer, car, or financial service. This lack of customer understanding is out of place in the 21st century.

> 'Gender balance is a strategic issue. That is because there is a real business case for it. It is an imperative. About 60% of college graduates are women (it is the same for the US and for China). Women are also the consumers who make the majority of the purchasing decisions in the household. 60% of the decision-makers for car purchases are women, and this is up to 70% in China; it is 50% for electrical devices; and 90% for food.'[10]
>
> Michel Landel, CEO, Sodexo

Women worldwide control about $20 trillion in consumer spending each year, a figure that may grow as much as 40% in the next five years. Women earn $13 trillion a year, a number that should also grow by up to 40% by 2015. In the US, women influence $4.3 trillion of the $5.9 trillion in consumers' spending decisions every year – meaning that 73% of consumers' outlays are influenced by women.[9]

Much of the world's new consumer demand from rising economies will also come from women, according to a recent report from Goldman Sachs. It claims that the middle classes in the BRIC nations (Brazil, Russia, India, and China) plus 11 other emerging countries will more than double from 1.7 billion people today to 3.6 billion by 2030.

By 2030, 85% of the world's middle classes will live in these nations. Goldman Sachs also expects that women's purchasing power will increase because of changes in healthcare, fertility rates, education, legal protection, and political involvement, as well as a slight increase in the proportion of women working (with fewer working in low pay sectors in some countries). It expects women's consumption patterns in those nations to mirror those in the West, with women making at least three quarters of the spending decisions in sectors such as childcare, education, and food.[11] This alone is a good enough reason for companies to wake up to the potential of women dominated markets and examine their readiness to tap into them to the full.

Talent

Women comprise the majority of the newly educated Talent in the world today, a trend that is set to continue upwards. Truly meritocratic systems will ensure that women are recruited in at least equal numbers to men and developed, retained, and promoted in the same proportion as they move through their careers.

 Female talent facts[12]

- Women are 54% of university graduates across the OECD
- Among the general population of 25- to 34-year-olds, on average 33% of women have tertiary education, compared with 28% of men
- In Europe, women earn 59% of university diplomas and 61% of PhD degrees
- In the US in 2002–2003, women earned 58% of all bachelor's degrees and 59% of all master's degrees
- In the US, women earned 47% of doctorates in all fields, and 48% of 'first professional' degrees (e.g. dentistry, medicine, and law)

'Gender balance is not a fairness issue, but a strategic business issue and it is evolving rapidly. Since the beginning of the century, the pace of awareness has changed. Six or seven years ago, a very limited number of business leaders would have said that it is a business issue. And you would even have had women executives who'd have said it is not. Things are different now. ... One of the reasons for this is the change in the Talent pool: There is

*a growing majority of women graduates. In the Talent
wars, we need to attract the top people.'*

Olivier Marchal, MD, Bain (EMEA)[13]

In addition, a recent report from the Higher Education Policy
Institute in the UK shows that women are more likely to get
places in the top universities and, once there, go on to get better grades. They were also shown to outnumber men in high
status subjects, such as law and medicine. Women have been
entering university in greater numbers than men in recent
years – with the participation rate for young women standing
at 49%, compared with 38% of young men.[14]

The trend looks set to continue ever upwards as the OECD
predicts growth of women graduates to 2020 (see Table 4.1).[15]

Table 4.1 Tomorrow's talent (%age of women graduates)

Country	2005	2015	2020
Australia	56	62	62
Czech Republic	57	55	61
Denmark	59	66	68
France	56	65	66
Germany	53	65	61
Hungary	64	66	73
Italy	59	68	70
Japan	49	49	54
Korea	49	54	56
Poland	66	63	62
Sweden	63	74	76
Switzerland	43	49	48
Turkey	44	35	37
United Kingdom	58	72	72
United States	58	61	57

OECD (2008), 'The Reversal of Gender Inequalities in Higher Education: An
On-going Trend' in *Higher Education to 2030 – Volume 1 – Demography*.

Innovation

There is growing evidence that gender balanced teams are more innovative. A recent report from management consultants McKinsey & Co, for example, revealed female leadership strengths that are instrumental in driving effective, creative, and innovative organisations. They include building a collaborative team atmosphere in which everyone is encouraged to participate in decision making; presenting a compelling vision of the future and inspiring optimism about its implementation; defining expectations and responsibilities clearly and rewarding the achievement of reaching targets; and spending time teaching, mentoring, and listening to individual needs and concerns.[16]

A recent study from the London Business School underlined this point by showing that the optimal gender balance for teams driving innovation is 50:50.[17] The study found that neither men nor women flourished when they were in a minority on a team. When in a minority, women tended to network outside whereas men tended to be less motivated. Having a slight majority of women on teams (about 60%) improved the self-confidence of the team.

Male team leaders were more likely to work 'significantly' longer hours than their female counterparts. As a result they were more likely to suffer from exhaustion. The report said it was 'crucial' that companies 'urgently consider' ways to combat the long hours culture. At the same time, women team leaders were six times more likely than men to perform the domestic labour duties at home. In all, 96% of the male team leaders who responded had children, against 48% of the female team leaders.

Reputation

Finally, a less obvious outcome for companies with a good gender balance is that they enhance their reputation with a wide range of stakeholders, from employees to potential recruits to investors. Conversely, companies dominated by all male leadership and management teams are increasingly likely to look outdated as well as less efficient and creative. And such companies will find it ever more difficult to attract and retain good female Talent.

Creating commitment at the top

Presenting to the Executive Committee

Since it is hard to get time on this team's agenda, cover as much ground as possible when getting the leaders together.

In some companies, getting a full day is impossible, in which case the different topics noted below get spread over several meetings. The advantage of this approach is that it gives the ideas time to mature and each individual has more time to digest a complex topic. The disadvantage is that it takes more time, and has slightly less impact when delivered in small doses spread over several months.

The CEO's role

The CEO plays a crucial role in this session. He or she needs to be carefully briefed to lead, on a subject where the CEO may not be entirely comfortable. A couple of hours of advance preparation with the gender expert facilitating the session will help to define the roles, objectives, and pacing of the session.

Awareness Session for the top team: The three key objectives

Objective No. 1: Find out who cares (and who doesn't)
CEOs often assume their senior teams are aligned on the importance of gender balance. However, the truth is that they have usually not debated the issue as a team and do not know what they think individually.

Objective No. 2: Understand the data
It is a good idea to show the executive team some key data relating to the external Talent pool, customer profiles, demographic pressures, and differentiated academic achievements by gender, coupled with relevant internal data on recruitment, development, and retention. The latter usually reveals that there is 'gender asbestos' (where women are leaving the company at a relatively low grade level) rather than a glass ceiling. Some education on the research on gender differences and their impact on both the customer and managerial experience helps executives to look behind the numbers to understand what is actually going on – and what can be done about it.

Objective No. 3: Make a plan
The day's discussions are followed by the crafting of an action plan and a decision about who might lead the initiative. It is wise to consider appointing a man to the job to ensure it is seen as a change management exercise of relevance to everyone.

Also, it is important for the CEO to lead the session 'from behind'.

In the interest of getting a real debate, and to encourage team members to express their real positions, the CEO should introduce the session by stating that objective. Many of the leaders who launch these initiatives are personally committed to the subject (and usually have a reputation for being so), and it is important that they avoid imposing a top down view on their team. The CEO needs to generate a robust and honest debate on the issue and the business case, from which the whole team can decide whether or not it is a strategic priority for the company.

One of the key objectives of this session is to align the team around the topic, while encouraging open discussion, including disagreements. The CEO will learn more about colleagues' positions and commitment on the issue if he or she spends plenty of time listening to the various arguments put forward.

The CEO's leadership in concluding the session will help to lay the basis for the success of the programme. The strength and conviction with which the topic is led from the top define its outcome. But that can wait until the end of the session, after the topic has been debated and the action plan defined.

Competitive advantage

Companies that pull ahead on gender will create a virtuous circle of loyal customers, top Talent, and excellent leadership teams, giving them first mover advantage. Enlightened leaders are convinced that better gender balance will release new organisational capabilities and open up new markets or deepen penetration into existing ones.

Still, some executives need more convincing. For them, there is a steadily growing body of research and opinion which supports the view that gender balance means better performance and more profitability in the long-term. Some of this is listed below. It is helpful to make sure that this kind of research is made available or is referred to during the debate on the business case. The leadership team will want proof, and you will want to have it on hand.

The proof: Leadership, Talent, and Markets

Leadership

The relationship between gender balance and corporate performance continues to be supported by the latest research. Below is a list of some of the research showing a link between gender balance and business performance.

Catalyst Research[18]

Fortune 500 companies with three or more women on the board gain a significant performance advantage over those with the fewest:

- + 73% return on sales
- + 83% return on equity
- + 112% return on invested capital.

Women Matter

- A McKinsey study of 101 companies[19] showed that those with three or more women in senior management scored higher, on average, for each organisational criterion[20] than companies with no women at the top.
- Corporate performance increased 'significantly' upon attaining critical mass (at least three women on management committees with an average membership of ten people).
- Another McKinsey study of 89 listed European companies showed that there is likely to be a correlation between the number of women in leadership and good financial performance:
  - 11.4% return on equity compared with an average of 10.3%
  - EBIT operating result of 11.1% against an average of 5.8%
  - Stock price growth of 64% against the average of 47% over the period 2005–2007.

Women Matter 2

A later McKinsey study, known as Women Matter 2,[21] produced in 2008, established five leadership behaviours where women performed better than men:

1. **Participative decision making:** Building a team atmosphere in which everyone is encouraged to participate in decision making.
2. **Role model:** Being a role model, focusing on building respect and considering the ethical consequences of decisions.

3. **Inspiration:** Presenting a compelling vision of the future and inspiring optimism about its implementation.
4. **Expectations and rewards:** Defining expectations and responsibilities clearly and rewarding achievement of targets.
5. **People development:** Spending time teaching, mentoring, and listening to individual needs and concerns.

Pepperdine Study[22]

A long-term study by marketing professors Roy Adler and Ron Conlin from Pepperdine University in the US reported in 2009 that the 'companies identified as being the best at promoting women outperformed the industry median on all three profitability measures [sales, revenues, and assets]'.

Data were supplied by 200 Fortune 500 companies covering a 22-year period. For 2001, the 25 best firms for promoting women outperformed the industry medians with:

- Overall profits 34% higher when calculated for revenue.
- 18% higher in terms of assets.
- 69% higher in regard to equity.

In 2008, Adler and Conlin examined a different list, the '100 Most Desirable MBA Employers' for women reported by *Fortune* magazine, and got similar results. For instance, in regard to profits as a percentage of equity, 59% of the companies listed ranked higher than the median performance of Fortune 500 companies in the same industries.

French companies with women at the top weathered the storm better

In 2008, research from Professor Michel Ferrary of Ceram Business School on companies from the French CAC 40 stock exchange index showed that the more women there were in a company's management, the less the share price fell in 2008, the crux year of the global financial crisis. The only large French company to record a share price gain in 2008 was Hermès – whose management was 55% women, the second largest share among French blue chips.[23]

Women improve oversight

Research from Professors Renée Adams of the University of Queensland and Daniel Ferreira of the London School of Economics,[24] based on data from S&P 1500 firms, showed that:

- Women are less likely to have attendance problems at board meetings than men.
- The greater the proportion of women on the board, the better the attendance behaviour of male directors.
- Holding other director characteristics constant, female directors are more likely to sit on monitoring-related committees, such as audit, nominating, and governance, than male directors.
- More diverse boards were more likely to hold CEOs accountable for poor stock price performance.
- Directors in gender balanced boards received relatively more equity-based compensation.

Taken together, these results suggest that gender balanced boards are tougher monitors.

More women in top management improves performance

Research from Cristian Dezsö of the University of Maryland and David Gaddis Ross of Columbia University, employing data on the largest 1500 public US companies from 1992 to 2006[25], found that companies with one or more women in top management 'just below' the CEO level performed better than other companies.

Women-led companies in India perform better

Nine Indian companies run by the most prominent women managers outperformed the 30 leading listed firms on the Bombay Stock Exchange (BSE), according to a SundayET study, in year on year growth rates.[26]

Over the five years through 2008, the nine companies averaged a compounded annual growth rate of around 35% in pretax income; the BSE-30 firms' CAGR was 21%. Profit grew by about 56% in that period, including a 64% rise in the last three years for the companies run by women.

Similar outperformance has been recorded in other emerging economies such as Vietnam.

Talent

At the end of 2008, in the midst of the biggest financial crisis since the 1930s, 17 leading UK businessmen, including the chairs of Anglo American, BP, and Tesco, called for faster progress in appointing women to senior positions, saying the economy needed the best Talent more than ever. They equated the urgency of the issue to that of climate change and poverty.

We are living through extraordinary times, and extraordinary times call for innovative solutions. We are convinced it is essential to accelerate the progress of women into senior positions, given the UK's need to deploy the best Talent available. This need is greater than ever in the current economic climate.[27]

As the world economy pulls out of the financial crisis of 2008–2009, businesses will once again face Talent shortages in key areas, and will be poorly placed to compete if they fail to tap into the ever increasing majority of Talent: women.

Feike Sijbesma, Chairman of the Managing Board of Dutch-founded life and materials sciences company Royal DSM, agrees fully with this view. He is driving a major diversity programme at the company with the aim of increasing the proportion of women and non-Dutch nationals in senior leadership positions. In large part, the rationale of the programme is to increase innovation by having a more diverse set of mindsets and behaviours.

The company's strategy is fully focused on providing new solutions to key global issues such as the need for alternative energy sources, addressing climate change, and providing food and health for all. People with the same views and perspectives won't come up with such solutions, says Sijbesma. He believes, therefore, that the company needs a diverse set of people to combat this myopia. In other words: DSM's focus on diversity is driven by a clear business need. Sijbesma recalls: 'We conducted some research several years ago looking into which types of diversity most effectively created an impact and we found that gender balance and national balance drove diversity the most in terms of behaviour and mindsets. Research showed that these two elements of diversity were the most significant in driving the change that we wanted to achieve, so we decided to focus (first) on these two and not on other areas of diversity such as age, religion, and ethnic background.'

 ## Stressing the *why*

At Dutch-originated life and materials sciences company Royal DSM, the diversity programme is centred on gender balance and nationality diversity, underpinned by a clear business case. It is connected to the company's goal to drive future innovation within the company. (See Chapter 7 for more.) 'It's very important to keep linking the reason why you wanted gender balance in the first place, which, in our case, is linked to our innovation strategy. If you don't do that, the initiative can easily get derailed,' says Chairman Feike Sijbesma. Royal DSM's diversity programme forms an integral part of the cultural change programme the company is going through. The company wants to further adjust its culture to the business (portfolio) changes made in the last decade. Sijbesma stresses again and again how important it is to make it crystal clear to all the staff *why* change is needed, *what* needs to be changed, and by *whom*. He indicates that if these three aspects are clear, the organisation and its management can relatively easily fill in the *how* itself. 'The risk is to go too fast to the *how*', he says.[29]

But it is also about Talent, as Sijbesma explains: 'I also link our gender (and nationality) balance initiative to the need to get the best of the available Talent in the world. Today, we are in a period of economic crisis, but baby boomers are phasing out and (in the long-term) we will have a shortage of labour in the world – I'm convinced about that. In that case, it would be pretty foolish to forget half of the world's population being women or 99% of the world population being non-Dutch.'[28]

In 2007, a McKinsey study predicted that Europe would face a shortfall of 24 million people in the most highly qualified jobs by 2040 if the employment rate for women remained constant. This figure drops to 3 million if the rate of employment of women were to rise to the same level as men's.[30]

Markets

Companies are generally failing to tap into the growing influence women have as consumers. Women are making the majority of purchasing decisions. In the US, for example, they make 80% of the purchasing decisions in hardware retailers and healthcare. In the UK, they constitute 63% of online shoppers.[31] Many small marketing agencies have sprung up – usually run by enterprising women – to help companies (usually run by men) market and brand their products and services more effectively to women consumers. Those companies that avail themselves reap the benefits of higher sales for little extra cost. It is a 'blue ocean' waiting to be discovered.

Leaders become more engaged in the issue when they understand the very powerful business case for driving gender balance in their organisation. This might be related to Leadership,

Table 4.2 Relevance of Leadership, Talent, and Markets

Why Leadership	Why Talent	Why Markets
• 73% greater return on sales • Significant improvement in corporate performance • Overall profits 34% higher • Better oversight	• 59% of EU graduates • 72% of UK graduates in 2015 • 76% of Swedish graduates in 2020 • Since 2000, women have filled six million of the EU's eight million new jobs • In January 2010, women made up the majority of US payrolls[32]	• Women's purchasing power = $20 trillion per year • Women's total annual earnings = $13 trillion in 2009 • Women influence $4.3 trillion of $5.9 trillion US consumer outlays

Talent, Markets, or all three (see Table 4.2). But a deeper understanding of the issue will make them aware of the way it can open up new revenue streams and new businesses, and create a much more sustainable positioning to take full advantage of the rising significance of women as Talent and consumers. Once the Executive Committee has discovered the topic, newly cast in an economic and strategic light, the Number One action plan item in my experience is the recommendation that similar Awareness Sessions be rolled out to their direct reports and to the entire leadership group. With the example of the top executives, the next tier down will understand, often for the first time, that no implementation of any of these issues will be possible without a shared understanding of the business case, and the compelling reasons for change.

Checklist

☐ *Have you prepared a powerful summary presentation of the Audit data for the Executive Committee?*

☐ *Have you won commitment from the CEO to book a day in the Executive Committee agenda?*

☐ *Have you found an external gender expert to assist in facilitating the debate, which will combine the internal review with a debate on the business case for your company?*

☐ *Have you prepared the CEO for the session, by ensuring that he or she understands the objectives of the session?*

☐ *Have you got the team to debate and design the company's own business case on gender?*

☐ *Have you ensured that the session ends with an action plan, with a designated person to lead it?*

Chapter 5

LEADING GENDER BILINGUAL

'What the research showed was that ... they were actually deselecting us.'

Rachel Campbell, Global Head of People,
Performance and Culture, KPMG

Once the members of the Executive Committee have become convinced of the need for action, it is time to roll out the Awareness Phase to their senior teams. This next phase will be easier because the Executive Committee went first. The topmost leaders now act as role models for the senior teams and the rest of the organisation, showing that they believe in a clear business case for gender balance, and that they are acting on this recognition. They can then credibly lead others to do the same. Other managers will be reassured by the fact that the Executive Committee is practising what it preaches.

Running gender bilingual leadership sessions for all the heads of business units, divisions, and country operations will allow the organisation's key leaders to become convinced *and* convincing about the company's business case on gender. This often involves from 100 to 300 people for large multinationals.

Those executives need to understand the main ways gender differences make an impact on the workplace culture and on customer experiences. If they do not make the effort to understand this, it is very hard to ask their managers to do so.

These Awareness Sessions need to be run by a credible and convincing expert who is comfortable debating the strategic business implications of gender balance at a senior level. The person will need to be able to respond objectively to all the different questions and arguments in a calm, non-defensive tone. Therefore, the facilitator should not be linked too closely to the end results. Using someone directly and internally invested in the programme could make it look like a lobbying effort.

Building buy-in

Frame the Awareness Sessions for the senior leaders like the Executive Committee meeting: as an open debate to define the business case and craft an action plan, if relevant. It helps if gender balance is not perceived, at this stage, as another rule coming down from the top with little apparent relation to business needs.

Having the sessions re-analyse fully the merits of the business case lets leaders fully engage, debate, disagree, and then align around the importance of gender balance for their business. Each session can then contribute to the formulation of the business case and the action plan, fuelling and reinforcing the arguments and plans that the Executive Committee made for gender balance.

The facilitator should be present at each of these sessions to gather the ideas, synthesise the debates, and start collecting the action points. At the end of the series of workshops, the action plan can be finalised, based on the input of all the organisation's leaders. This ensures that they are familiar with the reasons for the actions, and feel that they have contributed to the framing of them. It is of fundamental importance to get key organisational leaders (usually mostly men) to the point where they understand and believe in the benefits of implementing the final action plan in their own areas and teams. This approach may seem heavy-handed or slow to companies impatient for progress, and convinced that their leaders have heard it all before. But in my experience, moving forward before you have senior management buy-in is the main reason why progress is poor or even non-existent at most companies – not the usual suspects like reluctance, fear, stereotyping or willful resistance.[1] Gender balance does not work if leaders don't want it, and don't see why they should.

When the subject of balance is accurately framed, led from the top, and the top team is made accountable for the remedy as well as the result, both men and women in countries around the world readily and enthusiastically embrace the challenge. They see it as a major 21st century opportunity for business and a transformational lever in most existing corporate change efforts.

Senior executives often believe that they are very progressive on gender issues because they have committed to equality and fairness. But they have little understanding of what is going on beneath the surface. A Country Managing Director introduced a Leadership workshop I facilitated by asking his largely male team: 'How many of you would claim to understand women?' They laughed, but admitted that not one of them would dare venture such a claim.

When you deliver the research, reasoning, and data that help leaders understand how to better manage half their workforce, and how to better reach half their customers, the reaction is a mixture of amazement, relief, and disbelief. A typical response from one manager was: 'I thought I knew exactly how to manage across genders: by ignoring differences and treating everyone the same. I've learnt that this is not effective. This really opened my eyes, and there were some amazing insights.'

Designing, preparing, and running the session

An effective workshop must start with the hard facts, move into the subtleties of gender differences, and finish with action plans

 Outline for a gender balance workshop

The key themes of the Awareness Session are to cover the business case for gender balance for the company (the *Why*), the history and explanation of the company's approach and results so far (the *What*), and the best way to design and implement effective change (the *How*). These three themes should be clearly structured, relatively balanced in terms of time and attention, and each should make room for debate among the group, with clear outputs and exercises at each phase.

While this kind of workshop for senior leaders can be run in anything from four hours to several days, the minimum for sufficient impact is six hours. More time and space for interactive group discussion will generate more commitment and buy-in. Also, the amount of time reserved tells participants how seriously the company and its Executive Committee are taking the subject. Allow for a full day's session if the aim is to come out with a robust action plan.

1. Why gender?

- **Business case:** A macroeconomic view of the profit and loss and other business reasons for gender balance.
- **Where we stand:** The results of the Audit Phase, detailing the current situation at the company.

2. What differences?

- **What is going on?** Explanation of the gender differences that underlie the statistics.
- **Becoming bilingual:** Introduction of tools and tips for managers to create a better balance and manage across genders (see Chapter 6).

3. How to balance?

- **How we can advance:** An overview of recommended implementation steps, with some benchmarks from other companies including competitors, focusing on best practice.
- **What we will do:** Decision on the objectives, priority actions, and next steps for the company to take in the coming year.

and deliverables. Top teams are familiar with this format and pace, and it helps to handle gender balance in the same way as any other subject. These sessions also have other objectives: to find out who cares, to become familiar with the relevant internal and external reality and opportunities, to build awareness about gender among male dominated leadership teams, and to get commitment on an action plan. Below I outline some of the steps in designing the content, organising the session, and facilitating it.

Who invites, and what to call it

The Leadership Session invitation is often the first time the company has 'gone public' internally on gender balance. How the session is framed, what it is called, and who invites whom are key determinants of its success. Ideally, the CEO sends the invitations. The leader in any key market, where he or she might later be running gender balance sessions, should echo invitations sent to his or her team members. Avoid invitations

 What the CEO needs to say in the invitation – 21st century leadership

Outline the factors that have made the organisation a success, such as the ability to transform itself. Note how bringing in new ideas and perspectives is a key lever for dealing with changing Markets and/or stakeholders and/or Talent.

Challenges and opportunities

Outline the challenges facing the company, such as needing to adjust quickly to an ever changing environment, managing complexity, customer centricity, being solutions driven rather than technology driven, or dealing with ambiguity, globalisation, and heterogeneity.

Set the business case for gender balance with such facts as how women make up the majority of customers and Talent and how women are a fast growing proportion of shareholders.

The company's future

Describe what the leadership has set in motion to transform the culture, like creating a flatter hierarchy and a more networked, collaborative culture. State the type of organisational qualities the company hopes to develop, such as flexibility, customer focus, and a high performance culture.

Describe the success factors, including anticipating the needs of consumers, employee engagement, and achieving sustainable performance.

Conclusion

State that the Executive Committee wants the leadership to review its competitive positioning across businesses and markets to decide whether or not specific actions are required. Invite participants into a debate on strategy and solutions.

signed by HR, Diversity or a women's association. That would limit and label participants' view of the session before they even enter the room.

The invitation should introduce gender balance as a strategic lever for achieving other 21st century change initiatives.

Be careful not to describe the exercise in ways that could encourage defensive and mocking responses from the more sceptical men and women. For example, companies often unthinkingly launch what they call 'Gender Training' sessions, generating endless jokes before the first session starts. Instead, describe the session as a strategic debate, not as a training or awareness workshop. The invitation must start the communications campaign on gender balance, with the key messages, vocabulary, and positioning of the effort. That way, it will control how the issue is perceived and what responses it prompts.

Leveraging group dynamics

These sessions need to be highly interactive, energising, and eye opening. The style is as important as the substance. Getting the group to work together with a different tone can illustrate some of the benefits of new approaches and new thinking, wrapped up under a gender label. Most of the learning happens experientially, among the group, by executives watching, listening, and debating with their colleagues on a subject that is relatively far from their usual conversations. Interactivity is key. Break the team up into smaller groups to debate among themselves and then present back publicly to the full group. The underlying goal is to shift the usual dynamics of the group, by getting participants to debate a new subject in an open way. Frequently, companies introduce me in a boardroom, with a large, immovable, U-shaped table dominating the room. This creates a formal atmosphere where it is hard to get people to talk freely. Instead, organise the meeting using small round tables for groups of three to five people each, depending on the size of the group. Shift the hierarchies, mix the messengers, and get a variety of people to talk who would not normally choose to come together. The facilitator should change these groups throughout the meeting, to maximise debate among colleagues to keep people, information, and ideas moving. Appointing someone unexpected as the rapporteur of each group is a good technique to measure how comfortable each team member is in understanding and presenting on the issue. In implementing the programme, it will be essential that the company's leaders be both convinced and convincing about gender balance. This session allows the leaders to evaluate their colleagues on this subject.

To find out what each executive really thinks about gender balance, the facilitator can start by asking participants to rank anonymously on a Post-It note the priority level they would give the issue as a business imperative for the next five years. Use a scale of 1–10, with 1 being highly strategic and 10 being irrelevant. When the numbers are read out, they rarely align across the group. In the first 60 seconds of the session the facilitator will have revealed – visibly and unarguably – why the company has not made much progress on gender over the years. It's because its leaders do not agree that it should.

Next, show the executives the statistics, starting with the external ones: the reality of a shifting Talent pool, customer profiles, and demographic pressures. The Audit data usually reveal a shift in the ratio of women and men among customers, end users, and other stakeholders even as the proportion of women among senior managers is at best static. This leads the senior leaders to address the implications for the business – today and tomorrow.

SWOT exercise
Improving a company's gender balance

Strengths
What are the strengths we currently have that would facilitate improving the gender balance?

Weaknesses
What existing realities would make improving gender balance more difficult?

Opportunities
What business benefits, if any, can we expect if we become more gender balanced?

Threats
What are the risks, if any, in becoming more gender balanced?

A simple SWOT analysis focuses the debate on the business opportunities that lie beneath the gender balance issue. By analysing the strengths, weaknesses, opportunities, and threats that the company faces in improving, the executives start to see the issue in a sharper light. Applying this very familiar tool to gender balance will reinforce that the issue is a strategic one requiring the same sort of approach and analysis as any other business topic. The exercise will make it eminently clear who sees gender as a critical business case and who doesn't, and how relevant their arguments are.

If some teams or individuals are struggling, that may tell the company it needs more awareness and education before implementation becomes viable. They may require some additional follow-up or coaching, or may require sessions and data more tailored to their cultures or businesses. Finally, some form of action planning ends the session. The group must list the priorities the company should focus on in one-year and three-year horizons. This gets the leadership team to define the orientation of the programme. Usually, at this point, a top recommendation is that similar sessions be rolled out to all managers or even all employees. Because their eyes have been opened to the multiple facets of gender balance, the senior leaders know that such sessions are the foundation on which implementation will depend.

Structuring the session in this way leads almost automatically to the desired objectives. The senior executives construct the business case themselves, becoming convinced by their own analyses and data. They get new tools and research about gender differences to see afresh their company's culture and approaches to Markets and Talent, and to identify what needs to be changed. Then they construct the plan and the priorities themselves, guaranteeing buy-in as they implement these actions in their own divisions and teams.

Consciously or unconsciously competent?

Microsoft (APAC) used a simple methodology to discuss gender balance with its senior leadership team. Participants had to self-evaluate their own awareness of the gender balance issue in the workplace. The placed themselves in one of four categories:

- unconsciously incompetent,
- consciously incompetent,
- consciously competent, or
- unconsciously competent.

'In terms of the focused work we have been doing with our leadership team we have used the "Unconsciously Incompetent to Unconsciously Competent" format as a background model to "track" our progress as an APAC Leadership Team,' says Stephanie Nash, Senior HR Director at Microsoft. To determine the executives' levels, the Asia-Pacific branch of the software giant ran workshops, each about three hours long and each focused on one of the company's three pillars of Diversity & Inclusion:

- Representation
- Inclusion
- Market Innovation.

Nash's boss, Emilio Umeoka, President of Microsoft (APAC), wanted to get a clear understanding of the competency level of his APAC Board. Exit interviews told Umeoka that work–life balance was an issue for many women (something confirmed by

external interviews). In addition, the women leaving the firm referred to the importance of female role models and commented
on the cultural norms.

Umeoka made sure that his culturally diverse senior leadership
team went through this process. 'Out of 30 people, we are from
16 countries and can speak 40 languages.' Overall the team was
very competent. After the discussions about their own attitudes,
members of the group addressed what to do next.

'The women wanted to really build the business case and to
engage the next level of leaders. They wanted their next level of
leadership to do the same self-assessment and then follow this
with their own discussions about what to do next. The women
pushed very hard that instead of specific targets to track progress,
we have a set of aspirational goals. The next level is to take this to
the People Management community at Microsoft (APAC), which
will spark self-assessments and discussions.'[2]

Handling the debate

People have very strong opinions about gender. And they often
believe that they know all they need to know. This received
wisdom is remarkably similar across different cultures and
companies. It is, therefore, doubly important for the leadership to challenge their own and others' preconceived notions,
and base their deliberations on the facts and analysis produced
during the Audit Phase. This will root the discussion in what

is actually happening in the organisation and focus it on what needs to take place to seize the business opportunity.

Challenging the received wisdom: Markets and Talent

Tease out people's assumptions about why the company, their region, and the sector lack a healthy gender balance and check them against the facts – the data and feedback from the Audit Phase. There are usually quite a number of surprises. Below are some common misconceptions I have come across covering Talent and Markets, with handy retorts to them.

Talent – misconceptions

'Our sector is male-dominated; women are not attracted to it.'

Ask if any attempt has been made to target women in recruitment campaigns, and review how well this has been done. Check if any competitor has more diverse recruitment statistics.

 ## Looking at the facts

The professional services firm KPMG started to audit its gender balance in 2005. It discovered that the proportion of its female managers dropped off steadily the higher up they went (see Fig. 5.1). At the bottom management layer (Grade C), the balance was 38% women to 62% men, while one step higher it plummeted to 24% women. At Grade A, just below partner, the proportion

---

of women dropped to 15%. Only 11% of the partners were female at this time, which is hardly surprising given the fallout rate in the Talent pipeline. The chairman of KPMG Europe, John Griffith-Jones, later said, 'If you want to be the best accounting firm in the world, you need to take [the best] people from the whole population.' So, it was imperative to solve the problem, which the company started to do.

Many of the leaders in the firm assumed that women were dropping off because of family pressures. When they looked at the research, they discovered something quite different. Rachel Campbell, then the Head of People, KPMG Europe[4], recalled: 'What the research showed was that they were not leaving to stay at home and have kids. They were going to equally demanding jobs in other industries or other organisations. So they were actually deselecting us.'[5]

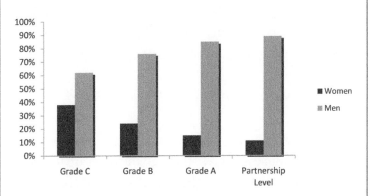

Fig. 5.1 KPMG gender balance management pipeline.

'There are no women engineers (or computer scientists, etc.) and we are a technical company.'

Check the university statistics. In Europe 25% of engineering, manufacturing, and construction degrees go to women, according to the latest EU figures based on the reference year 2006[3]. At the least, the company's statistics should reflect the population of graduating classes in the region. And does the company really want to recruit only engineers? For example, according to the same data, 41% of graduates in science, mathematics, and computing were also female.

'Women drop out because of children.'

Maternity is one of the biggest perceived obstacles cited by male managers. It is not the major obstacle cited by women – it is not even in the top five. Check the statistics and interviews on when and why women leave, compared with men. And go beyond the easy exit interview report, where women will often say (because it is easier) that they are leaving for family reasons. See how many of them actually ended up at another firm.

'Women bump into a glass ceiling at the top.'

In most companies, the glass ceiling is a misperception. People assume that women progress through the ranks up to a certain level – and then suddenly get blocked. The harder reality is that the percentage of women drops off at every grade level, almost from the first rung of the ladder, as KPMG discovered. I call this phenomenon 'gender asbestos', meaning that the problem is not a momentary, limited issue, but a perennial, widespread problem that needs to be removed from the corporate DNA.

Check where the percentages of women start to drop. Then ask why. Remember that only the right analysis creates the right solution.

Markets – misconceptions

'Women don't buy our products.'

That's what the hardware stores and carmakers said until they looked at the numbers and discovered that women had become the majority of their customers. What does the market segmentation say about the significance of gender? Has the organisation broken down the data by women and men? How has it evolved over recent years?

'We do target women; we have a whole line of products dedicated to them.'

Companies often underestimate the potential value of female consumers in their markets. They assume that they can capture this customer group by isolating women into specific product segments or categories. We have all seen pink products such as phones and computers. This is too narrow an approach to reaching a hugely diverse group. Check the gender analyses and audits. Do most women appreciate your 'pink' products? What is the Markets opportunity of rolling out some 'women friendly' ideas to all your clients? Is there more innovation potential in this topic? (See Chapter 10 for more detail.)

'We know women; we have been focused on them for decades.'

Check the facts when you hear this statement. Some companies that have marketed to women for many years have seemingly failed to update their definition and understanding of the word. Women are changing fast – has the company kept up? Again, look at the Audit results, and ask, Do women customers trust and adore the brand? If not, more progressive approaches may be needed.

Leading change

Leaders have a particularly crucial role to play in implementing change initiatives around topics like gender balance. They have to be able to understand the topic, and act as a role model

 Femme Den designs what women want

The US marketing agency Smart Design's radical unit Femme Den[6] brings new value to its clients by designing products for women. Femme Den emerged in 2005 after an all male marketing team at Nike had trouble selling a range of watches to women. Two female designers from Smart Design discovered that the target market was begrudgingly opting for clunky men's watches because they wanted that line's more athletic features. (Armed with this information, Nike produced a sporty, aesthetic range aimed at women.) Agency co-founder Dan Formosa, who is known as 'Femme Dan', pushed the new unit, knowing that women's needs and wants are different from men's. 'If you talk about the differences between men and women at a corporate human resources meeting, you'd be fired or sent to diversity training. But when we cover the same ground with large corporations, the discussion just lights up.'[7]

Yvonne Lin, one of the Femme Den women, explains: 'Men will walk into an electronics shop and look at the white cards that list the features. Women will pick up the cameras, flip them around, and look at the buttons. They want to know: "Is it intuitive?"'

At the Consumers Electronics Show in 2006, only 1% of women surveyed felt that gadget makers kept them in mind during the design process.[8]

Products designed for women as a result of Femme Den's work include:

- A more intuitive camcorder from Pure Digital Technologies which put ease of use at the top of its design agenda. The Flip camera, with just seven buttons, sold 1.5 million units in its first 18 months.
- Pyrex bowls with built in spoon and lid rests from World Kitchen designed for quick clean ups.
- Scrub suits designed for women, who make up 70% of the healthcare population but had had to put up with scrubs made for men. The Cardinal Health outfits have V neck instead of stretch collars, and kimono sleeves to increase range of motion. They have straps and snaps for adjusting the hem and rise, as well as breathable mesh at the back and knees.

to their teams, with the appropriate language and behaviours. This is harder than it may seem. Self-awareness and gender bilingualism are prerequisites.

BC Hydro's former CEO, Bob Elton, gender balanced his entire leadership team (see Chapter 4). Below are the rejoinders he learned to offer, with a gentle sense of humour and an even handed familiarity, to issues raised by sceptics of both genders.

 Bob Elton, British Columbia Hydro, responds to sceptics[9]

'Are you saying we're not going to hire the best person?'
'We will focus on hiring the best teams. I never said you have to hire a woman. You just have to evolve towards a gender balanced team.'

'No women apply.'
'We all know that by now. Men who aren't qualified will apply and women who are won't. So let's find out who should apply and encourage them to do so.'

'Not this role: There is 80% travel, and a woman can't do that.'
'Why is there 80% travel? Is it really necessary? Are there other ways of designing and doing this job?'

'No quotas?'
'We use aspirational targets, not quotas.'

'Women lack technical backgrounds – there aren't enough female engineers.'

'How much of the role is actually technical? That may be absolutely required for a line manager in a remote area. But elsewhere, do you really have to understand the work itself, or do you have to understand the people doing the work, and how to manage them? I put a woman in charge of our modelling engineer team – a bunch of hugely brilliant people. Nobody understands what they do. But she understands how smart people need to be led, and enables their brilliance to shine.'

'We women don't want to be hired simply because we are women.'

'If I think about this too much, we get tied up in knots. Men *never* have this concern. It would never even cross their minds. And you only get this reaction for the first two or three senior women appointed. By the time you have five or six in any group, these comments disappear.'

'Men feel left out.'

'There are still many roles for men. The bigger challenge is for guys who expected to be promoted. How do you manage unrealistic expectations?'

'What about flexibility?'

'If you believe, as I do, that there is a Talent shortage, the question is, "How can I keep people?" And you make the necessary adjustments.'

'*It's not gender but diversity of thought that is important.*'
'The fact that you are all white 50-year-old men does not preclude diversity of thought – but it certainly makes it less likely.'

'*Women need more time off.*'
'Women are more likely to tell you what's going on, especially in terms of personal issues. Then they are very good at figuring out how to deal with it. And we all need to be able to do that. Here, we could really learn from each other.'

'*What about company culture?*'
'Yes, it definitely changes when the gender balance changes. The conversations about work are different. And there is a lot more talk about values.'

'*Will it last?*'
'I don't know. The people on [the] organisational chart, how will they be doing in a decade? For the women on the chart, they may go on to be leaders of boards and non-profits. For the men, I think they will remember having learnt something about 21st century teams.'

Be the change you want to see

Most of today's leaders, around the globe, have not been raised and educated in a context of gender balance. There are many good intentions, which are sometimes unfortunately harmed by misjudgments around implementation or communication. Male leaders need to challenge their own assumptions and be willing to learn afresh. They should be curious and take the time to learn the language and culture of women, examining how it differs from that of men. Women leaders, who have risen in male dominated companies, also need to challenge some of the assumptions they have taken on board. A few tips to keep in mind when leading a gender initiative:

- **Be courageous**: It takes personal courage to lead change programmes. They involve delicate issues that demand strong, consistent, and resolute leadership. Don't compromise. Make the principles clear, and then stick to them – visibly, and vocally.
- **Be convinced and convincing**: If you don't really believe in gender balance, take the time to be convinced. If you don't believe, no one else will. Without that conviction, it is better not to spend time and company resources on the effort.
- **Watch the vocabulary**: Become conscious of using military and sports metaphors that are a constant in today's business world. They do not have the same impact on women as they may have on (some) men. A recent advertisement, for example, in *The Economist* magazine for a two-day management programme at the University of Cambridge's Judge Business School opened with the following quote from the 17th century poet George Herbert: 'Skill and confidence are an unconquered army.'[10]
- **Become a minority**: Male leaders can understand what being a minority feels like by having lunch or meeting with a group of women, or speaking at a women's conference. Most women leaders have this experience every day. Many men are astonished to discover what it feels like. Listen for the different tone and culture that these meetings

may have. And watch for how hard or easy it is to connect. Self-awareness is an important building block of gender bilingualism. Senior women can also organise this sort of meeting with younger women to watch for generational differences and to be accessible as potential role models.

- **Check your track record**: Are you promoting women who are as similar as possible to men? Are you valuing and welcoming different leadership and management styles from female staff? Are you assuming that men and women are equal and the same? Do you believe that this is the definition of being progressive?

 ## Where to go to understand women better

- Women's Conferences:
  - **Forbes** – *Forbes* magazine holds an annual conference for women executives, usually in the US.
  - **Fortune** – the publisher of *Fortune* Magazine runs a two-day summit linked to its Most Powerful Women survey, usually in the US.
  - **Forum for the Economy & Society** – annual three-day conferences held in Deauville, France, usually in October, and in Beijing in May. They aim to bring together leading women from public and private organisations to discuss 'building the future with women's vision'. Male leaders are welcome contributors to the debate, but are definitely the minority. More information: www.womens-forum.com

---

- ○ **WIN** Conference – Women's International Networking runs an annual three-day global conference for women in business aimed in part at middle management and younger women. It includes a half-day corporate session on best practices. More information: www.winconference.net
- ○ **Women Mean Business** – a new women's conference in India, launched by the Cherie Blair Foundation for Women. More information: www.cherieblairfoundation.org
- ○ **Business Schools** – watch for annual conferences run by Women MBA Associations at business schools that draw women students and alumnae.
- ○ **Awards** – plenty of bodies such as the US organisation Catalyst and the UK group Opportunity Now hold meetings and conferences to encourage women friendly organisations. More information: www.catalyst.org and www.opportunitynow.org.uk
- • Professional Women's Associations such as:
  - ○ Europe: the European Professional Women's Network, www.europeanpwn.net
  - ○ US: Catalyst Women, www.CatalystWomen.org; National Association of Female Executives, www.NAFE.com; and the National Organization for Women, www.NOW.org
  - ○ Japan: Global Enhancement of Women's Executive Leadership, www.GEWEL.org
  - ○ Your company's internal women's network (formal or informal).

Global gender contexts

National culture plays a significant role in the gender issue (though the reality of corporate gender issues relating to both Talent and Markets is remarkably consistent across countries).

So it is important to integrate the cultural dimensions from the start and be sensitive to the cultural reality in which a business is operating. The top down approach suggested here allows the leadership team in each division and each country to discuss both the global framework and principles of the approach, while localising the key drivers in a particular business or country, and crafting a culturally relevant approach.

But businesses should be aware that culture is often used as an excuse for inaction. A multitude of cultural barriers will be raised in many industries and in many geographies. Nonetheless, companies have improved their gender balance even in some of the more challenging areas. Such areas often provide some unexpected and unexplored opportunities.

Variations across the globe[11]

United States – The United States is often considered (mostly by itself) as more advanced on the issue than it actually is on a global scale. With very little public policy, gender is an issue sometimes more driven by legal precedent and stringent compliance issues than by business strategy. The subject has been pushed by individual private sector initiatives, with some of the most progressive companies achieving some of the best global results with very proactive internal policies. However, it is a cultural approach that mostly allows women to succeed if they conform to the masculine culture shaped by decades of business life, often forgoing family completely, or simply reversing traditional gender roles. The US is one of only four countries in the world not to have legislated national, paid maternity leave. And despite several decades of extensive corporate efforts to bring gender balance to management, there is an unsustainable piece to the American puzzle: The majority of senior women in the corporate world in the US remain in staff jobs as opposed to operational roles.

Europe – Europe is a highly diverse region with some of the most advanced countries and policies (in France and the Nordic countries) and some of the most conservative (German speaking Europe). The difference in Europe comes from the public policy frameworks that recognise and facilitate the 21st century reality of dual income families. This includes tax systems, public daycare, school hours, and policies on household employees. The former Communist countries of Eastern Europe keep the legacy of a gender egalitarian ideology, with a highly educated and experienced female labour force much appreciated by international companies. Norway has introduced quotas of 40% at corporate board level, and Sweden and more recently Germany have replaced maternity leave with parental leave that can be taken by either parent, with fathers required to take a minimum of three months or that part of the leave is forfeited.

Asia – Asia is even more split than Europe, with some of the most gender balanced countries in the world (the Philippines, China) and some of the most conservative (Japan, South Korea). The Philippines is practically at parity in management ranks, while fewer than 10% of managers in Japan and South Korea are women. In the conservative North of Asia, women are still expected to leave the workforce once they are married. This may explain why relatively few young Japanese women choose to marry, and birth rates in these countries are among the lowest in the world. India remains a challenge, with a highly educated female workforce but strong cultural expectations for mothers to focus on their families over their careers. But this is set within a fast changing context, including very strong female leadership role models in both business and government.

Middle East – The Middle East is one of the more challenging regions of the world on gender issues, yet a region that is beginning to shift. In the United Arab Emirates, the government is pushing the topic proactively and 70% of university graduates are now women, followed by 60% in Iran and 60% in Tunisia.[12] It is different again in Israel where, for example, four in ten board seats in government owned companies are held by women.[13] Women in Israel are ahead of other nations in the region in terms of participation in the workforce. And just over 30% of legislators, senior officials, and managers are women, according to data from 2007.[14] Israel is ranked at 45 in the 2009 Global Gender Gap report from the World Economic Forum and was 31st in terms of the number of women participating in the labour force. Turkey was ranked near the bottom at 129 overall and at 125 for labour force participation, though a 2009 survey found 22.8% of 'top level administrative staff' of the leading 111 companies to be female.[15] Still, only 6% of the most senior executives in Turkey are female and only 24% of women are in the workforce.[16]

Latin America – Despite a strongly macho tradition in many Latin American countries, the education and competence of the female labour force is beginning to shift things. Colombia has the region's highest percentage of female managers and is among the leading nations by this measure in the world: 75% of management positions and 38% of top management positions are held by women[17]. In another study, Panama scores well, with women representing 43.6% of the legislators, senior officials, and managers.[18] Several countries have the benefit of more readily available household help and family support networks, so the major challenge in companies in this region remains traditional male mindsets. In Brazil, 83% of businesses have some women in senior roles and women make up 35% of legislators, senior officials, and managers.[19]

This global overview is simply a reminder that gender initiatives must take cultural realities into account. As several multinational companies have shown in countries like Japan and even Saudi Arabia, becoming proactive recruiters and promoters of female Talent offers a strong competitive edge, letting companies cherry pick the very best female Talent in challenging countries, while creating true meritocracies in more advanced countries that yield loyal staffs with above average corporate performance.

Once the full leadership population is well briefed and on board on gender as a strategic business lever, the momentum is enormous. The change will broaden corporate transformation into the 21st century.

Gender will move from a traditionally divisive and politically correct compliance issue to a powerfully motivating human force that benefits all employees, customers, and stakeholders – often for the very first time. Now it is time to roll out this energy to the broader management population, so that all managers can learn to work gender bilingually.

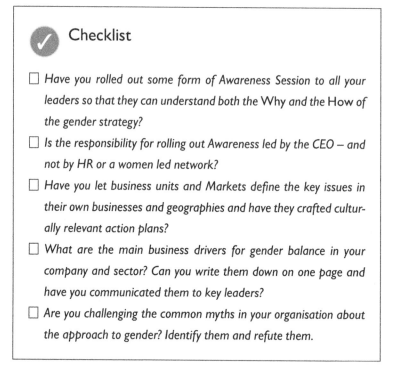

✓ Checklist

☐ Have you rolled out some form of Awareness Session to all your leaders so that they can understand both the Why and the How of the gender strategy?

☐ Is the responsibility for rolling out Awareness led by the CEO – and not by HR or a women led network?

☐ Have you let business units and Markets define the key issues in their own businesses and geographies and have they crafted culturally relevant action plans?

☐ What are the main business drivers for gender balance in your company and sector? Can you write them down on one page and have you communicated them to key leaders?

☐ Are you challenging the common myths in your organisation about the approach to gender? Identify them and refute them.

Chapter 6

WORKING GENDER BILINGUAL

'I now realise that we should work differently, that we should manage Talent differently.'

Jean-Marc Duvoisin, Deputy Executive Vice President, Human Resources and Centre Administration, Nestlé

Acknowledging (and celebrating) gender differences in the workplace is the first essential step to getting the best out of both men and women. Without going into a scientific treatise on gender differences, this chapter describes the ones most relevant for managers. There are a few key, career-related differences that hugely affect the gender balance statistics in most organisations. I am convinced that if these areas were better understood and handled, by both male and female managers, companies would be well on their way to a better and more sustainable balance between men and women.

What's the difference?

Peter Drucker, the 20th century's most eminent management guru, said, 'Knowledge workers, whatever their sex, are professionals, applying the same knowledge, doing the same work, governed by the same standards, and judged by the same results.'[1]

So we've largely educated everyone, especially managers, to believe that treating people equally means treating them exactly the same.

And that's the problem.

The need to comply with equal opportunities legislation may have contributed to the notion that the best way to promote equality is to treat women just like men. This is neither necessary nor helpful, although it may have been an unavoidable phase in the earlier stages of equalising basic rights and recognition before the law.

Today, companies can uphold their commitment and obligation to fair employment practices without having to act as if there are no differences between the sexes. It is time to recognise that men and women are different in ways that are full of opportunities for business, and that not recognising these differences can create unintended obstacles or misunderstandings that have a detrimental impact on customer responsiveness as well as management effectiveness (not to mention the careers of half of the Talent pool).

A host of recent research has illustrated some of the physiological, psychological, and especially neurological differences between the sexes. It is fascinating material, but I think managers would be sufficiently gender bilingual if they were aware of, and attentive to, the more career-related differences listed below.

The question as to whether men and women are really different is controversial, particularly in some cultures and countries (in others it is so obvious it does not need underlining). Many men, particularly the most progressive ones, would prefer considering every person as an individual human being. Many business leaders believe passionately in the power of meritocracy and are deeply committed to ensuring that women are managed exactly as men are, maintaining that as long as you offer men and women the same opportunities, they will flourish equally.

'I thought before that by treating [men and women] as the same we would make it possible for things to happen,' says Jean-Marc Duvoisin, Deputy Executive Vice President, Human Resources and Centre Administration, at Nestlé. 'But I now realise that we should work differently, that we should manage Talent differently, that we experience differences, and that we should manage Talent in a diverse way.'

Duvoisin knew about some of the differences but there were others that he learnt about during the company's gender balance journey. 'For example, there were weaknesses in the way women networked and there were issues relating to [a lack of] self-confidence. In general, women did not ask for higher positions and they did not argue aggressively on salary increases.'[2]

Damien O'Brien, CEO of head-hunting firm Egon Zehnder International, agrees that there are significant differences between men and women. 'A lot of the men we deal with are aggressive managers of their careers. Young guys will come into my office and they know what they want their résumés to look like in 10 years' time. They know which boxes they want to tick and they are seeking help on how to tick them. They proactively build their careers around those objectives. I have rarely met a woman who looks at her career that way.' Their interests are very different. 'Most of the women I deal with are more interested in the quality of their work experiences, the quality and richness of the challenges they face, and they're more interested in balance in their lives.'

Difference No. 1: Career cycles

Careers traditionally start when people are in their 20s, accelerate in their 30s, and peak in their 40s and 50s. Women don't necessarily fit this linear, unbroken career pattern. It was not designed with them in mind. It was built by men in the 20th century for men with stay at home wives. By and large, this design has not been revised since. Now that the majority of the educated Talent is female, companies are faced with the choice of adapting their systems – or losing their women.

The rhythms of women's lives – and those of modern men – are different from how the majority of 20th century male breadwinners lived. The difference is particularly obvious for women in families with children, not to mention the growing number of households headed by single parents. The complexity of managing parenthood and work simultaneously usually takes some time to learn. And that complexity arises at *precisely* the same time that most companies begin identifying their high potential Talent.

This is a classic example of an outdated policy in need of change. The age at which people are first identified as 'high potential' and selected for more focused leadership development is quite precise in most organisations – often, written human resource policies set it between 30 and 35 years old. Being 'fair', companies apply the policy to men and women in exactly the same way.

The approach certainly wasn't introduced to discriminate against women – it was created before there were many women in the workplace. Yet probably no other single policy has done more to eliminate generations of women from the leadership pipeline. The single worst period of a woman's life to be identified (or not) as high potential is the few years when she is typically having one or more children … and not usually sleeping through the night.

As young fathers become more involved with the early years of childrearing, this is increasingly affecting male careers as well. Parenthood is something that companies have been able to ignore for many decades. No longer.

Ambitious young women tend to marry later than they used to. They also tend to delay childbearing. Then they do both of these things, rather suddenly, usually somewhere in their early 30s. This reality – and its impact – differs from country to country, mostly depending on how much public or private sector infrastructure is available to help smooth out the demands of this period. Fig. 6.1 provides international comparisons. The graphic shows how the labour participation rates of women drop in different countries during the crucial 30s, and usually pick up again later. This 'M' curve, as it is known, is most

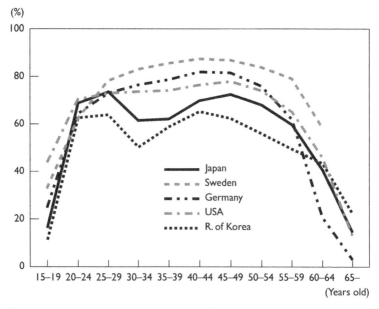

Fig. 6.1 International comparisons. Source: Gender Equality in Japan (2007), Gender Equality Bureau, Cabinet Office, Government of Japan.

pronounced in Japan and South Korea, and least felt in the most gender balanced countries like Sweden.

This makes the 30s a decade that is characterised by some of the most exciting and time-consuming moments of a woman's personal life. Unfortunately, it coincides exactly with the moment in corporate life when competition heats up at work and key Talent begins to be selected for development. Companies must recognise and adapt their career management cycles to women's different career patterns, particularly their management of the 30s. Otherwise, women will keep falling into this hole, many never to get back out, sidelined and squandered as 'mothers'.

Increasingly, ambitious young men find themselves married to ambitious young women. And, except for a handful of countries and cultures, they are increasingly involved in the early years of childrearing. This means that the career management timeframe that is not very relevant to 30-year-old women is increasingly problematic to *both* halves of a dual income couple. Most corporate cultures punish men even more than women if they dare ask for parental slack or flexibility, let alone time off. But unless companies want to rely on the minority of men who don't help at home (a dubious criterion for leadership potential), they will need to manage men and women in their 30s who have significant family responsibilities.

It is not just babies that affect women's careers. Generally, most male managers conclude that the reason women do not make it to the top is maternity or work–life balance issues. Most women disagree.

There is another issue that underlies the crucial 30s decade. Different skills are developed at each career phase, and companies seek the emergence of new skill sets at different ages and career phases. These shifts in expectations are not equally apparent to everyone.

Career cycles: The company's perspective
20s: The doer

In their 20s, young graduates recruited into management are expected to produce. Companies want hard work, intelligence, discipline, and productivity. This is very similar to the skills developed by students in school, where girls excel, increasingly outperforming their male peers. So women tend to do well in this phase of their career.

30s: The networker

By the time managers are in their 30s, companies are on the lookout for key Talent to groom for leadership, through developmental jobs and, often, international mobility. They are looking for more than just basic performance. They want individuals to become better at initiating projects and ideas that drive innovation, supported by the ability to motivate and lead staff and build coalitions. This is a different set of skills than were needed previously, and this stage has very different rules of the game for promotions and development.

These new rules are unwritten and they are not particularly transparent in most companies. This kind of information is usually passed on orally, through networks and informal mentoring relationships. Women are often not included or informed in this transmission. Neither are all men. Essential career management information is, more often than not, transmitted from like to like by managers who feel close to or are comfortable with a certain profile of young person, most often resembling themselves. This creates an unwitting, and largely involuntarily, replication of similar people.

A key criterion for individuals in their 30s to be identified as high potential is the ability to manage one's image, to be known and visible to more senior executives than their direct manager. This gets people on Talent lists and high potential lists, which bosses choose from for developmental assignments.

Women, research proves, are uncomfortable with self-marketing. They are much more recognised for managing teams well (managing down) than for managing their managers and their own images (managing up). While companies pride themselves on their meritocratic Talent management systems, they still rely on 'who you know' and other subjective evaluations of performance.

Some companies have started shaping more effective corporate cultures that bring out the best in all their people, men and women (see Chapter 12). In some companies promotion is now based on team development as well as personal performance – resulting in a sudden, huge boost in female advancement. (See 'The hard soft skills where women score well' for P&G's case.)

A small number of other companies never had to relearn how to value employees – they have always been that way. At W.L. Gore, the US company famous for Gore-Tex, its waterproof fabric, the founders of the company, Wilbert (Bill) Gore and his wife, Genevieve, deliberately set out in 1958 to create a company based on trust in the human instinct to do good. As such, the Gores rejected the fashion for rigid, military style hierarchies controlling staff in favour of a culture in which the leaders had to earn their spurs by their actions as judged by their colleagues. That culture persists to the present day and has put the company in a very good position to capture the spirit of the times and motivate all of the Talent it employs. Interestingly, its current CEO is a woman, Terri Kelly.

The hard soft skills where women score well

What happens when a company evaluates its managers on how well they develop their teams? Procter & Gamble found out when it changed its senior management evaluation process to include more measures that reflected the importance of motivating and developing large teams known as 'organization teams' (such as the cross-departmental Market Development Organization tasked with marketing in one country or a set of countries). This was linked with employee survey questions, which included sections on diversity and inclusion, relationship with colleagues, empowerment, relationship with the person's manager, and work–life effectiveness. This change rewarded all managers including women with strengths in developing the 'organization teams' and getting the best from people's talents, and encouraged others to make this a higher priority. This approach also demonstrated that it is not enough to set an objective on diversity, businesses also need to look at all key processes, measures, rewards, and policies to improve gender balance. For example, P&G also learned that changes in policy and positive management attitude to more flexible working arrangements was an enabler for better gender balance.[3]

 ## New management model invented in 1958

In his book *The Future of Management* (Harvard Business School Press, 2007), Professor Gary Hamel picks W.L. Gore, manufacturers of the rainproof fabric Gore-Tex, as one of the companies best placed to bring the best out of its people – one of the competitive differentiators in the 21st century, which will be about less control and more autonomy. Hamel explains the background to this unusual company.

Inspired by his time at DuPont, where he worked in self-governing R&D teams, Wilbert (Bill) Gore and his wife wanted to create a company that was free of bureaucracy. Gore's vision in the late 1950s, very much ahead of his time, was influenced by Douglas McGregor's *The Human Side of Enterprise*, whose Theory Y posited that human beings were self-motivating problem solvers who found meaning in their work.

The structure that persists today has no management layers and no organisational chart. The core units are self-managing teams devoted to making money and having fun. Gore saw it as a 'lattice' structure rather than a hierarchy connecting every individual to everyone else.

The lines of communication are direct – person to person and team to team. In this system employees serve their peers, not their bosses, and don't have to work through channels to collaborate with their colleagues. Associates become leaders when their peers judge them as such, and those who make a disproportionate contribution to team success attract followers. Teams can fire their chiefs, so they must maintain support.

That is how current CEO Terri Kelly was chosen. When her predecessor retired, the Board of Directors supplemented its decision by polling a wide cross-section of Gore associates, asking them to pick someone they would be willing to follow. 'We weren't given a list of names – we were free to choose anyone in the company,' Kelly recalls. 'To my surprise, it was me.'

Professor Gary Hamel stresses the importance of unleashing more human ability in his recent book on the future of management. He writes that companies must do more to motivate the people they employ if they are to win in an increasingly disruptive world. 'To safeguard their margins, they must become gushers of rule-breaking innovation.' To do this they 'must learn how to inspire their employees to give the very best of themselves every day.'[4]

Post-40s: The Leader

When managers are beyond the age of 40, the leaders have usually been picked and have already gained valuable international experience and significant operational responsibility over large teams. But many women are just re-energising after a few years of relative balance between personal and professional roles. Around 40, they are ready to step back fully into professional roles – only to discover that there are no longer opportunities in those roles.

In most organisations, the career train passes only once, and if you miss it, you can't get back on – ever. But companies need to re-evaluate that track, keeping in mind the female part of their Talent pool. The 40s is the decade when female careers step up, if the women are offered the opportunity. Men's and women's careers have differed by about a decade, with the peak of women's careers coming later than men's, on average.

In this century, companies that want to optimise Talent will have to adapt their career management and Talent identification systems to take into account the different rhythms of dual career

Management innovation at Nestlé Japan

Nestlé in Japan was used to the reality that most women in Japan quit their jobs when they married. That was the accepted cultural norm. But when an American, Chris Johnson, arrived as the Market Head in 2008, the global corporate mandate was to create gender balance worldwide. So Johnson seized on the idea that women at the age of 40 and above might be ready to re-integrate into the workforce once their children were older. He started a recruitment campaign aimed at former Nestlé employees. Bringing back those women recouped the investment in training and development that had already been made.

couples and parents – not just for women, but increasingly for men as well.

Women are not the only ones asking for flexibility and non-linear careers. The demographics of many countries are pushing retirement ages back. How will companies manage people into their 60s? This older generation will have some of the same flexibility needs as parents of young children. The younger generations, Generation Y in particular (those born in 1979–94), have little interest in the unbroken, linear careers of their elders. They want flexibility, lifelong learning, and variety.

Whatever the pressure point, career management in the 21st century will evolve, pushed by a Talent crunch in many developed markets. Some companies, such as Deloitte and Schlumberger, are already experimenting with concepts like

'Mass Career Customisation', which entails building structures that support careers that move both horizontally and vertically, with strong and regular doses of flexibility, sabbaticals, and lifelong learning.

Difference No. 2: Communication styles

Much has been written about how incomprehensible one gender is to the other. Deborah Tannen has spent a lifetime on the differences in communications styles. For managers who seek to become truly gender bilingual at work, I recommend her book *Talking From 9 to 5: Women and Men at Work*[5] as an eye opening introduction to understanding the differences that language both hides and deepens. This section is a very succinct summary of her ideas.

Boys seek to shine

Some basic differences in males and females can be witnessed as early as the playground. Little boys tend to play in groups. Their play seeks to establish who is the best, the fastest, the biggest, and the smartest. The most successful boy is accorded leadership status.

These childhood rules of the game do not need to change much as boys grow into men. They compete at work instead of in the playground. Who is making the biggest contribution to the business in profits, new business, or innovation? Who got the biggest contract? Many men (not all) are familiar with this natural form of routine competition. Those who are particularly good at it find it a lot of fun. And this is the kind of masculine style most favoured by today's corporate cultures.

Girls seek similarity

Girls prefer to play in pairs, listen to one another, and share experiences and fears about things that they have in common. They are essentially trying to find common ground with the other girl. They learn not to be boastful or arrogant, behaviours that are frowned upon by other girls. Girls (and later women) who try to put themselves above other girls are not much appreciated (to the great bemusement of women who get promoted).

This dichotomy creates challenges in corporate life, as the rules of the game have been designed by men and are therefore normed to men's preferred styles. Women's relative modesty (in communication terms) is rarely seen positively. In fact, it's often interpreted as a lack of leadership, charisma, or vision.

Hierarchy hurts

In one company, a manager told the story of a team that he had created, where he had purposefully recruited and developed a dozen high performing women, with a smaller number of men. When he was about to move on, the manager sought to promote one of the women to head the team. None of them wanted the job. This was interpreted as a lack of leadership ambition. The manager finally convinced one of the women (whom he admitted was probably the one with the most masculine characteristics) to take over. The result was a disaster. The smoothly running group dissolved into a mass of people asking to be transferred out. None of the men watching this dynamic had any idea what was going on. It became a classic 'women just don't get along together' interpretation. Yet the women got along beautifully until the relationships they had built among themselves were disrupted by an imposed hierarchy they did not find necessary.

Leader or lost?

In one gender training session I ran, a woman presented a report to a group of peers. At the end of every sentence were a question mark and a lift of her voice. She seemed somewhat unconvinced about her presentation, and seemed to invite affirmation from her colleagues. When her communication style was debriefed by the men and women in the group, many found it weak and unconvincing. Only one man suggested that it was actually a superior style: rather than imposing and 'selling' one person's opinion, it invited teamwork and collaborative problem solving.

This is the 'sharing' style typical of women in groups. Male dominated groups and cultures often perceive it as lacking impact. The traditional response has been to train women to be more 'assertive' and adopt more masculine communication styles. But that eliminates exactly the difference that may bring value, as suggested by the man in the anecdote above.

Managers should instead be more aware of these differences, and learn to listen appropriately. International managers have learned to modulate their communication styles to more modest and consensual Asian modes of communication. It requires acknowledging that these differences exist, and becoming familiar with how to read their undertones and meanings.

As companies seek increasingly collaborative, team oriented cultures that depend on sharing knowledge across business units and geographies, this female culture could offer a powerful antidote to the competitive and divisive tendencies in many companies. If you want to bring more 21st century styles to work, creating more gender balanced teams may be a fast and highly effective way of allowing for complementary ways of working and being.

It is important to bear in mind cultural differences when discussing differences in communication styles between men and women. Asian cultures tend to be more 'feminine' in terms of communication styles and will be positioned less far to the left on the chart (Table 6.1). But within those cultures, the same spectrum of male–female differences still exists.

Table 6.1 Gender differences in communication

Masculine	Feminine	Impact on career process
Power/status orientation	Rapport orientation	Talent identification
Who's best?	All the same	Performance appraisals
Women judge men: *Boastful*	Men judge women: *Lack of confidence*	Readiness for responsibility
Minimise doubts	Downplay certainty	Ambition assessments
Direct	Indirect	Constructive feedback, motivation
Different approaches, e.g. Questions when knows	Different approaches, e.g. Questions when unsure	Visibility, image management

Power versus rapport

Anaïs Nin wrote that 'we don't see things as they are. We see them as we are.' Nothing could be closer to the truth in the way men and women interact at work. The problem is often in how they judge each other across gender lines, without realising that part of what they are judging comprises characteristics common to many people of the same sex.

At a typical business conference, after an expert panel, men are more likely to ask a question they can already answer. They are challenging the experts in a display of their own expertise. Women are more likely to ask a question in order to learn something new. Men may be genuinely baffled if a woman stands up in front of 300 people and reveals what she doesn't know, while women may roll their eyes at the parading of knowledge to the crowd. Yet such reciprocally negative judgements cover the potential benefit of using both approaches flexibly and relevantly, rather than simply unconsciously.

Most large corporate cultures are positioned somewhere on the 'masculine' side of the chart. Listen to the vocabulary of leaders, read the annual report, look at management presentations, or review product advertising, and you will find a common preference for 'performance' language. Becoming bilingual means becoming aware of how the corporate culture sounds to women and how the culture and its leaders perceive women. Until we become far more cognizant of these crossed perceptions, it is very hard to manage them effectively.

The objective: Bilingual management
The challenge is not to push women to become more masculine in their working styles (which is what we have been doing for the last 30 years), or to make men more feminine (a more

recent but growing phenomenon). It is to ensure that managers and leaders understand the differences in order to optimise the Talents of both halves of the Talent pool and be better able to read and respond to both halves of the market. As well, it could enable them to appreciate the benefits that the other side brings to the table.

These differences not only result in contrasting career behaviours. They also – and especially – affect how these differences are interpreted and perceived. The information in Fig. 6.2 comes from a study carried out by IPSOS and a network of France's Ivy League-level schools (Grandes Écoles). More than 8000 alumni and alumnae from these schools answered a survey asking about women's use, relative to their male peers, of behaviours in seeking promotions, like self-marketing, pursuing power, and participating in informal networks.

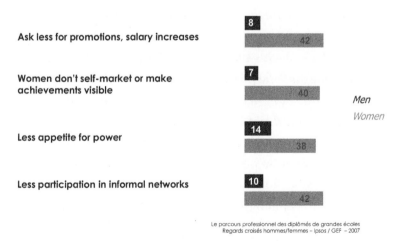

Le parcours professionnel des diplômés de grandes écoles
Regards croisés hommes/femmes – Ipsos / GEF – 2007

Fig. 6.2 Key career behaviours illustrated by the Accenture Study Grandes Écoles.

Only a minority of women were aware that their male colleagues take a very proactive approach to managing their own careers, while men were largely oblivious to the fact that women do such things less.

Most women remain convinced (for the first half of their careers) that promotion is based on job performance. So, if the average male manager is expecting the next mover and shaker in his company to be self-promoting and aggressively pushing for power, he is unlikely to find these behaviours among his female staff. It may be deeply counterintuitive for him to consider pushing women who have proved themselves as capable as their male colleagues but who are not pushing themselves forwards. For many male managers, expressed ambition is a major underlying assumption they have of leadership potential.

> *'I have found that men are usually ready to go forward when you encourage them to strive to reach new goals, even if they are not really fully prepared for the challenge. But women seem to feel they need to be 102% ready before they will be prepared to go beyond their comfort zone. I still have women Country Managers who say that they would not have accepted the role if I had not encouraged them because they didn't think they were ready. And you're never ready for a role like that!*[6]

Emilio Umeoka, President, Microsoft (APAC)

These behaviour and communication differences between men and women affect every aspect of corporate life. They have a particular impact on issues of Talent identification, succession planning and performance evaluations. They also affect how companies relate to women consumers, and how open they are to hearing customers express themselves in a very different way.

Difference No. 3: Power and political competence

For the first part of their careers, a majority of women are largely oblivious to the political realities underlying their organisations. This kind of information can be made more transparent through a formal mentoring programme – which is why many companies have implemented such programmes.

It could also simply be more explicitly stated in management development. As it is, for both men and women, the knowledge is accrued only gradually through the first two decades of work, through experience, bosses, and management coaches. This is too late for many women, who then have to scramble to make up lost time, frantically filling gaping holes in their networks.

Some companies have introduced leadership courses aimed specifically at women. In my experience, these are geared to senior women, who are already switched on to the realities of modern corporate politics that exist in most companies. The real issue is to make this kind of information available to all managers, men and women, much earlier in their careers. For women, the focus should be around 30, before they enter their childbearing years. That way the playing field is levelled, and the rules of the game become more transparent to all. This broadens the Talent pool not only to women, but also to many men who have not understood the system quickly enough.

Women may have to accept that company politics have been shaped by men and that if they want to change the situation, they need to join the club first. Too many women opt out of corporate politics and view the whole endeavour with suspicion, as though it were corrupt or unnecessary. Women need to make their views and voices heard if they want companies to evolve in their direction.

But companies may want to think twice about whether or not they really want to encourage women to become more political. Or, on the contrary, should they use this transition moment to encourage men to become less so? The answer that most of the leaders in my workshops give is a resounding yes. Senior leaders are often very tired of men jockeying for power in their organisations. But they have not always been aware of the gender component to this behaviour. And even those who do not much appreciate the behaviour often implicitly expect it of future high potential leaders.

It is often considered a 'risk' to promote a woman who is not avidly pushing for a higher position. And this feeling remains in place as the first few women are promoted. Once there is a critical mass of women in key roles, companies begin to realise that there is little correlation between hunger for power and the ability to actually exercise it. And for companies increasingly seeking to develop leaders who win the respect and loyalty of their colleagues and staff ('followership') across diverse, cross-cultural teams, these more inclusive and collaborative forms of leadership behaviour, often exhibited by female leaders, are much appreciated by many of the people expected to be followers.

Managers can pass on information to women about the evolving rules of the game, and how to develop effective networks and build key leadership skills. They can encourage them to build their influencing skills and networks without having to act like a man. They can also push them into operational roles and developmental jobs. Many men also find this 'risky', forgetting the potential risk to the company of not having enough women in leadership at all.

Most successful women today acknowledge that there was at least one extraordinary manager on their career path who really pulled them into a position they were initially unsure about or intimidated by. This is equally true for men, but there are more senior men ready to take a risk on young men based on their perception of their potential. There are fewer who are able to accurately evaluate and appropriately promote a talented woman. This makes the Talent identification skills of managers particularly important. And it is a skill that needs to become far more gender bilingual.

More effectively and more radically, companies need to rethink their criteria for promotion and leadership.

- *Are you increasingly looking to build flat, global, knowledge sharing organisations?*
- *Do you want employees who embrace change and collaboration and who can work in a collection of informal, ad hoc networks to get work done?*
- *Do you prize innovation and creative problem solving that comes from as many bottom up, customer-driven ideas as possible?*

Shifting value systems

Businesses need to challenge their old assumptions if they are to build new corporate cultures more adapted to the modern realities. And these outdated assumptions can be eliminated only after they have been made explicit. Gender balancing initiatives can help here, as many of the gender differences overlap with many of the shifts in management that companies are increasingly intent on developing.

Much of what needs to be changed is linked to the three themes mentioned in regard to gender career cycles, communications, and power and political competence. Companies that understand the meaning of these areas in terms of gender are also more likely to be better at adapting all of their Talent processes for the modern worker. Flexibility, innovation, customer focus are all affected by the ability of employees to manage their lives and careers with some degree of control and understanding. They are the heart of the matter in terms of adapting the company to women. They are also the heart of the matter in terms of adapting the company to the new century (Table 6.2).

Table 6.2 Comparison between 20th century/21st century

20th century	21st century
Individual – subjective	Individual – collective
Competition	Collaboration
Difference	Tolerance
Domination	Co-existence
Winners and losers	Winners
Performance	Teamwork
Reason – logic	Reason – intuition
Exclusion	Inclusion
Opposition	Supportiveness

Tips for bilingual managers

Here are ten essential tips for managers wanting to understand the language and culture of women as well as men.

Know thyself

In managing across genders, you need to know what parts of your thinking, reactions, and emotions are influenced by your gender and gender assumptions. All of us, men and women, make assumptions in our minds. We need to become more conscious of what they are. Without knowing who you are, and why, it is hard to manage people who are not like you.

David Loughman, MD A/S Norske Shell and VP Commercial Europe, Shell Upstream International, describes the state of many men's minds on this issue: 'I think most of my male colleagues would say they fully understand the case for diversity, that they see it and that they understand why we need to promote it. But they are still carrying around in their heads very deeply embedded mental models of what the balance between the sexes looks like. It is not easy to shift. It remains below the waterline of visible differences between individuals, and is a very big barrier to moving things on.'[7]

Learn the differences

Good managers pride themselves on their egalitarian credentials. They pride themselves on treating everyone as human individuals. Unfortunately, this approach does not usually work, unless the manager is already very gender bilingual (maybe he was reared in a female dominated household). It is one of the root causes of why women's progress into leadership has been so slow. Managers are often challenged in identifying female Talent, which may look and sound different from what they are looking for subconsciously. Women and men are not the same in countless interesting and complementary ways. Know what they are, and make sure you get a full set of complementary skills and styles on your team.

Don't assume anything

Many managers make assumptions about women without asking them directly. For example, one manager admitted that he had not offered an international transfer to one of his direct reports because she had just had a second child. He learned afterwards that she had very much wanted such a move, and was so upset when he gave it to a male colleague that she almost left the company. The old models and ideas that we all have in our heads may no longer be relevant. Do not assume you have the answers or know what is best for someone. Ask instead.

Don't take 'no' for an answer

Women sometimes turn down promotions, to the great consternation of their managers, who are seeking to push them ahead. Do not take the first 'no' as your answer. Try and find out what is behind it. It is often a concern about being able to do the job, or about the time implications. Reassurance and encouragement are often the only missing ingredients.

Push, support, 'risk', promote

One of the least understood roles of gender bilingual managers is to pull women into management. Very few successful women (or men) have not had at least one exceptional manager who pulled them into a big growth phase, giving them that crucial

Profile of a woman leader – power behind the throne

Women leaders do not at all like to self-market in the way that many men are seemingly very comfortable doing. Even when they are in positions of power, they can seem unusually modest. For example, Angela Ahrendts, CEO of British luxury coat company Burberry, came across as very humble when interviewed by the journalist, Richard Milne, for a video in the View from the Top series on the *Financial Times* website. In spite of the company's entrance onto the FTSE 100, a relatively strong position in the midst of a global recession, with the company worth an estimated £1 billion at the time, she talked in quiet tones about the foundations of success and the need to 'let the team perform'.[8]

In another case, the formidable businesswoman Safra Catz rose to become Larry Ellison's Number Two at business software giant Oracle without anyone apparently understanding what she did exactly. In fact, Catz became increasingly important in the business from her arrival in 1999 to when she was finally named co-president in 2004, reflecting her true status. A recent article described how she could be grossly undervalued and underestimated by male colleagues: 'A senior executive from the Oracle unit that sells to the federal government arranged a meeting with Catz to figure out what she did. "I'm here to help Larry", Catz said, according to an attendee. "Does that mean you're getting his laundry?" the executive responded. Catz, no one's gofer, was not amused.'[9]

and formative 'big break'. Some consider promoting a woman a 'risk'. It is time to start seeing that *not* promoting women might be riskier.

 ## Andrea Jung, CEO, Avon Products

Andrea Jung describes how early in her career at Avon Products she was encouraged and supported by Jim Preston, then the CEO and Chairman of the company. At the time, Jung was working in marketing and had started to develop some radical new ideas for the business, 'forcing globalisation of brands across an organisation where everything was very decentralised.' She says it was a very unpopular idea and she knew that the 'antibodies' would 'come out and kill the concept'. She says she worked many nights trying to figure out how to present the new idea to senior management. Because Preston was such a 'great sponsor' of hers, Jung says she did get the ear of senior management, who on hearing her pitch, wanted to understand more.[10]

Draw the line in the sand

In some organisations (depending on the corporate culture as well as the country they are based in) sexist jokes or comments are not uncommon. In corporate hierarchies, it is up to the most senior person (not the lone woman in the room) to draw the line in the sand on what are acceptable comments. Remember, anything that is not visibly rejected becomes acceptable.

Setting the right tone

Saad Abdul-Latif, President, SAMEA (South East Asia, Middle East & Africa), PepsiCo, describes how he and other leaders set the right example, challenging old prejudices in male dominated workforces. 'There have been some challenges, specifically in relation to jobs which were historically dominated by men such as the sales force – the people who drive the trucks or run sales teams. Bringing women in was a bit odd for [them] at first. How do we get [the women] in? What do we need to adjust? For example, for the first time, the men had to pay attention to what they were saying because there was a woman present. So, in some cases there was some resistance.'[11]

Sell diversity (and buy it)

Gender balance is not the easiest topic to sell. Most managers have not thought a lot about this topic, even as they feel that they have been hearing about it for far too long. The data and figures on the significance of women as leaders and Talent and women as consumers have become so compelling as to make the argument easier and far more convincing. (See Chapter 9.) But managers still need to be persuaded. And that requires being convinced yourself first.

Vet your partner

Many managers subconsciously assume that people of the other gender share some of the characteristics they have observed in their partners or spouses at home. Nothing could be further from today's realities. Men, women, and gender roles have all become highly diverse, and can differ dramatically among these turning point generations. Managers should be consciously careful in making any assumptions about what colleagues at work want that are based on what their spouse wants.

Choose to choose

Promoting gender balance is not an HR issue, not a diversity issue, and not a women's issue. It is a business issue. It is up to you whether you decide this is an issue that is worth investing time, effort, and interest in. The data suggest that your team, your company, and your bottom line will benefit. The rest is up to you.

Become bilingual

Most international managers have understood the importance of learning the language and culture of the Brazilians, the Russians, the Indians, and the Chinese to take full advantage of trade with the growing economic power of the BRIC countries. Yet studies show that women worldwide are a bigger market opportunity and have a greater impact on global GDP than these countries combined. In the 21st century, leadership will also require learning the language and culture of women.

The process of becoming fully gender bilingual means understanding the differences between the sexes in order to optimise the talents, complementarities, and opportunities of both men and women. My experience shows that this is a very popular and easily received message. Men do not feel accused, women discover that many managers are far more enthusiastic about the idea of balance than they had thought, and the conversations shift.

These are the building blocks of the culture and mindset changes required to make organisations ready – and even welcoming – for the new Markets and Talent realities. Once managers and employees have been made aware of the business case for gender balance, and once they have been given a sufficiently in-depth understanding of what that might require, they are ready to accept and work with the action plan that many of them will have taken part in crafting. This is when the investment in preparing minds and hearts will pay off, with managers ready and willing to do their part in implementing an action plan that they both understand and support.

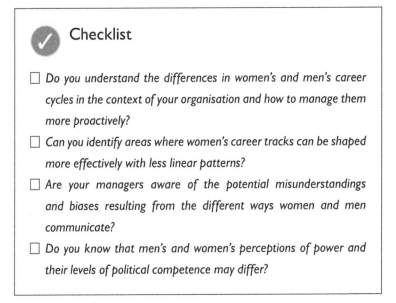

✓ Checklist

☐ *Do you understand the differences in women's and men's career cycles in the context of your organisation and how to manage them more proactively?*

☐ *Can you identify areas where women's career tracks can be shaped more effectively with less linear patterns?*

☐ *Are your managers aware of the potential misunderstandings and biases resulting from the different ways women and men communicate?*

☐ *Do you know that men's and women's perceptions of power and their levels of political competence may differ?*

Chapter 7

THE ACTION PLAN

'Why have too many gender initiatives missed the mark? One reason is that too many gender initiatives focus on changing women.'

Catalyst

At last the moment has come to frame an action plan. The foundation stones have been laid and the business units will, by now, have a clear idea of why they are investing time and money into gender balance. Their leaders will be aligned and committed. Knowing *why* they want more gender balance and *what* they need to focus on will enable them to define *how* to implement the programme most effectively when they turn to designing an action plan.

Ideally, companies will take the time to complete the Audit Phase properly and use the initial part of the Awareness Phase to win understanding and buy-in, first from the Executive Committee. In this way, the top managers can avoid these pitfalls.

Claire Martin, who started Renault's company-wide Audit Process in late 2009 (see 'Auditing Renault', Chapter 2), was patiently awaiting the results. 'When we get the diagnostic, we will use this information to create an action plan. I'm sure lots of sudden initiatives will spring up to deal with any shortcomings – people will realise when they are involved in the diagnosis that they could be better at something and they will initiate something to deal with it. We will use this kind of movement to build a plan adapted to the different issues it raises.'[1]

The head of the initiative can consolidate the suggestions and ideas made by managers during the Awareness Sessions to create a full plan suited to the company. The added strength of this approach is that the new plan will be based on the ideas set out by the leaders who represent all divisions and functions, not just HR or Diversity & Inclusion. This ensures that the plan will cover all the opportunities gender balance offers the company as well as determining that the managers have bought into it.

At Schneider Electric, the French-based global electrical equipment supplier, HR manager Mai Lan Nguyen explains that the company did not adopt an action plan straight away. 'From the beginning, we chose not to take the issue to the Executive Committee. Our CEO, Jean-Pascal Tricoire, is a passionate supporter of the initiative. He was keen to push forward with an action plan, whether there was good awareness among managers and employees or not.' Of the need to create gender balance throughout the company, Tricoire expresses his commitment succinctly, 'I don't see why I would deprive our company of half of the brains of the planet.'[2]

Tricoire and Nguyen discussed the issue further and decided that it was critical to get a greater level of awareness first. Otherwise, recalls Nguyen, there could be significant 'pockets of passive resistance' to any initiative adopted by the top executives. They decided to run Awareness Sessions for the leadership teams of each of the company's five business units. Each team would then define the action plans for the business unit. After that process, Nguyen says, they'd be able to go to the Executive Committee with a 'more accurate sense of what we need to do next'.[3]

With the results of the Audit, the enhanced awareness of leaders, an in-depth understanding of the issues, and the action plan recommendations from the leadership Awareness Sessions, the team is ready to define an achievable and realistic objective that makes sense for the business.

Setting the objective will define the pace, the resources, and the communication required to achieve it.

What do you want?

The Awareness Phase heightens leaders' awareness of the business potential that can be harnessed with a strategic approach to gender. Managers will have become more aware that they can tap into leadership and governance performance, into customer understanding and responsiveness, and into global Talent management.

There are many potential business benefits to creating a more gender balanced and gender bilingual organisation. Prioritise which ones to focus on. In most cases, they will be come under one of the following headings:

- *Market opportunities* – realising new marketing opportunities and profits as a result of a better understanding of female consumers.
- *21st century leadership* – having modern, progressive executives who know how to manage workforces and a wide variety of stakeholders consisting of women and men, in a way that integrates and responds to the needs and styles of both.
- *Talent management* – attracting, developing, and retaining talented women with similar understanding and effectiveness as with men and becoming known as a good employer for both women and men.

Exploring these options can start businesses on defining what success means and what it looks like to them. Rather than being a general and vague reference to balance everywhere in the company, the gender initiative can be defined more accurately and tied to the organisation's specific goals and broader strategies.

Internally, is the aim to achieve gender balance among the company's Talent across the board, at all levels, and/or across all functions? Would it include both operational and functional roles? These details need to be worked out.

On the external Markets side, where companies are looking to improve their approach towards women consumers and customers, they need to refine the gender balance goals in regard to their market, product, and customer-related teams

Building gender balance, not promoting women

While most people think that gender programmes are automatically about women, I underline that the objective should be achieving gender balance, not just focusing on promoting more women into leadership. This means that sometimes it is more relevant to increase the number of men working in a particular unit than the women.

L'Oréal, for example, has had no problem attracting women to its marketing division, though it is tougher to do so in the industrial research and engineering side, says Sylviane Balustre-d'Erneville, Europe Diversity Manager at the cosmetics company. But marketing is a whole other matter and the growing men's market for cosmetics and beauty products means that the company will need more men in the marketing function in the future. 'We have too many women in marketing – we have to balance it and attract more men into the marketing function and more women into the industrial part.'[4]

For many other companies, there is a functional imbalance along gender lines. HR and communications departments are often dominated by women, while sales and engineering roles are dominated by men. Evening out these roles between men and women becomes the priority for many companies that would like to see more gender balanced teams across the board.

and departments. Should the project be aiming to get a better gender balance in the organisation's customer bases and/or its sales forces, or should it focus on the adaptation of its products, services, or marketing and sales strategies?

At this stage, it is important to think about metrics. They will be critical later when driving the programme and maintaining momentum. What criteria will be used to measure its success? How will they be tracked? (See Chapter 12 for more on metrics.)

The other issue to take into account is the time set for the task. The timeframe will affect the resourcing options. Set the programme's pace in a realistic way with achievable goals. But don't make the goals too modest. Shifting from an existing ratio of 90:10 men to women to something like 85:15 over five years won't impress stakeholders. Targets like that destroy the credibility of the issue.

To quota or not to quota

In 2008, Norway introduced quotas to create gender balanced boards on publicly listed companies. Companies that did not staff their corporate boards with at least 40% women directors would be summarily delisted from the stock exchange. This legislation was introduced by a male, conservative government Minister, Ansgar Gabrielsen, quite the opposite of the liberal, female Minister most people would have expected to be the sponsor of such a bill, says Sven Erik Svedman, the Norwegian Ambassador to Germany.[5] Gabrielsen provides a very good model for the kind of leader most companies need to lead on gender balance. It is often better to have a senior male executive propose and roll out a gender balancing effort. Another

'Break up the alpha male club'

At the turn of the century, the then Norwegian Economics and Trade Minister, Ansgar Gabrielsen, shocked the nation by putting legislation onto the agenda to force companies to ensure they had at least 40% of either gender on their boards. The idea was introduced in 2002 and put into law in 2005, after which companies had to comply with the quota law by the end of 2007 or face possible delisting. The scale of the change was huge. In 1993 Norwegian corporate boards had 3% women members and by September 2008 the number was at 43% – the highest in any country in the world.

By his own admission Gabrielsen was an unlikely person to lead such a change, but clearly he turned out to be the right one. 'I am a conservative. I am practical, rational, and I want Norway to flourish.' He also knew that it would take such a person to make the change. 'In October 2001, I was made Minister of Economics and Trade. In six months, I decided for myself, "I will be the one who makes the difference." I knew that the person who would make a difference had to be a conservative man from business – or a minister of trade – not a female or a female advocate.'

But why did he develop the view that this change was needed? He recalls his own distrust of the lack of diversity on typical boards. 'Too many Boards have seven, nine, 11 people who are made in the same factory, very often with the same education, very often in the same year. They go sailing, boar hunting, and salmon fishing together. They dine in the same restaurant. They are very alike. I believe in the opposite. It is important that people think their own, different thoughts, and get to say what is needed, not what is wanted.' Diverse boards were likely to improve business performance and therefore boost the economy.

He also believed that women bring important new perspectives and qualities to the table. 'I believe that women are equal to or better than men. Why? Women don't take high risks. The big international scandals such as Enron – the people who got them in trouble were men. The whistle-blowers were all women. I wanted to break up the alpha male club. We had educated 50/50 boys and girls. The women had the experience. There was no reason why they should not advance to the highest levels.'[6]

interesting point about the Norwegian quotas is that they are gender neutral. That is, they define a minimum quota of 40% of board director seats for each gender. 'That guarantees that men will always have some seats,' Ambassador Svedman reassures with an ironic smile.

Since then, the debate on quotas in the private sector has escalated in Europe, particularly since the economic crisis. Several other countries have advanced similar legislation, including Spain and France. The media in Europe have spent much time debating the issue, and it is a favourite question of many journalists.

Most men and women do not like quotas. Men suspect that they lead to unfair competition, and women often worry that the promotions they finally achieved were not merited (or not perceived as such).

But the discussion should be almost obsolete, just at the same moment that it is gaining ground in public opinion. The economic business case for gender balance is so strong that smart companies the world over are already adjusting. And the debate focuses on quotas at board level, which can have little relation to the gender balance within the company itself. So whether or not board quotas are implemented, the issue of gender balancing the company remains. A recent study comparing countries showed that in 2009 Norway had a relatively low percentage of women legislators, senior officials, and managers in spite of the boardroom quota. Only 31.2% of these positions were filled by women, unexceptional for Western Europe, where Germany topped the list at 38.2%. Countries such as the Philippines, Panama, and the US had much higher percentages of women in these positions: 57.1%, 43.6%, and 42.8% respectively.[7]

Instead of quotas, the best route is through aspirational targets. That's how companies work on almost every other measure – there's no need to make an exception on gender.

How to get there and stay there!

Now that leaders are gender bilingual, and objectives have been set, reaching the end goal requires rolling out and aligning the entire organisation with a similar but pared down version of the Awareness Sessions given to the top leadership teams. It requires cascading Awareness training, followed by a more focused close-up of particular issues. As it broadens in scope,

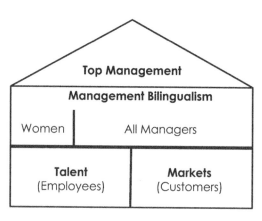

Fig. 7.1 House diagram 1.

the initiative needs a careful and strategic communications accompaniment.

As the company prepares its Action Plan, you want to ensure that you cover all the different segments displayed in the first house diagram (Fig. 7.1). The top layer of the house, getting top management to commit, has been covered in previous chapters. The middle layer is the work of cascading this Awareness throughout the organization, making all managers gender bilingual. The bottom layer of the house, which I often refer to as the 'plumbing', is the systemic issues which underpin the Talent management side of organizations and the customer-facing Markets side. Each is covered in more detail in Chapters 8–10. They are:

- *Gender training for managers and specific functions.*
- *Reviewing processes on both the HR and Sales & Marketing sides of the organisation.*

- *Focusing on the development of the existing female Talent pipeline.*
- *Focusing on the specific needs of female customers.*

First, the organisation needs to enable all managers to become gender bilingual. They are the day to day implementers of the change programme, so male and female managers must receive some kind of education on gender balance. Mainstream this training into the company's existing management and leadership development after the initial roll-out has got most of the existing managers on board.

Second, companies often accelerate progress by reviewing all the women in their existing pipeline. This can be helpful in the short-term to ensure that the Talent identification process is working without bias. Many companies use this list to review their promotion trends by gender, and to question their promotion and succession planning criteria.

Third, the company must check the systemic side of the organisation's processes affecting Talent and Markets to see what changes are needed to achieve the gender balance programme's goals. This is equally applicable to the internal issue of Talent and the external one of customers.

Focus on females

Companies often start their gender initiatives with a focus on the lack of women in management and leadership positions. This often leads to the conclusion that a lack of women in the Talent pipeline is one of the key obstacles to improving the numbers of women working at senior levels. Yet many of the executive level workshop debates centre on the argument that there are excellent women in the company – they just don't seem to get identified and put in the talent pool. So an early step for a company is to create a database of its top several hundred women. The leaders can then review all the women in the company above a certain level. Thereafter, at succession planning meetings, they should discuss the names on this list, checking why the women may not have been included in the succession planning lists and how to optimise the women's identification and development.

This can be done either at a global level or decentralised to the national and local levels. Damien O'Brien is the head of Egon Zehnder International, the global head-hunting firm. The consultants and partners at the company's 63 offices worldwide work together in a collaborative manner, each individual consultant and local office operating without centralised control. It would not be appropriate for them to have processes or policies coming from the top.

Instead, O'Brien aims to inculcate a cultural transformation over a period of a few years. 'The way we achieve these outcomes is by providing a value setting and establishing the tone. So, when I speak and communicate at partner meetings and telephone conference calls with our office leaders, there are certain messages that I drive home. This is one of them.' There are no quotas, targets, formal agendas, or positive discrimination initiatives. 'But we will continue to reinforce a culture which promotes greater gender balance and more flexibility. It's not a revolution … it's more organic.'[8]

At Nestlé, Jean-Marc Duvoisin, Deputy Executive Vice President, Human Resources and Centre Administration, realised early on that the cultural differences in various countries meant that gender balance processes needed to be approached in a relevant and receivable way. He knew that the explanations for the gender balances in different countries were shaped by their different markets and cultures. It was not wise to impose a one-size-fits-all model. 'This convinced me that we need to look at this issue on a country by country basis, with a reliance on local action plans.' This meshed well with Nestlé's decentralised corporate model. At the same time, central HQ needed a way to maintain a connection with the local action plans and drive progress. So every country manager now presents his or her action plans on people, which include gender criteria, in the annual strategy reports given to the head office, along with the progress made.[9]

Table 7.1 The action plan

Audit	Awareness	Align	Sustain
Analyse current statistics	Facilitate Awareness Sessions with top managers and other leaders across the organisation	Train specialist functions	Communicate internally and externally
Audit internal and external gender statistics		Provide support resources (toolkit, webinars, etc.)	Celebrate success
Audit external communications	Build business case		Report regularly against KPIs
Benchmark	Develop detailed action plans by function/geography	Adjust Talent/HR policies	
Present synthesis of findings to top management	Cascade awareness	Adjust Markets approach	Reward success
		Focus on existing pipeline	

Systemic reviews

Companies next need to look inside themselves, reviewing processes that may hide subconscious gender biases, from Markets to Talent (Tables 7.2 and 7.3).

On the Markets side, companies often needs to work with the sales, marketing, and product development teams to review how they can achieve a sharper understanding of female consumers and enhance customer relationship building skills to develop a more sophisticated gender bilingual perspective. Do their campaigns, products, sales pitches, advertising, and so on, appeal to both men and women? Are there ways to improve the attraction or retention of women customers? Do they need to attract more male or female customers? Do they know how?

On the Talent side, organisations need to ensure that their HR teams are fully gender bilingual, as they are the key interface for everything to do with attracting, retaining, and promoting female as well as male executives. They will also need to review HR processes and approaches in all countries to see where there are subconscious biases.

Each of these phases addresses the four areas referred to above. The 'house' diagram can be used again in laying out the action plan to ensure that all the key areas have been addressed, as illustrated (Fig. 7.2).

Table 7.2 Gender bias – Talent

Bias	Updated
Recruitment: Women are not attracted to our industry/company, only men apply	Industry/company has not adapted its image and communication to connect with women
Retention: Women choose to prioritise family over career	Modern companies will eliminate the issue of choice for both men and women, and make conciliation possible for both parents
Promotion: Women are less ambitious than men. Only men are asking for/accepting promotions	Men and women are equally ambitious, but women expect to be promoted on performance, not because they push for promotion. Companies and managers need to review talent identification criteria

Table 7.3 Gender bias – Markets

Bias	Updated
Customers: Men and women are the same; we can segment our markets by other, more significant factors	Men and women are different, and gender is the primary and most impactful segmentation. It goes first, other dimensions second
Communications: Women like pink and soft, men like black and tough; design women-focused ads and products, with lots of flowers	'Women' is not a segment, it is an entire market, to be segmented by age, career phase, family status, and socio-economic profiling. Don't think pink!
Products/services: Men and women buy in the same way and focus on the product when they choose between options	Women look at a holistic customer experience, including websites, relationships, messaging, retail and user interfaces, ads, image, and service. Men may focus more on product specifications. Evaluate the whole customer journey

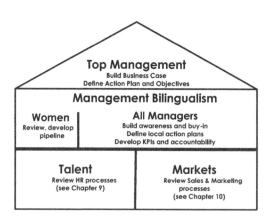

Fig. 7.2 House diagram 2.

Communicate

Communications is an absolutely crucial part of any gender balance initiative. I devote Chapter 11 to it, as it also merits a very separate and specific strategy. A useful rule of thumb, adopted by the more successful companies in this area, is to minimise communication about the gender initiative until managers have been through the Awareness Phase. And then largely confine communication about it to an internal audience until there are firm results.

What not to do

Learning from what does not work can sometimes be just as useful as learning from what does work. Here are a few suggestions to help you avoid some pitfalls:

Brand bilingually: Don't brand and present a gender initiative as a 'women's initiative' – this effectively excludes the very people who are the key to making gender balance happen – the men currently doing most of the promotion and succession planning as well as the product development and design.

In fact, I suggest eliminating the word 'women' from anything to do with an internal, corporate gender initiative. While it is useful in external environments and events, inside companies it has the unintended consequence of making men feel excluded. Companies have a found a variety of other ways of presenting gender as a strategic business issue, usually by bundling it into other broader change initiatives. So, '21st century Leadership', 'Customer-driven Innovation', or 'Solutions-Driven Flexibility' have all been umbrella 'change' brands under which gender balance fits quite comfortably.

These steps also serve to avoid two misunderstandings common to gender balance initiatives. First, that they are restricted to HR issues, and second, that they concern only women. So don't have HR visibly run the initiative unless the action plan is completely focused on the Talent side of the gender equation.

It is imperative that companies avoid any suggestion that men should simply 'support' the initiative. Instead, they must be seen as the key drivers of the initiative, motivated by a clear and strong business case for doing so. Men must be comfortable leading on this topic, be seen to be doing so, and held accountable for the results.

Lead seriously: Avoid appointing the company's most senior woman to head up the initiative. Ideally, the initiative should be led, very visibly, by the CEO. If not, it is better to appoint (at least at first) either a senior and respected man or a gender balanced team of men and women. Whatever organisations do, they shouldn't make it appear as though women are pushing for their own advancement. Most men don't appreciate the push when it is presented that way. In such cases, they generally will feel as though the entire project has nothing to do with them, or that it is posing unfair competition for the next promotion.

 ## Make men lead players, not supporters

A recent report from Catalyst, the American non-profit devoted to women's professional advancement, breaks new ground by expressly including men: Its title is 'Engaging Men in Gender Initiatives'.[10] Catalyst astutely asks: 'Why have too many gender initiatives missed the mark? One reason is that too many gender initiatives focus on changing women.' The report underlines that in their 'exclusive focus on women, rather than engaging men, many companies have unwittingly alienated them' – that is, the men.

The report presents an analysis of the main barriers to men's involvement in gender initiatives: apathy (74%), fear (74%), and real and perceived ignorance (51%). 'More than having an awareness of gender bias,' Catalyst suggests, 'men must have a strong commitment to the ideal of fairness – a strong personal conviction that bias is wrong and that the ideal of equality is one for which they should stand up.' The rest of the report focuses on involving men as 'champions' and 'supporters' of gender initiatives.

Yet I think the more subtle issue is that most male managers *have* a strong personal commitment to fairness. It often strikes me as rather insulting to suggest they don't. They are doing exactly what women have asked them to do for a century or more: They are treating everyone equally and the same. And they are made to feel very uncomfortable with the accusatory tone of some gender experts who focus on 'stereotyping', 'discrimination', and 'glass ceilings'. While these may be there, they are largely subconscious, and will not be overcome until both men and women are convinced that there is some business benefit in doing so.

Andrew Cohn, a leadership consultant, stresses the importance of not blaming men in discussions about how to shape more gender bilingual organisations. 'I believe that all of us – but particularly men – are much more willing to engage in a constructive conversation if we are not being blamed for the existence of the challenge we are addressing.'[11]

Also, men should not be asked to *support* equality. They should be made responsible for implementing gender balance. If the company has set an action plan in place with a clear objective, all its managers should not just be supportive of gender balance – they should be accountable for it.

Communicate credibly: Many companies want to enhance their images and employer branding by trumpeting their gender credentials. Make your claims credible. Otherwise it just looks and feels like manipulation. Women (and men) are getting better at seeing through this.

Target wisely: Companies would also do well to avoid substituting 'pink' products for a strategic rethink of a new overall product and marketing approach to appeal to women consumers, who they may have discovered to be a more significant portion of their market than previously thought. Women may not appreciate brands that categorise their wide complexities into stereotypical 'female' responses.

Once companies have crafted their action plans, they need to align the organisation's processes and systems to support their objectives and deliver on their targets. This is the subject of the next section, which looks at how the organisation can be shifted in various ways to maximise its ability to develop a more balanced approach in terms of marketing and the management of Talent.

Checklist

☐ *Has the company prioritised which benefits from gender balance are most important to it?*

☐ *What metrics will the company use to measure success?*

☐ *Has the programme been rolled out carefully, first to managers, then to the staff as a whole, and then, and only after achieving set goals, outside the company?*

☐ *Does the company have a training programme in place to develop gender bilingual managers and prepare in-house Talent to lead future gender awareness programmes?*

☐ *Have subconscious management biases related to women been identified and addressed?*

☐ *Is the leader of the initiative the right person? Ideally, it should be the CEO. Barring that, it should not be a senior woman or, if focused on anything other than Talent, HR. Those choices would send the wrong signals.*

Part III

ALIGNMENT

How do we build
gender balance
into our
corporate DNA?

Chapter 8

TRAINING

'The workshops were a turning point, a pivotal event in the life of the firm.'

Douglas M. McCracken, former CEO, Deloitte Consulting

The Alignment Phase involves looking at the systemic side of organisations and identifying where and how gender balance could be improved to support the business. The best people to carry out these reviews are the people who run and staff these areas, whether R&D, Product Development, Sales & Marketing, or Human Resources. Before they can effectively analyse their own functions and processes from a gender perspective, they will need gender training. This should be adapted to each function or group. This chapter takes a broad overview of these different forms of training, and the subsequent chapters look in more detail at the specifics of the processes that can make these groups gender bilingual.

The managers

A company that has passed through the Audit and Awareness Phases is now ready to broaden training to all managers. Their action plans are in place, the leadership is behind the initiative, and the systems are being reviewed to support the change.

Now, the organisation needs to take the initiative to the next level, which means cascading it down to all the managers and even every employee, especially in the key areas of consumer R&D, product development, Sales & Marketing, and HR.

Gender training should also be mainstreamed into the company's management development programmes.

Training sessions for managers can be similar to the one developed for the executive teams. Remember, managers may be more sceptical about the need for a gender initiative than their bosses, and they are usually less informed about the macroeconomic shifts affecting the subject. Therefore, lead with the business case for at least the first part of the training. Managers may not need to have the same level of discussion as the executives, but they need to understand why the gender initiative is important and where it fits within the company's overall plans and goals. To make clear how critical the issue is, many companies tie the gender balance initiative firmly to a wider change programme. That way, gender is part of the organisation's efforts to change and become more competitive.

Information about the business case must be as relevant as possible to the local team being trained. Shape it to the team's current situation to maximise the impact and immediacy of the issue. Also, compare the local business with other operations in the company.

Explaining the different ways that professional and working life plays out for men and women remains a key element of the training, supported by detailed case studies and tips on how to manage adeptly across the gender divide. The example from Deloitte below shows how these kinds of sessions can be revelatory to managers, many of whom are unaware of the subconscious biases that exist in everyday corporate life.

Douglas M. McCracken, a former Deloitte Consulting CEO, described one typical scene[1]: 'One partner was jolted into thinking about an outing he was going to attend, an annual "guys" weekend with partners from the Atlanta office and many other clients. It was very popular, and there were never any women. It hadn't occurred to him to ask why. He figured, "No woman would want to go to a golf outing where you smoke cigars and drink beer and tell lies." But the women in the session were quick to say that by not being there, they were frozen out of informal networks where important information was shared and a sense of belonging built. Today, women are routinely included in such outings.'

McCracken recalled the importance of holding gender awareness workshops for 5000 people (Board directors, management committee members, and managing partners). It cost the firm $8 million but, in McCracken's view, was worth it: 'The workshops were a turning point, a pivotal event in the life of the firm.'

Using discussions, videos, and case studies, people's subconscious biases were challenged. Some attendees discovered they were unwittingly prejudicing women's chances by judging women according to performance criteria while judging men according to their 'potential'. Other examples included managers being tougher on women over men when both turned up late because of childcare problems, and women being passed over for certain assignments because their managers assumed they would not want them.[2]

Similarly, Julie Gilbert, formerly a Senior Vice President at Best Buy (2000–2009), recalled that the senior leadership team and certain high-potentials were selected to go on intensive three-day store visits around the US by the electronics retailer. They were jetted around without advance notice to the stores concerned. Cries would go out from the store personnel when the plane was spotted, followed by the words, 'The jets are up!' when they left. It was a prestigious group to be included in and many key strategic conversations took place there, affecting decisions about future projects and appointments. But, Gilbert recalled, women were rarely included.[3]

Recognising success

Being gender bilingual should be viewed as a key component of being an effective manager and leader in the current century. Reaching gender goals should be recognised and rewarded. It should be one of the reasons managers are promoted to senior leadership positions. I address rewards and the motivation they foster in Chapter 13.

All employees

Reaching all employees and communicating the relevance of gender can be highly effective, with even a little education going a long way. This is especially the case in customer-facing roles, in operational contexts like factories, and in traditionally male industries that are changing quickly. The challenge here is in delivering effective training that goes beyond a superficial

Employee training

The business case

- Why the company believes that better gender balance is good for its business
- Overview of the Talent realities today in terms of gender ratio of graduates, performance, and profiles
- Overview of Markets realities, with analysis of the evolution of the customer base and trends
- A top line summary of the current situation in the company: gender balance among employees and customers

The differences

- Major differences between genders that affect working together, and communicating with customers
  - Staff: communication styles, flexibility, working in mixed gender teams
  - Customers: shopping, product, and communications preferences

Working bilingually

- Divide teams by gender and facilitate an analysis of working and communication styles within the company and externally with customers
  - Internal: How gender differences affect teamwork
  - Adapting styles to become a bilingual colleague
  - External: Gender impacts on customer interactions and preferences
- What male and female customers may expect and prefer in terms of service, contact, and follow-up

treatment of the issue to a large and diverse number of people. In general, training sessions for employees contain the same basic messages and structure as the managers' workshop. This usually covers the business case for gender balance (the *Why*), the current situation at the organisation (the *What*), the differences between men and women in the workplace context, and how a gender balance can be achieved (the *How*).

Training gender bilingualism – going online for mass impact

Well-designed e-learning helps employees (and their managers) understand and apply tools and concepts. In a cost-effective way, e-learning modules can present a wide variety of multimedia supports, such as videos, interactive sessions, audio podcasts, checklists, and so on, which serve to anchor and deepen the messages and learning.

At the global electrical equipment supplier Schneider Electric, Mai Lan Nguyen, the HR manager responsible for gender balance, decided to supplement the company's gender awareness workshops with an e-learning tool initially targeted at Schneider's 15,000 managers. The interactive tool lets users explore the issues via a series of interactive questions and exercises. If they replied to a question incorrectly, they were shown the right answer. In this way, they were made aware of the business case for gender balance and the specific situation at the company, as well as why the leaders of the company felt it was a crucial business issue. The gender balance e-learning module was delivered to all managers along with modules on corporate values and energy efficiency, which were the other key components of the company's strategy moving forward.

'You can work on the e-learning tool in stages,' Nguyen says. 'But most people who started the gender balance e-learning package finished it in one go. Out of the 3000 managers who took it, more than 2000 finished it immediately. 10,000 started the values module, but only 3000–4000 finished it. This shows that the topic and the way it was presented really raised people's interest.' In fact, the feedback was so positive that many of the managers called for Schneider to make the gender balance e-learning module available to all 115,000 employees.[4] The company agreed to start doing so in 2010. I have now adapted this popular product to a variety of other companies and sectors that appreciate its wide appeal and impact.

Sales and marketing staffs

If the Awareness Phase made it a priority for the organisation to release new revenue streams or discover new markets by becoming better attuned to the female consumers in its market, then it is critically important to implement a training programme for the Sales & Marketing functions as well as such functions as R&D and product development. They need to understand the opportunities afforded by a more bilingual approach to their markets and to start analysing their strategies against the gender balance benchmark.

- *How do men and women view the customer experience in retail outlets or online, for example?*
- *Are women as satisfied as men with the company's products or customer service?*
- *If there are differences, what are they?*
- *What drives customer loyalty to products and services in the industry, and what are the gender differences?*

For companies that don't even look at their key metrics and feed-back in this way, starting to do so usually generates realisations. It will show opportunities to become better attuned to men and women as distinct customer groups and to no longer sell to them as if they were a homogeneous whole. Most marketers can also benefit from devising accurate and effective customer segments for women as well as men, encapsulating the many and varied differences in these two groups (see Chapter 10 for more detail on female customer segmentation).

A Harvard Business Review article revealed how the US computer company Dell got it wrong when marketing to women precisely because the teams involved had not thought their approach through carefully enough. 'Consider Dell's short-lived effort to market laptops specifically to women. The company fell into the classic 'make it pink' mindset with the May 2009 launch of its *Della* website. The site emphasised colors, computer accessories, and tips for counting calories and finding recipes. It created an uproar among women, who described it as "slick but disconcerting" and "condescending".' The authors of the article, 'The Female Economy', found from their own survey of 12,000 women that companies constantly failed to meet women's needs in a direct and compelling way. 'They have too many demands on their time and constantly juggle conflicting priorities – work, home, and family. Few companies have responded to their need for time-saving solutions or for products and services designed specifically for them.'[5]

So, the purpose of training the personnel in customer-related positions is to avoid basic gender blind spots. It is not that hard to find out more about the gender differences in shopping,

Table 8.1 Gender differences in shopping[6]

Men	Women
Make purchase decisions in less than 60 seconds	Average purchase decision takes 4 minutes
Tend to focus on lead items at front of shop	Organised, purposeful; process more information
Pay little attention to environment	Sensitive to pricing, design, and selection
Try to find what they need without help	Expect detailed information and thoughtful help from assistants
Shop by a list	Explore based on set of criteria

buying, service, information needs, and so on (Table 8.1). There is a growing body of books and research devoted to the subject. But most companies have not even started sorting through their own data with the appropriate lens: looking at customers and customer satisfaction by gender. That's where the biggest business opportunities lie today. Only managers who are gender aware and constantly seeking to anticipate customer needs can seize those opportunities. Doing so requires research-based information on gender differences. It also requires a deep-seated empathy and understanding of both sexes, rather than just one.

Training allows consumer researchers to ask the right questions and evaluate the right metrics. Too often, market research has not been carried out with gender as a key focus.

An example from science illustrates the staggering mistakes that can result. In North America 30 years ago, heart disease was thought to be a male disease that did not affect women. It was not until more women became doctors and medical researchers that this assumption was questioned. What these women found was that all the studies leading to these conclusions had been carried out on men. When they started to include women in the research, they discovered that women suffered just as much from heart disease as men, but that they displayed completely different symptoms of the disease. How many times did women get sent home with a Valium when they should have gone into the emergency room? And how many companies make similar assumptions, simply extrapolating data and research on 'people' and assuming that men and women are the same?[7]

 ## Sales and marketing training

The business case
- The business drivers behind better gender balance
- In-depth presentation of the Markets realities today in terms of the gender ratio of consumers and end users generally in the market
- The current situation and statistics on the company's customer base, and any trends that are emerging

The differences
- Major differences between genders that affect their experience with the user and retail experience
- Shopping styles, user experiences, retail preferences, communication and advertising messaging, internet usage patterns

The market impact
- Focus on major sales and marketing areas that require adapting to gender balance
- Divide teams by gender to analyse the key facets of both male and female customers' perspective on the company, its products, and services

User experience
- Holistic approach to products, employer brand, and relationships with company
- Review the entire customer journey from start to finish, with gender preferences in mind
- Review customer satisfaction surveys by gender

Retail experience
- How do men and women rate the retail experience?
- Review the survey questions themselves for gender biases
- Review retail outlets with gender preferences in mind: Are they tailored to women as well as men?

Communication
- Review product advertising, packaging, naming
- Review website functionalities and ease of use
- Check the blogosphere for customer feedback that may not be officially tracked

Gender initiatives focused on exploring the external Markets opportunities will succeed only if they have the full support and commitment of Sales & Marketing. The task of the training at this stage is to get the people in these operations to reflect on how they have worked up to now, and to think, from a gender perspective, how approaches could be improved and where any subconscious biases may lie. In addition, effective training for these teams focuses on in-depth analyses of systemic obstacles to progress and potential opportunities that specifically involve sales, marketing, product development, after-sales service, and relationship management. It involves getting the teams to review and explicitly describe where there may be gender impacts as well as analyse current and projected customer bases and key trends. It facilitates the reviewing of sales and communications materials through a gender lens and gets male and female staff members to react to products and services to see if there are significant differences. It also trains customer-facing staff in some of the preferred modes of communication and client relationship management between men and women.

Human resources staffs

HR staffs are a key community in implementing gender initiatives. They are the practical implementers of the meaning and processes behind the messages. They manage many of the gate-keeping processes that must become more proactively gender bilingual – from recruitment to performance evaluation to succession planning.

The success of gender balance initiatives that focus on improving the balance of men and women in the Talent pool clearly depends on the HR function for both support and implementation. While managers are the key drivers in developing individuals, HR staffs are central in identifying and eliminating systemic bias. Remember though to run the gender initiative across the company lest HR focus it entirely on Talent issues.

It is tempting often to expect HR to automatically respond well to the introduction of a gender initiative. In many companies, it has become an increasingly feminised function, leading many to assume that the women in HR will be the most open to gender initiatives. However, oftentimes women can be just as subconsciously biased about gender as men. Women have had to adapt to the male dominated workplace. Therefore, it would not be surprising to find that they have also accepted some of the gender biases and have learnt to think, to some degree, like organisational man. Many managers have stories about how women can be harder on other women than their male colleagues. We all share assumptions about what leadership looks and sounds like. It takes conscious awareness of these issues to move beyond them.

Sir Mike Rake, BT Chairman, described to a journalist how he had had a run-in with HR when he was the head of the professional services firm KPMG. The reporter wrote: 'He said that, to begin with, only about 9% of KPMG's UK partners were women. And when he had tried to tackle the issue, women partners had told him they felt isolated. "I became concerned the HR function was not delivering. I was really shocked that, when the best employer table came out, we weren't on it and the HR people didn't seem to care. HR is so important that it should not be left to HR professionals." He then appointed a woman, Rachel Campbell, to head up HR. She came from outside the function. He told the newspaper: "I got enormous resistance but, to cut a long story short, it made a dramatic difference.

KPMG became the best employer of the year for five years in a row. We had to force the issue but, when we did, we found it had significant benefits".'[8]

All of these subtle issues make training and understanding that much more important for the HR function. Getting the department to appropriately champion the initiative should be a key upfront goal.

Training specificities

The HR training session should focus on more in-depth analyses of the systemic obstacles to progress that involve the HR function. It should get the HR teams to review and debate actual HR processes, and explicitly describe where gender may have relevance, such as recruitment, retention, and development.

- *What is the gender balance of the company's interview panels?*
- *What are the high potential identification criteria and are there any gender biases implicit in them?*
- *Does recruitment advertising appeal to women as well as men or is it geared very much to the male mindset, such as the desire to be powerful and at the top of the hierarchy?*
- *Do retention processes take account of the different career cycles of men and women, and do they subconsciously exclude high potential women because they are not as mobile as men (or they are less prepared to say that they can move around the world for the job before they actually have to make the decision)?*
- *How do you brief executive search firms to provide more gender balanced shortlists? Very often, executive search*

companies fish in the same pond for Talent and need to be pushed into looking further afield to find more female Talent.

 HR training

The business case
- The business drivers behind better gender balance
- In-depth presentation of the Talent realities today in terms of gender ratio of graduates, performance, and profiles
- The current situation and statistics in the company

The differences
- Major differences between genders that impact careers
- Career cycles, communication styles, power and political competence profiles

The HR impact
- Focus on major HR areas that require adapting to gender balance

Recruitment
- Recruitment methods, the gender balance of interview panels, the use of assessment centres
- Explicit and implicit candidate evaluation criteria
- Recruitment advertising, website messaging
- Executive search and the management of head-hunters

Retention

- Career cycle management
- Mobility, international experience, dual career management
- Management practices relating to employees with children, dependent care issues, leaves, and returns
- Flexibility, part time, teleworking, etc.

Development

- Talent identification, talent pool management
- Profiles of leadership competencies
- Promotions, succession planning
- Training and development opportunities
- Operational versus functional staffing

This process of training, if done well, will help to spread awareness and understanding of the gender issue to critical parts of the organisation. It will motivate and direct key players to drive forward and improve the gender balance, knowing why they are doing so. The next stages are to develop deeper processes and policies in the key areas of Talent and Markets, depending on the specific goals of the gender initiative.

As the Awareness Phase showed, rolling gender awareness across the company must be done in waves, from the top down. Many companies want to educate their own people to become internal trainers to roll out the same approach more broadly. This may be included in the existing management development programme and/or integrated into the company's e-learning platform along with webinars so the maximum number of

Management bilingualism – rolling it out

Top management
- Face to face sessions with an expert on gender issues
- Integrate into leadership development programmes

All managers
- Train the trainers for internally run programmes
- Integrate into general management development programmes
- Online toolkit and resources

All employees
- E-learning modules focusing on explaining gender balance opportunities
- Online toolkit and resources
- Integrate into on-boarding programmes

employees can understand the issue, its potential, and its solutions.

There are a variety of delivery mechanisms for doing this, more or less quickly, and more or less globally. Here are the ones that I have had success with:

- **Train internal facilitators**: Design an Awareness Session aimed at all managers or employees, or have it designed for the business, and then accredit internal change agents to deliver the session for you. Depending on the focus of the gender balance initiative, it may be best to have these sessions delivered by line managers rather than by HR. The advantage of this approach is that it keeps the focus clearly on gender balance, and is also a way of communicating to others the company's defined action plans and how they fit in to the overall company strategy.

- **Mainstream into management and leadership development programmes**: Whether or not you develop a specific session, it is important to have a focus on gender that becomes part of the company's management and leadership development programmes. This ensures that the issue is framed as a basic managerial competency in the company, and is framed by other key issues. As in the rest of the roll-out, think about where this module is situated in the overall programme. It is better to position it around change management or customer-centric issues than automatically framing it in a diversity context.

- **Go online**: Some companies have successfully developed online resources to raise awareness and give in-depth tools to support gender balancing – everything from basic business case arguments to slide presentations for managers to brief their teams to back up research on specific customer or Talent management issues. Intranet sites, or resources like my own 20-first Online Toolkit, offer case studies, benchmarking of other companies' initiatives, detailed Q&As, and stories where companies and managers have attained the desired balance.

- **Offer e-learning**: Finally, for communicating as widely, cost-effectively, and multilingually as possible, I've had excellent results with e-learning modules. In short, focused, and interactive sessions, they can deliver much of the content and key issues that managers need. They monitor how many managers actually took and completed the sessions, and aggregate their feedback and results. Managers can also test their own knowledge on these issues through the tool.

Whatever the method of distribution, these sessions should equip managers with the tools and competencies to manage bilingually across genders. The idea is to give a pragmatic, solutions oriented approach to the differences between genders that have an impact on Talent management issues or on customer relations. Both of these subjects are covered in more depth for specialists in Chapters 9 and 10.

Many companies offer 'diversity and inclusion' training, which usefully focuses on becoming more self-aware and more inclusive of all different kinds of thought, behaviour, and style. But such training never spends enough time on the specific differences between men and women that must be understood to be effectively managed. Managers know that it takes a lot of specific education to understand the language and culture of, say, the Chinese, the Brazilians, or the Russians. Similarly, it takes focus and attention to learn the language and culture of women, especially if one has grown up in a male dominated corporate environment.

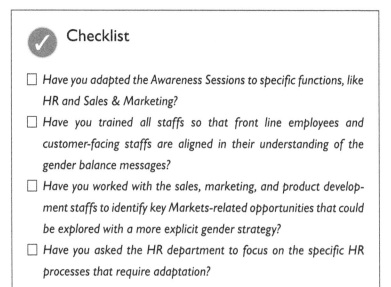

Checklist

☐ *Have you adapted the Awareness Sessions to specific functions, like HR and Sales & Marketing?*

☐ *Have you trained all staffs so that front line employees and customer-facing staffs are aligned in their understanding of the gender balance messages?*

☐ *Have you worked with the sales, marketing, and product development staffs to identify key Markets-related opportunities that could be explored with a more explicit gender strategy?*

☐ *Have you asked the HR department to focus on the specific HR processes that require adaptation?*

Chapter 9

TALENT

'No decision and certainly no succession planning decision is made without the perspectives of both men and women.'

Bob Elton, former CEO, BC Hydro

Women will be the majority of the educated Talent for the foreseeable future. Six or seven out of every ten graduates entering the job market are women. Within a decade, companies that have not learnt to attract, develop, and keep women will face the ire of their shareholders. It is likely that it will be seen as a major management issue. Plenty of leaders today recognise that they cannot hope to recruit and keep the best Talent in the world if they don't draw on this particular pool.

Human Resources policies are an essential lever in embedding gender balancing programmes into the DNA of the corporation. All HR processes must take account of shifting gender ratios among the workforce. Talent management must shed subconscious gender biases and adapt to the realities that 'Talent' may look and sound slightly different depending on whether it is male or female.

HR policies reflect corporate choices

Many HR policies are legacies of 20th century management approaches, based on large corporate hierarchies and linear, male, single-earner career models. In many companies, the leaders have spent much of their careers with the company and their rise has been charted along a carefully designed, and largely uninterrupted, course. This usually includes operational experience with P&L responsibility, managing steadily larger teams, some international mobility, and regular doses of management development coupled with a total commitment to the company.

Men and women have become used to certain leadership styles based on examples of leaders that they have grown up with. The majority of these models are male, which can make it difficult for both genders to recognise the different leadership styles that women may bring – or their value.

When women first started filling management ranks in larger numbers, companies tended to retain and promote the women who adopted the existing career models. Naturally enough, many of the women who became managers in this first big wave tended to adopt masculine traits in an effort to fit in with the cultural norm, often sacrificing their desire to have children on the altar of their career ambitions.

The next generation of women is much more comfortable in the workplace and is consequently less likely to accept this trade-off. This more confident attitude about working where they want is why many companies are now experiencing serious difficulties in retaining mid-career women.

Companies are at a fork in the road. They can choose to continue to ignore any gender specificities among managers and, when they can't, respond to them on an ad hoc, individual basis. This will continue the trend of a small group of relatively masculine women making it through to leadership positions, while the others depart. The business will miss out on the benefits of gender balance, since the women who are allowed to filter through will simply echo male perspectives and styles.

Or, companies can overhaul and adapt their system to 21st century Talent realities. That requires consciously enabling women's different behaviours, styles, and voices to affect almost everything that the company does and thinks. Those who 'get it', as women like to say, will be rewarded with the very best of that Talent. The others will soon find that the dearth of successful female role models at all levels in their organisations creates a self-fulfilling cycle that makes it ever harder to recruit other women. Below are some of the policies that need reviewing, and some of the common issues that companies discover in reviewing them. This chapter focuses on what needs changing to allow companies to unlock the power of a huge wave of female Talent arriving on the shores of the corporate world.

Recruiting

Many companies say they would love to recruit more women, but 'we just can't attract them'. Attracting one gender or another is a gender bilingual management issue. Companies – from aerospace to oil field services – that have really focused on becoming more attractive to women have usually succeeded. It requires a commitment to balance and the understanding of what would be considered attractive (or not) by the target audience.

High-tech companies often compete hard for the best female engineers and management trainees. 'Many of them want to work for companies like L'Oréal,' says Catherine Ladousse, Executive Director, Corporate Marketing & Communications (Europe, North America, Japan, and Australia) at PC company Lenovo. 'We need to show potential recruits that we are an open and flexible company and that we will facilitate a woman's career.' Being a relatively young company with a 'pioneer spirit', women can be promoted faster at Lenovo than elsewhere. 'We are all building this new company so a woman with the right skills and competencies can probably be promoted faster than in other companies.'[1]

Laurent Blanchard, VP, European Markets & General Manager, Cisco France, is dealing with a similar issue. He says: 'I believe we can make the employer brand more appealing [to women] by putting more stress on the human element of our work, connected to our company-wide campaign around the "Human Network". As a company, we position ourselves as enabling people to work in the Human Network.'[2]

Companies that want to attract a balance of male and female Talent need to ensure that their recruiting processes, messages, and people are rooted in an understanding of women as well as men. Issues of employer branding also need to be reviewed through a gender lens. Is the company attractive to both women and men? Are there role models that show that women as well as men can progress and be given fulfilling roles? Do websites and recruitment ads appeal to both genders?

Here are six ways to make a difference in the area of recruitment, including a list of pertinent questions to ask.

Six ways HR can make a difference

1. Employer branding

What kind of reputation does the company have on gender? Does it have a history of supporting women internally, or innovating in terms of products and services that connect with women? What about the sector overall? Are the products, brands, or activities as well known to women as men? Has the company analysed brand recognition by gender?

Companies usually have sections on Diversity & Inclusion on their corporate websites and annual reports in which they promote their progressive approach to potential recruits. These sections almost always include a reference to the desire to encourage and develop women in their careers. Often the companies include some metrics to show how much progress they are making on increasing the proportion of women in senior positions. Companies have become much better about communicating around gender issues. Corporate brochures show far higher ratios of women in the photos than there actually are in the company's management. And, increasingly, advertising campaigns feature a politically correct mix of diverse people, usually including at least one woman.

This is not enough to create a gender balanced employer brand. There are risks to having very proactive communications messages about gender balance that are not reflected internally. More important is whether or not the image is supported by reality. If not, how should an organisation present the image? Will a case for gender balance be credible with the image that exists or will it require a fresh new approach, challenging the older, more traditional brand?

2. Role models

Having strong role models is important for both men and women, and it motivates managers to grow by learning from people they admire and wish to emulate. In male dominated organisations, identifying and profiling female role models is extremely important in attracting female candidates. This is a challenge for companies that have few of them.

Julie Gilbert, formerly a VP at Best Buy, the very macho IT retailer, recalls two things about the times she visited stores (where she was the most senior person in her group). First, the male managers in the stores always came up to shake the hands of her male colleagues and never shook her hand. 'This kind of thing knocks women's confidence,' she said. The other odd thing that happened was that women workers in the stores always gave her a hug. Eventually, she asked why and they told her that they had always seen the organisation as a male one, and felt uncertain that they could develop their careers there. Then when they saw Gilbert coming in, they were greatly encouraged. It made them believe it was possible for women to advance in the company. That was why they were so pleased to see her, hence the hug.[3] (See Chapter 10 for more on Best Buy.)

Companies often underestimate how essential it is for women to see successful women in the organisation in order to believe in their own opportunities. So showcase the women role models in the company to recruit some more female Talent.

But choose role models carefully (see Chapter 13). Publicise both men and women who truly reflect the aspirations of the Generation Y who are now graduating from university. In this generation, both men and women are looking for more flexibility and life balance than the generations that preceded them. Young women are looking for companies where they can have a career without having to ape men or give up the chance to have a family. Many women at the top of organisations today have had to fight their way to the top in a heavily masculine working environment. Often, they are perceived, fairly or not, to have developed a masculine management and communication style. Some may also appear to have made big personal sacrifices to get where they have, such as choosing to remain unmarried or to forgo having children.

As it was internationalising, EDF, the French electricity company, took out a series of full page ads in *The Economist* showing a range of employees, men and women. The ads showcased the company's female engineers and scientists, in alternating spots with men, focusing on how they were contributing their passion about science to energy conservation, cleaner energy, and a range of environmental issues. The ads were effective because they featured real employees, in a balanced 50/50 sampling of men and women, sharing what they loved about their jobs and how what they did helped the world. This bundled several objectives and key messages without being specifically female-focused: that among the company's passionate, committed staff there were strong, scientific female role models, and that they were focused on the company's stated mission of improving the environment. This is gender bilingualism at its best. Using messages that appeal to both men and women, engaged together in a larger mission.

3. Websites and job ads

Another area to consider is websites and job advertisements. It is surprising how often, even today, the planners and creative teams fail to think about how women might react to the images and words they create. They need to take into account how men and women can have different expectations and reactions to recruitment advertisements, and to employer branding more generally.

Some research from the UK marketers Jane Cunningham and Philippa Roberts describes how women often are driven by different desires and needs than men.[4] For example, men may be motivated by products that draw on their desire for power or performance, whereas women are often driven by motives such as the desire to create a better world. Recruitment advertising campaigns can tap into this 'utopian' impulse with messages suggesting 'join our company and help make the world healthier, greener or more equitable'. By contrast, many men may prefer more 'performance-based' messaging, along the lines of 'join our company and you will become stronger, richer, more successful'.

Vocabulary has an impact too. Performance oriented words that imply competition, battle, and conquest may be less well received than more 'gender neutral' terms that accentuate themes like innovation, wellness, learning, or curiosity.

HR should review all recruiting communications, both online and off, with these gender differences in mind. It should review the corporate website, and the leadership teams represented there. Does it 'speak' to both women and men?

Research has shown that women will not apply for jobs if they feel they don't fulfil all the criteria listed in the posting. Men are more likely to apply if the job sounds interesting and they meet some of the criteria. One company calculated the comparative response rate from men and women on internal job announcements and found that women responded only if they met 100% of the criteria listed, while men responded if they had 60% of those stated perquisites. So, if job advertisements feature a long list of criteria, they unwittingly exclude female candidates who self-select out for missing even just one or two of the items listed.

Bilingual recruiters will therefore be aware that a given advertisement is likely to elicit applications from women who are relatively over-qualified compared with the men.

Very often, job ads are dry and uninspiring. They have no 'soul', and many are technical descriptions of jobs, with very little mention of the mission and vision of the company. They often lack colour or design. This is not very attractive to most women, who are more attuned to the values and purpose of the organisations they work for and the manner in which this purpose is presented. Companies are not always focused on getting their story across in a compelling way in recruitment communications. Women respond better when there is some focus on ad design.

Companies that I have worked with find that when they adapt recruitment advertising to make it more attractive to women, the profile of the men who apply is often closer to the kind of profile they have been redefining for future leaders. This is a general comment across the board. When processes are adapted to become more women-friendly, they generally become more human-friendly by encompassing both rational and emotional reactions and considerations, playing to both the right and left sides of the brain. As leadership becomes increasingly a balance between emotional intelligence and intellectual capacity, processes that speak to both bilingually draw in people who are more attracted to balanced recruitment messages. This brings in a lot of women, and it also brings in a slightly different profile of men.

4. Interview process

Beware of the tendency many of us have to hire someone in our own image. Recruiters' perceptions are often influenced by striking characteristics or similarities to themselves, and this may influence a decision in either a positive or negative way. Jaspal Bindra, CEO (Asia) at Standard Chartered Bank, says: 'There is a tendency for a recruitment panel to choose people who resemble them. So, we insist that there must be a senior woman who sits on the selection panel as well, and that supports greater diversity.'[5]

Gender awareness training for recruiters is essential. There are a number of differences in the way men and women communicate, particularly in job interviews, that interviewers may not know well and thus interpret as personality traits. One senior director at the OECD remarked after a gender Awareness Session for recruitment: 'We need to become far more familiar with these differences. What I've learned is that the person we put at No. 2 or even No. 3 on the list may actually be the one who should have been at the top.'

For organisations that have interview panels, many underestimate how daunting it can be to have a row of men interviewing a lone woman. Turn the tables on this sort of experience by having a man interviewed by a panel of women.

Having a single woman on a panel of several men is useful, but does not really help shift the dynamics of the group. To get a more bilingual analysis of candidates, ensure that at least 30% of interviewers are of either sex.

Take notes with a specific evaluation criteria grid so impressions and personal feelings don't later get in the way of the factual data that were recorded.

5. Post-interview pointers

Track by gender which candidates have been eliminated at what point during the process, and why. If there have been more men or women eliminated, bring this up with recruiters. Create a post-interview evaluation tool that is gender neutral and does not privilege male or female features. Try to have both men and women in the final shortlist and see who best fits the skills set out initially. In recruitment communications, it helps to remember the general rule that progressive business leaders never insist on hiring an individual man or woman. But they do insist on teams evolving towards becoming gender balanced. So check if, over time, certain functions, divisions, or managers are consistently recruiting a single sex.

6. Use of external recruiting agencies

While it is relatively simple to establish gender balance at graduate recruiting level, it is harder at more senior management levels. Companies that seek to gender balance relatively quickly and that don't have a well stocked pipeline of female Talent will need to use external search firms. These firms often require some training on the subject of gender as well to ensure that they provide balanced lists of candidates.

Klaus Holse Andersen, Area Vice President, Microsoft, Western Europe, and Corporate Vice President, says that he is very clear with head-hunters that their lists must reflect accurately the availability of female Talent in the market. Some of the agencies get it immediately, he says, while others need to be 'coached a few rounds'. He adds, 'They do have to look harder.'[6]

Damien O'Brien, CEO of head-hunting firm Egon Zehnder International, agrees that clients expect search firms to pitch diverse teams, ensuring they find the available female Talent. This makes business sense, as the companies get the Talent they need for creative solutions. But there is also an ethical point. Clients would see his company as 'socially irresponsible', he adds, if it did not get better at fielding female candidates.[7]

Most head-hunters use an old style career template, says O'Brien. They look only at people who have pursued a linear career path to the top. Many women don't fit this pattern, so they get missed. 'Our task is to challenge the traditional template,' says O'Brien, 'and recognise that there may be some candidates who don't tick all the boxes. But they may be qualified because they are outstanding on a number of other dimensions.' This opens up opportunities for women who may have taken time for family reasons or pursued other interesting non-corporate activities. 'Because of these experiences they can also develop some really interesting and valuable perspectives and outstanding qualities that could add a lot of value to our clients.'[8]

 ## A gender balanced search firm

In Egon Zehnder International's London office something has happened to create a good gender balance at the consultant and researcher levels. About 45% of the female consultants there are women, a balance that is a benchmark for the rest of the group. In the last few years, says Andrew Roscoe, head of the London office, the office hired six consultants, five of whom were women. 'I genuinely feel there has not been a conscious effort to recruit women rather than men,' says Roscoe. 'I personally think it is more individual than gender. I can think of very good men and women who do the job very well and in different ways. The key requirement is building strong relationships with our clients.'[9]

So, if that is the case, what explains the gender balance success at the office? There are two possible reasons related to the long-term way in which the company views its consultants. Typically, it recruits senior level candidates in their 30s from other fields of work. Instead of developing people up and weeding out the weaker ones, it hires people for senior positions, expecting them to have a long career at EZI. For this reason, the company is happy to be flexible in its approach to the individual consultants. 'We can look at things over a longer timeline. So, the fact that someone might be out for a few months in a 20–25 year career, it doesn't seem very relevant,' says Roscoe.

As head of the office, Roscoe will discuss with each individual man or woman when she or he needs greater schedule flexibility to manage outside issues. 'One female consultant wanted to take some time out to help her two children get through a period of exams. The arrangement was that over the year, she would work 70% of the time and the 30% off would be spread in different ways. We designed it together.'

The other reason the company allows for greater work flexibility relates to the way it measures individual performance. Instead of assessing people by how much money they bring to the firm, it focuses on a set of behaviours known as 'What Good Looks Like'. 'It is much easier to take a longer term view if the starting point is not related to numbers. For example, in the case of the woman who takes 30% off, I'd be looking at the level of her relationship with her clients. The reduction of her working time won't affect the quality of the answers she would give.'

This kind of support does not apply to women only – it is applicable to the whole culture. 'We have a male employee going through a divorce and we chose to be very flexible. And he said he'd never forget how much the firm stood by him. This is more a feature of how we see employees rather than how we see women and men,' says Roscoe.

But why has London stood apart from the rest of EZI? What has made London different? Roscoe suggests it might be a quirk of fate. 'Perhaps it was because the first few women who joined our practice turned out to be very good. So, immediately it became impossible to question the strength of a female candidate purely because she had a family, for instance. You just could not say it, because there were very successful female consultants in the office who had shown this really wasn't an issue.'

Level	% women	% men	Total number
Partner	30	70	20
Consultant	46	54	37
Researcher	71	29	31

Retaining

For a majority of companies, particularly professional services firms, retention is a major issue. This is often caused by rigid career cycle policies and 'up or out' cultures that firms are reluctant to change. Companies often underestimate the difficulties women can face in entering very masculine style organisations and having to adapt their natural working styles.

For example, Siân Herbert-Jones, the Chief Financial Officer at Sodexo, believes men and women tend to have very different approaches to meetings. 'Women do not feel comfortable with the male way of running meetings, for example. The male approach is to make all the decisions beforehand. Women need to be encouraged more to assert themselves. Their confidence can be knocked down by little things.'[10]

Recognising women's career cycles

As was mentioned in earlier chapters, companies that have been traditionally male dominated often have fairly standardized career cycle management. The more this is true, the more these firms tend to have issues retaining women, particularly women in their 30s. Retaining women successfully requires not ignoring or suffering through the differences in women's career cycles – it means embracing and proactively managing them. Companies that manage these cycles well will benefit from women's strong loyalty. But to do so requires understanding the cycles.

Women's career cycles tend to have three major phases across three age groups – the 20s, 30s, and post-40s, taking them in stages from being single usually in their 20s, to having children in their 30s, through to their 40s, where they are ready to turbocharge their career (this is covered in greater detail in Chapter 6). The HR team should study the differences between men and women in terms of their career patterns, and sketch out specific policies to improve the way in which they approach women's careers. In general, organisations have been designed by men for men, and women usually have been expected to fit into the male norm. So, HR can make great inroads into changing things for women by looking at some of these processes and systems in the light of women's careers.

Managing by objectives – modern management

One of the key differentiators of a gender bilingual employer is their commitment to facilitating and encouraging flexible working conditions. For a majority of companies, retention of top Talent is a major issue. Giving people increased flexibility in their working conditions, whether in terms of time or location, is a great way to retain Talent.

Busy women are particularly loyal to companies that reward performance rather than presence. However, it is important to stress that flexibility is also an increasingly important driver of men's career satisfaction.

It is essential to allow and encourage flexibility and autonomy for both women and men. It's true that flexible working conditions are often highly appreciated by talented, busy women, who routinely juggle multiple responsibilities. Providing flexibility around schedules or working location can be a powerful way to retain top female Talent. However, it is essential to recognize that men also benefit from this cultural shift. Once the benefits of flexibility – and the empowerment that comes with it – are clear, it creates great motivation and loyalty among male Talent as well.

In today's society, men are often eager to have greater flexibility in their working conditions. For example, in the UK, where full time men work some of the longest hours in the European Union, recent research has found that 52% of men and 48% of women would like more flexible hours.[11] It is therefore critical to position the discussion about greater flexibility of working conditions as something that can benefit both men and women, not as a 'women's issue'.

Lenovo has moved to a new management model that allows its staff greater flexibility over where and how they work, as long they get the tasks done. This approach – known as managing by objectives – is a very powerful way to motivate leaders, both men and women, in fast-moving markets.

It sounds easy but few companies operate this way, preferring to stick to the old management methods of strict rules, office hours, and control. Isla Ramos Cháves, Lenovo Director of Strategy & Business Optimisation, Western Europe, explains why it matters. 'This, I think, is a massive, massive leap, because going from a presence approach to an objective-based approach is absolutely critical for women.'

Managers like Ramos Cháves have to be able to set clear objectives and motivate their people to do the work. She has 107 people reporting to her, dispersed across different locations. 'Flexibility is not just about time – it is about really understanding that you give people the means to enable them to work from wherever they are.' In her own case, she would not have taken on her present senior position if she had worked for an old style company. 'I would never have accepted this job if I had been asked to move from Madrid. My manager let me work from where I wanted. In that sense this is a massive quantum leap.'

A woman with children, for example, has no trouble working at her best in such an environment. 'I have had a woman at Lenovo work for me who has six kids. The first time I discussed things with her, she said, "I don't think I can make a career here because I have six kids." And I said, "I don't understand." She said, "I have to leave at five." And I said, "Okay, you have to leave at five," and she said, "Oh, you're okay with that?"'

Ramos Cháves operates in one of the toughest, fastest moving markets and has managed to skilfully operate and manage people in this way. She stresses again that this helps to retain competent women. 'I remember having a very talented girl work for me when I was a Spanish GM and when she left the company it broke my heart. She went to work in the cosmetic sector.' But then things took an unexpected turn. 'Six months later she called me and said, "Do you have a job for me?" She had shifted to a great job with better pay and I could not understand why she wanted to change again. Then she told me that she could not stand it because at her new job she got asked what time she would be in, what time she would be out, when she might need to go to the dentist, and so on. She felt totally constrained.'

A flexible way of working makes all the difference for highly talented, busy women. 'For a woman, this is a massive difference. It is *the* difference. They feel valued and appreciated – working in an organisation where you feel you are equal.'

Men also benefit from this cultural shift. 'They see the generic advantage of flexibility,' Ramos Cháves says. 'Once they get in the swing of things they would never walk out – it gives them a sense of empowerment.'[12]

Recognise that men have children too

In the same way that flexibility is an issue for both genders, so is parental leave. Companies usually still focus almost exclusively on maternity leave, yet one of the more innovative approaches to becoming gender bilingual is to move from maternity leave thinking and the association of children with mothers, to parental leave thinking and the recognition that most children have two parents, not just one mother. It is important not to make children and maternity a women-only issue.

Companies will be able to retain and develop women as leaders only when they also allow men to be fathers. Companies welcoming women as full contributors and partners at every level in the workplace will make it easier for men to fulfil their responsibilities as parents. The same applies the other way round. Those which accept that men are full partners in parenthood will make it easier for women to fulfil their potential at work.

Most new fathers no longer see their key role as the breadwinner, according to a recent report from the UK Equal Opportunities Commission (now called the Equality and Human Rights Commission). Four out of five of respondents to a recent survey say they would be happy to stay at home alone to look after a baby.[13]

Development

Companies lose female Talent the farther up the management hierarchy you look. There are many reasons for this, most of which have to do with how Talent is identified, encouraged, and developed. The more companies and policies try to treat men and women exactly the same, the more women are effectively eliminated from the leadership pipeline. Successful long term retention of Talent requires a genuine appreciation of the differences that women and men bring to business – and policies that guarantee that these differences are optimised.

In September 2009, Benoît Potier, Chairman and CEO of Air Liquide, discussed the issue at an event run by the Grandes Ecoles au Féminin.[14] He recalled that when he started his career in research there was a good balance of men and women and that it felt very natural to have women in this environment. Moving into project management, he began to notice that it was much harder for female colleagues to gain credibility. It was all about defending results against budgets and timelines. He believes that men and women have different but complementary styles, with men being more rational and women tending towards the more relational and intuitive. However, organisations, he felt, were very masculine.

With a greater understanding of the gender differences, Air Liquide was able to change some of its development policies to give women an equal chance. For example, the age limit for identifying high potential leaders was increased from 40 to 45 in the case of women only, to allow for the fact that many of them would take some time out, usually for family reasons, in their 30s or early 40s. By recognizing the different career cycles of men and women, the company was better able to offer a level playing field. As a consequence, the company had been able to increase the pool of identified high potential women by a significant margin, from 28% in 2006 to 34% in 2008 (see Chapter 12 for more).

Professional services, the partner problem

Professional services firms (law, accounting, and consulting) face a conundrum. The average gender balance among partners in most of the leading firms is around 85/15 men to women. Most firms are trying to increase their gender balance amid growing pressure from clients. For instance, many of the women who have left law firms over the past decades (realising they would never 'make' partner) have gone into corporate legal departments. Ironically, they then become clients of law firms, and these women do not necessarily appreciate the all male teams firms send in to advise their companies.

The firms' attempts have been well meaning but inefficient. The single-model career path and relentless 'up or out' cultures in highly homogeneous partnerships, particularly in law, will never become more gender balanced until the model itself changes.

Yet nowhere in the business world are the people who lead the system so clearly invested in the status quo. The partnership model is based on a pyramid structure. A very small group of highly paid partners has clambered up a very difficult path, largely based on 24/7 commitment to slaving away in service of a senior partner. Once appointed partner, remuneration is entirely based on the productivity of the new junior staffers. Therefore, partners have no incentive to change the system to accommodate women – at least while they can still find men ready to do what they did.

Most of this is unintentional. We are all, for the moment, what Professor Gary Hamel calls the 'unwitting prisoners of a paradigm'.[15] These partners may truly believe that women aren't making it to partner because of something they lack (time, competence, style). Many managers in companies believe the same. They need to stop asking what is wrong with women that keeps them from reaching the top and ask what is wrong with the organisation that wastes so much of its Talent and the investment it made in that Talent.

Companies and the people who run them are committed to promoting competence. Yet, in many cases, the persistent drop in the percentage of women through the leadership pipeline calls into question the existence of a real, performance-based meritocracy. The issue is that 'best' is often a more biased concept than we realise, and it operates at a largely subconscious level. Fixing it requires taking a fresh look at the processes. The checklist (below) indicates the areas where HR can make a difference.

Leadership – identifying potential
The loss of exceptional women at each level of advancement in hierarchy means fewer women to choose from at the

highest levels. Why are women not there? When you scratch below the processes and cultures, this often comes down less to how leadership potential is defined than how it is actually interpreted and practised by the managers doing the identifying. Getting gender balance into high potential identification usually involves reviewing two major issues: the criteria and the interpretation.

Re-examine the written criteria for leadership potential that has been communicated to managers, looking for any implicit biases in some of the characteristics listed or some of the vocabulary used in describing them. Are tomorrow's leaders being selected on criteria that were successful yesterday but may not be entirely what the future needs? As many cultures have traditionally been run by male leaders, how much of their styles and profiles dominate the thinking about 'what it takes' to lead in the company?

The mobility criterion

Multinationals like Nestlé and Standard Chartered Bank commonly insist that candidates for high potential leadership pools be ready and willing to work anywhere in the world to gain valuable experience. This is obviously important. But women are sometimes less willing to commit themselves to mobility, so they are simply excluded from the identification process.

Nestlé changed this by separating the mobility criterion from the high-potential identification stage. Marie-Thérèse Burkart-Arnoso, responsible for Talent and organisation development at Nestlé Corporate HQ, recalls: 'We have always had a strong expatriate culture at the company. Senior managers work in different markets, gaining experience, and then are brought back into the HQ.' There they can draw from their newly rich understanding of different cultures to help the business grow. Mobility became a key criterion for the people marked out for Nestlé's Executive Management Board. 'If you had not been mobile, you could not be placed in this identification process. It was not designed to discriminate against women. It just reflected the reality that mobility was a core criterion for advancement.' But mobility had nothing to do with potential. 'Once people understood this gender bias, they immediately agreed that the identification process should include all those people who had made it to the relevant level.'

It is still too early to tell what effect this change will have, says Burkart-Arnoso. But the shift is important in opening up the process to more high potential women.

In addition, Nestlé offers new mentoring for 90 high potential women by Executive Management Board members or those just below that level. 'The level of awareness about gender balance is very high,' says Jean-Marc Duvoisin, Deputy Executive Vice President, Human Resources and Centre Administration. 'There is complete buy-in.' The challenge, he adds, is in seeing how quickly the company can deliver. 'How long will it take before we see the first results? Will it be fast or slow?'[16]

Standard Chartered found that as it grew bigger, its businesses in certain markets such as London and Singapore were large enough to give its leaders full, in-depth training of the whole business, and therefore, mobility was of less importance to leadership development. The bank's CEO (Asia), Jaspal Bindra, recalls the effect this had on women's chances. 'Mobility was a very important criterion in furthering your career [at Standard Chartered] and we used to have international mobility listed as a requirement to be high potential.' As women addressed their likely ability to be mobile, they tended to rule themselves out. 'Because of family circumstances or the fact that men's careers often come first in some cultures, women were more vulnerable. Also, the women were probably far more honest in admitting they were not mobile. The combination of these factors didn't support women's progression within the bank, and this was a big issue for us 10 years ago when we had only two to three big markets.'

With far-flung postings no longer necessary for in-depth training, that dynamic has changed. 'What we have seen is that the number of women who were classified as part of the high potential category significantly increased.'[17]

Acting on the criteria

If the criteria for leadership potential have been updated and truly reflect the new century's challenges, the next issue to examine is whether managers are actually identifying and promoting people based on the desired criteria. Often, managers have a subconscious preference for 'masculine' behaviours that they do not ever consider as gendered in any way.

The most obvious gender difference often overlooked is that men are more likely to push for progression and recognition than women, who expect to be recognised for performance. Managers need to become far more aware of the precise components of what they mean by potential, and they need to be able to report on these components in a written, objective, and performance-based way.

Businesses need to openly discuss the fact that women tend not to push themselves forward for their next career move, expecting their bosses to recognise their suitability for promotion based on their past performance. In essence, managers need to push women more aggressively to take up the next challenge.

Mind your language

I asked three CEOs recently what principal characteristic they looked for in a future leader to replace them. They said it was to be 'hungry' for power. One of the CEOs used this language when talking to a group of his top 150 women. When he left the room, the women were asked how many would define themselves as hungry in this way. Not one raised her hand. So the CEO had unwittingly just told his top female Talent (united at considerable cost) that they would not be in the running for his position. As long as companies have a very specific image of what leaders look and sound like, based on traditional models, they are unlikely to find many women that match their expectations.

Women at the top

Getting gender balance at the top of organisations depends on developing the pipeline. It also depends on promoting a few key and visible women into leadership. Research has shown that it takes a critical mass, around 30%, of women on a top leadership team for the impact to be felt on performance.[18]

David Loughman, MD A/S Norske Shell and VP Commercial Europe, Shell Upstream International, agrees with this view. He strives for at least two women on a leadership team to make a real difference. In describing what he has seen women bring to a team when there is a critical mass, he says: 'Women listen to what people actually say, they test for understanding, and they look for the collaborative solution. You also get a lot of discussion on the emotional side. What is the mood in the company on this? How do people respond to this in terms of feelings and motivations?'[19]

I found in my survey, WOMENOMICS 101, that only 12 out of 227[20] of the world's largest companies had this critical mass of women on their executive teams – just 5% of the total (see Chapter 2).

Here are three areas to think about when promoting women at senior levels:

1. **Lead by example**: Managers often look to their Executive Committee for leadership on this issue. When they are checking for commitment on gender, they expect to see

this group lead by example. This means promoting women to the top levels of the company.

2. **Token is not enough**: Promoting one token woman is not usually enough to make the commitment to gender balance credible. The value of gender balance comes only when the complementary skills and views of both genders are fully expressed and listened to. This usually requires critical mass.

3. **More women with P&L experience**: Too many women on leadership committees are in staff or support roles rather than operational roles. To stand a greater chance of promotion to the very highest positions, including CEO, leaders need operational profit and loss experience. Companies that promote women into leadership only through staff roles such as Communications or HR demonstrate that they have not yet worked out how to gender balance their leadership development systems and their Talent pipelines, affecting their ability to understand the gender opportunities in their markets and among their customers.

Women leaders often bring a very different approach to management, which some might say is better attuned to the challenges of the 21st century. Hamel has argued in his latest book, *The Future of Management*, that companies need to do much more to inspire their employees if they are to realise the true value those workers can bring. In his view, companies must better harness the 'human imagination' to remain competitive in the fast moving and uncertain business environment of modern times.

Management practices devised in the last century emphasised rules, control, and direction of people. They very rarely appealed to the 'human' in their staff. Such human values as Beauty, Truth, Love, and Service have inspired people through the ages to do great things, Hamel says, and yet businesses talk in a much duller language. 'These are the moral imperatives that have aroused human beings to extraordinary accomplishment down through the ages. It is, sad, then, that the vernacular of management has so little room for these virtues. Put simply, you are unlikely to get bighearted contributions from your employees unless they feel they are working toward some goal that encompasses bighearted ideals.'[21]

 ## Laura Roberts – school teacher turned entrepreneur[22]

Laura Roberts, co-founder and CEO of North American chemicals company Pantheon Enterprises, recalls the difficulty she had trying to get her all male management team to buy in to her more values-based mission to create a sustainable chemicals business that produced environmentally sound products at competitive prices. Roberts acquired the company from her mother in the late 1990s and set about hiring 'big guns' from companies like Procter & Gamble and Dow Chemicals for her management team. They were all men, and they seemed to Roberts to be steeped in the old 'dog eat dog' style of management that she wanted to avoid. Trying to persuade these corporate males that the company existed in part to help create a better world felt like 'I was hitting my head against a wall', she recalls. 'For them it seemed to be just rhetoric, whereas to me it was real.' She talked about the triple bottom line of people, planets, and profits and how chemical firms needed a third scorecard to show at what cost they were achieving their profits. 'We'd be arguing over these points and some of the men would say there was no global warming crisis and another would say I had been watching too much liberal news. I was depressed that being a leader and succeeding to get employees to buy in to a vision was so hard.'

This all changed when Roberts started to mentor women in her company. 'They understood what I was thinking and aiming for. It resonated much more with them.' Later she made sure that the women lower down in the management chain were included in 'brown bag sessions' where she led group discussions. She found that the women who did well and rose to the top were 'long term thinkers' and wanted to make a difference in the world. 'We have major global problems as a society, which have to be solved fast, and we could talk to the women about this. They understood. Many of them had children and the fact that these issues were going to impact on their children in their lives tended to tug at their hearts more strongly than the men.' The current balanced management team of four men and three women are now all 'good little sustainability soldiers'. But the value of the women in the company was instrumental in Roberts' getting the leadership behind her green vision.

Women leaders

Organisations can try to promote women who will serve as role models to other women in the Talent pipeline, and make sure that their culture and processes allow them to be themselves. It also seems often to be the case that women promote other women, especially when they are in top leadership positions. Three of the companies of the 12 that have achieved 30% female representation on their Executive Committees are run by women CEOs: Archer Daniels Midland, Kraft Foods, and WellPoint. This is impressive given the fact that only 15 Fortune 500 companies, or just 3%, are run by women CEOs.

 Leading the way for other women in Africa

'If you understand the history of South Africa, women have not been allowed to develop, particularly in mining, and black people were never allowed to become involved in business prior to 1994. I thought that if South Africa holds 80% of the world's reserves in manganese, why not use it to show what women can do?'

Daphne Mashile-Nkosi, Chairman of Kalagadi Manganese, recounted this story in 2009 after she had achieved her goal of setting up the first South African mine run by a woman with a significant percentage of women shareholders. Mashile-Nkosi, a former African National Congress activist who had been incarcerated by the old apartheid regime, was determined to create a precedent for women to follow.

When a new law in 2005 opened up mining to newcomers, mining of manganese, a mineral that is needed for steel production, was dominated by BHP Billiton and Assmang (Associated Manganese Mines of South Africa). Mashile-Nkosi attracted the steel major Arcelor-Mittal, which paid $432.5 million for half of the company so it could secure a supply. Ten percent of the company is owned by a government-backed investment fund, and the remaining 40%, known as Kalahari Associates, is 68% owned by women, which allows women to participate as shareholders. They use the dividends to pay for school fees and improve community living standards.

Mashile-Nkosi is also determined to make sure the Chair remains a woman. 'I realised that the vision of [encouraging] women must continue even when I'm not there. I don't know what tomorrow will bring. I then said as part of the charter of this company, this company will forever be chaired by a woman.'

The mine eventually will employ 2200 miners, some of them women, and 1200 people in the smelter. 'We strive to make sure we involve as many women as possible in our project, not only as employees but in procurement opportunities.'

Mashile-Nkosi also imposed her views on gender balance to her new partners. 'I said to Arcelor-Mittal that they would have to make sure that any Board they had that represented an interest in my company would have a woman.' Arcelor-Mittal duly appointed a woman as its South African CEO.[23]

Christina Gold rose to become CEO of Western Union, apparently without a plan to do so (see case below). At the helm, she has built a gender balanced executive team. Of this phenomenon, she says, 'Women are often the catalyst themselves for bringing other women into the organisation.'

 ## Christina Gold, CEO, Western Union

Christina Gold has managed to create a perfectly balanced executive management team at the billion-dollar money transfer company Western Union.[24] She has six women executives, including her, and six men. A Dutch immigrant to the United States, Gold developed her early career at Avon where she rose to become President of its North American business. She was not offered the CEO position at Avon, something that was initially disappointing for her, and she subsequently left the company to head up the e-commerce services provider Excel Communications. She then joined First Data (the former parent company of Western Union) in 2002 and four years later was put in charge of Western Union.

Like many women who have reached the top, she is modest about how she got there. In a recent website interview, the FT journalist Richard Milne asked her to describe her journey to the top. She said: 'I was always looking to do the next thing, to learn something new. But clearly to be a CEO was never really part of my plan. Working at Avon was a great opportunity for me where I started as a clerk and ended up running the North American business. I guess I was always curious and I was always competitive.'

Ümran Beba, President, Asia Pacific Region, PepsiCo, is also an impressive role model as a female leader, helping to drive gender balance as a business issue throughout the organisation. When heading up the company's office in Turkey, the percentage of women executives rose to 56%. She used this as a platform to share best practice with other business in the SAMEA region, which covers South East Asia, the Middle East, and Africa. She believes that women bring complementary skills and perspectives to teams, which should be encouraged. For example, they tend to be more open to new views in discussions. 'It is less about winning and more about making the right decisions,' she says. She believes that women should use their 'natural styles' in work and not try to become more masculine. 'We would help to introduce a warmer and more caring style.'[25]

Take a big first step

Nestlé Canada is the most gender balanced of all of Nestlé's national organisations. Why? In part, because 15 years ago a male CEO promoted a very successful and visibly very pregnant woman to the Executive Committee. This sent out a very loud and inspiring message to all the other women in the company: that pregnancy and parenthood were not career issues at Nestlé. Today, Nestlé Canada's Executive Team is gender balanced.

In another example, Emilio Umeoka, head of Microsoft's APAC division, is very comfortable working with women, recognising the value they bring. 'If you ever get the opportunity to work with good saleswomen, you find that they are exceptionally good. They bring something more intuitive in the way they engage with customers and they are better prepared.'

Now Umeoka is calling on his people management staff to dig deeper into the cultural depths, looking at such issues as job design to figure out ways to shape an organisation for the 21st century that attracts and develops women and men in equal measure.

Once organisations have started to tackle some of the systemic and process-driven blocks to gender balance, they begin to make substantial progress.

✓ Checklist

☐ *Have you reviewed your Talent-related processes (i.e. recruitment, retention, development) to see if they fit with the new goals on gender balance?*

Recruitment

☐ *Have you assessed your reputation as an employer – your employer brand?*

☐ *Do you recruit a balance of men and women across all functions and business units?*

☐ *Is this true in both functional and operational roles?*

☐ *Are your current leaders attractive role models for the next generation of both men and women?*

☐ *Are your job ads and web communications 'gender bilingual'?*

Retention

Career management

☐ Are your retention policies geared to the different career cycles of women?

☐ Get managers to discuss career management and prospects with their teams while being aware of career phases. Planning and preparation are very helpful for both the company and the individual.

☐ Decide what the company's and individual's expectations are for careers and personal life balance.

☐ Don't write off women who have children. Give them time to adjust and then re-engage them.

☐ Use mentoring programmes to help women (and men) understand how to continue to build their careers and networks during each of these phases.

Flexibility

☐ Allow and encourage flexibility and autonomy for both women and men.

☐ Don't consider parental leave an issue for women only. Encourage men to be fathers in equal measure to your encouragement of women to be leaders.

☐ Measure output, not input.

Development
Identifying talent

☐ Measure and track the gender balance of the company's formally identified Talent pool. If there is a lack of balance:
  - Review the criteria used for the identification of high potential Talent.
  - Review the process of how people are selected, and by whom. Ensure some degree of gender balance in the selection committees.
  - Discuss setting targets for the gender balance of the Talent pool.

☐ Measure and track the gender balance of all developmental and leadership training as well as key developmental positions.

☐ Develop a separate list of all top women in the company globally, and measure and contrast it with the formally identified Talent pool.

Succession planning

☐ Ensure that every succession plan contains a minimum degree of gender balance and define what that should be.

☐ If no women are ready to be on the succession list, systematically identify the most qualified woman for the role – and the development plan to ready her for the job.

☐ Develop targeted, individual strategies to accelerate development of long term potential female successors (job assignment, targeted training, mentoring, coaching, networking, etc.).

Tracking promotion statistics

☐ Track how many women and men actually are promoted from the succession planning lists.

☐ Many women are placed into the pipeline, but never make it into the 'ready now' category. Monitor for such drop-off.

☐ If there is a gender imbalance in promotion from the succession list, have the selection committee explain why.

Talent pipeline

☐ Are there any implicit biases?

☐ Are tomorrow's leaders being selected based on criteria relevant for the future?

☐ Is the accepted leadership style 'masculine'?

Chapter 10

MARKETS

'Understanding and meeting women's needs will be essential to re-building the economy; therein lies the key to breakout growth, loyalty, and market share.'

Michael Silverstein & Kate Sayre, in *Harvard Business Review*

Once a company understands how to manage women as well as men in terms of Talent, it's time to look at women as customers, clients, and end users. That is, if the company wants to tap the vast opportunities that await those that respond to the growing power of the purse around the world. In most of the Western world, women already make a significant majority of consumer decisions, even in a growing list of sectors traditionally considered male bastions, like cars, computers, or DIY.

Women are set to become equally significant in consumer markets in the rising economies of the globe, from the BRIC nations to Vietnam and Mexico. By 2030, a Goldman Sachs report predicts, 85% of the world's middle classes will live in these nations.[1] Empowered women in these countries, with more money to spend, will have, as in the West, most of the purchasing power and they will influence an ever wider variety of spending decisions.

Table 10.1 Talent and Markets in the 20th and 21st centuries

Talent		Markets	
20th century	21st century	20th century	21st century
'Fix the women'	Bilingual leadership	'Marketing to women'	Bilingual business
	Women are majority of Talent		Women are majority of Markets

The idea is not to suddenly add 'women' as a new segment, and deliver specific topics with specific 'marketing to women' approaches (see Table 10.1). This approach is no more effective in the Markets space than 'fix the women' approaches are in the Talent area. The size and breadth of the female impact on the economy is so huge that it requires adapting our definition of 'the economy'. This requires that all management thinking and processes geared towards customers become as gender bilingual as the managers and processes geared towards Talent.

Adapting to female customers requires building gender fluency in everyone from R&D staffs, consumer researchers, product developers, account managers, call centre staffs, and after-sales services personnel. So once you have looked at how much women may mean to your business, it's time to adapt the different ways you connect with customers. Typically, this will include:

- **The customer:** Analysis of your customer base – and customer satisfaction scores – by gender. (For the Audit side of Markets, see Chapters 1 and 2.)

- **The product and user experience:** Research, product development and how customers interface with your products.
- **The service and retail experience:** The channels used to sell products and how customers experience online and offline shopping, customer care, and after-sales relationships.
- **What you say:** Advertising, communications, and PR.

Each of these areas requires review and adaptation to female customers, who will put different priorities on different aspects of each one. The Audit Process called for breaking down customer satisfaction surveys by gender. Examining these four areas in terms of gender and acting on the findings leads to new markets, more customers, more loyalty, and more business.

Women *are* the market – worldwide

'A focus on women as a target market – instead of on any geographical market – will up a company's odds of success when the recovery begins,' says a 2009 *Harvard Business Review* article, referring to the financial crisis. 'Understanding and meeting women's needs will be essential to rebuilding the economy; therein lies the key to breakout growth, loyalty, and market share.' It estimates that women worldwide control about $20 trillion in consumer spending each year.[2]

One news magazine predicts how marketing patterns will change when companies tap into this new opportunity. 'The female propensity to save may fuel growth of banking services in countries such as India, where roughly half of all household assets are currently held in physical categories like land and machinery,' it reports. 'The vast unmet desire among Western women for more simple, understandable financial products and services could also help make retail investing in countries like the US more accessible and transparent.'[3] (Table 10.2.)

Table 10.2 Sectors that stand to benefit

Developed markets[4]	Emerging markets[5]
Financial services	Financial services
Apparel	Real estate
Beauty	Household goods
Cosmetics	Personal care
Food	Food
Healthcare	Healthcare
Fitness	Education

Middle classes in the leading emerging countries are expected to more than double from 1.7 billion people today to 3.6 billion by 2030. Where the middle class grows, there are significant improvements in the status of women, especially in the proportion of women working but also in healthcare, fertility rates, education, legal protection, and political involvement. That increases women's purchasing power, offering enormous potential in certain sectors in these countries. Female spending patterns in emerging markets will be comparable to those in developed nations such as the UK, where women are responsible for three-quarters of consumer spending on childcare, food, and education. 'Taken together, more income – and more income in the hands of women – will significantly affect consumer demand,' the Goldman Sachs report states.

So it is no wonder that companies are increasingly looking to female consumers as a way to maximise their current potential as well as create new markets.

Nestlé CEO Paul Bulcke is clear that improving the gender balance will lead to a better approach to the company's main customers: women. Nestlé's initiative, he says, 'is about understanding our consumers. ... Who can understand female consumers better than women? I am not saying men cannot understand them. But again it is about having a complementary perspective. Above all, it's the business opportunity that will drive the gender balance initiative at Nestlé.'[6]

To the East, Nissan, under the leadership of Carlos Ghosn, is determined to increase the proportion of women in its management ranks as well as in its sales teams. Why? Because the automaker's research found that women make 60% of purchasing decisions in its sector. Renault, also headed by Ghosn, is emphasising the customer experience for women. Claire Martin, head of Corporate Social Responsibility at the automaker, thinks it is outrageous that some car dealerships make women feel unwelcome. 'Someone is entering your dealership, possibly to buy one of your products, and you neglect them!'[7]

The customer: Do you know who your customers are?

The question may sound silly, but a surprising number of companies have not yet taken the first step of profiling in detail their client and user base by gender. This is particularly true for companies that have considered themselves traditionally 'male' or in male dominated sectors. This ranges from IT and medical devices to automaking and a variety of industrial companies.

Usually, they offer one of several rationalisations for this:

- **There's no difference**: The first is that they think men and women are 'the same', so differentiation by gender is unnecessary, and may even be discriminatory. Companies need to root out this major error, disproved by much research (see Bibliography for latest research), and communicate new thinking internally.
- **It's a sub-issue:** The second rationalisation is that gender *is* included in customer profiling segmentation, but is simply one of a long list of criteria. But that hides the actual gender impact or spreads it across a large number of different customer types. Make gender the very first segmentation feature in customer analysis at least once, to test the gender impact and opportunities in the business.
- **We've no female customers:** A third is that 'all our clients and customers' are men. But there are no more male-only products. Women buy 40% of male underwear[8] and are a significant segment of the home weight-training market.[9]
- **Men buy from men:** Another claim is that male customers are probably resistant to female client account managers or salespeople who are female. This approach assumes that women sell better to women, and men to men. Yet cross-gender selling can be highly effective. Take Nissan, for example, where internal research demonstrated that more male as well as female customers preferred to be served by saleswomen.

It costs relatively little to test the sceptics' claims. For instance, measure the performance of your salespeople and account managers by gender. Many of my clients have found that women outperform, even in the most male dominated industrial sectors.

Assumptions that are not fact-based kill the business potential of the gender issue before it is even tested. Unless a company can prove that gender has no impact, it is ignoring a potential windfall.

Who are you calling a customer?
The other issue that needs internal definition is who are you actually calling a 'customer'? Is it the name on the credit card that pays the bills, the purchaser, the person who actually decided what to buy, or the end user of the product? Each of these categories requires defining and reviewing by gender, as there will be implications across each population. And these categories are all evolving.

For example, in the food industry, the end user is usually a woman, but the producer's client is usually a supermarket or some form of intermediary. Some food companies will decide they are in a male dominated, B2B business where their customers are margin focused men who control the distribution channels. Yet the end user has the ultimate power of whether or not the product sells. She is likely to be a woman with an entirely different set of priorities. Power in many sectors is shifting from the intermediaries to increasingly well informed end users. That shift will require companies to reconsider who they consider their customer.

A growing number of purchasing departments in companies are headed by women, so women are also involved in major contract negotiations. As women are increasingly appointed to senior political positions and major ministries from Germany and Finland to Argentina and Canada to the Philippines and India, they are fast becoming key influencers in markets from energy and health to defence and education.

Companies need to review their own customer and end user markets, current and potential, in this light. Would women bring new and different approaches to contract negotiations and male customers and clients? Are women a growing share or even a majority of the customers or end users? If so, are businesses specifically designing products and services tailored to their needs? Have they appropriately staffed and trained salespeople and customer research teams? Are they advertising and marketing to both women and men in the most effective and gender bilingual way?

Sectors that stand to gain

A number of studies have pointed to different sectors that stand to gain from women's growing purchasing power. Here are some examples from recent research[10]:

1. **Financial services**: Banking wins the prize as the industry least sympathetic to women, even though women control about half of all private wealth in the US and many other countries.
2. **Apparel**: Women are ready and willing to spend money on clothes, but say it is a trial to do so. 'Trying on clothes is

often an exercise in frustration that just reinforces women's negative body images.' Imagine automakers marketing cars in a way that makes men think they look weak. Offering consistent sizes and a good range of cuts would help. Too many retail businesses think they've learned everything there is to know about women. They need to listen better to the female consumer in their sector.

3. **Beauty**: Cosmetics are largely marketed to women, but poorly, including excessive choice. Many cosmetic companies are staffed by a majority of women, but most are still run by men. In December 2009, L'Oréal's top executive team, for instance, was composed of 11 men and two women. A good first step toward gaining market share might be to put more women at the top levels of management, where they can help make key decisions and provide input about what does and doesn't resonate with customers.

4. **Food**: Women make the bulk of food purchases, but women sure are not happy with the stores where they make these purchases. For example, researchers found that women want a more welcoming and safer environment as they arrive and want the goods laid out so they can be found quickly. They want more fresh food available and more prominent display of healthy food. They want natural light and soothing colours and not elevator music.

5. **Health care**: Women report high dissatisfaction with medical professionals, and the more specialised the doctor, the more annoyed women are. Plus, women generally pay significantly more than men do for health insurance.

6. **Fitness**: Women's oft-stated desire to be more fit, coupled with society's pressure on women to look good, mean

that effective marketing in this sector (such as less he-man emphasis) would bring big payoffs.

7. **Education**: In the growing emerging markets, women are more likely than men to spend discretionary family income on education for their children, thereby contributing to the family's future earning power. As women in these markets become wealthier, they will spend ever more of their income on tuition, books, exam preparatory classes, etc.

There are huge opportunities in emerging markets as well. Goldman Sachs reports that 'as women gain more household bargaining power and influence over savings and spending decisions' in the rising economies they will direct more and more of their purchases to health, education, and welfare of the household.[11]

But there is potential in every sector, including those less identified with women consumers and where women's customer satisfaction levels are significantly poor. Table 10.3 shows just some of the top offenders.

Table 10.3 Level of customer satisfaction among women by sector

Sector[12]	% Women satisfied
Car dealers	27
Airlines	33
Insurance companies	36
Exercise/fitness clubs	36
Computer makers	36
Alcoholic beverage companies	40
Hospitals	45

'Women' is not a single segment

When first aiming to reach out to female customers, many companies make the mistake of thinking that women are a new or additional segment to their business that can be addressed in a single step or with a single approach. For instance, phone manufacturers have brought out a range of pink phones, some with screens that turn into mirrors, some with 'girly' packaging and accoutrements. While this may tap into a niche sub-segment of the women's market, most women do not respond to these efforts, any more than all men want a phone with a sports team's logo.

Women are a complex half of the world, and a majority of the market in a myriad of sectors. Companies need to know them better in order to better anticipate and respond to their needs. How to approach such a broad-based subject? As in the Talent issues of the previous chapter, age and life cycle are a good place to start.

Life cycle issues

Just like each decade of a person's life has a particular impact on career management, each age decade reflects a different customer stage as well. While this is obviously true for men as well, women's lives are more marked by these cycles, which have a deeper impression on everything they do – and buy. For example, a man will buy a phone for himself at every age. A woman also will buy a phone for herself, as well as a phone for her kids, then a phone for her ageing parents; all of these being purchases based on her age.

Table 10.4 provides a quick look at age life cycles as they relate to Markets.

Table 10.4 Age life cycles as they relate to Markets

Age	Markets
Children	Despite progressive parents' attempts to give dolls to boys and balls to girls, the children's market remains one of the most distinct by gender. In this huge and growing market, women decide the lion's share of purchases for their children, both boys and girls.
Teens	Electronics and clothes dominate for both girls and boys. Perhaps one of the more unisex times of life, in the teen years mothers still dominate the actual purchasing.
20s	Young working women in many countries worldwide are delaying marriage and childbearing, which often increases disposable income in this age bracket, even as they leave home for apartments, with accompanying needs and spending.
30s	Weddings, children, and work–life tensions characterise one of the most challenging decades for the modern woman, pulled between dual roles at work and with family. At this stage, she is often particularly time-pressured, typically in a dual income couple but also often a single parent. Spending is now focused on family with young children and the home, including real estate to accommodate the family.
40s	Working women with teens are slightly less time-pressed than young mothers but are often hugely taken up with growing career responsibilities even as they increase their focus on educational choices for children and have growing pressure to care for older relatives. The average US elder carer is a 46-year-old woman.[13]
50s	Post-children, more leisure time, more money, still working. More time on elder care and healthcare issues and retirement planning. Managing menopausal health. Downsizing to a smaller home.
60s	Retirees have leisure time, disposable income, and fewer dependent issues. Self-focus, fitness, self-care, diet, and nutrition. Travel. As grandchildren arrive, spending on children renews.
Post-70s	New fitness, health, and leisure needs, often including moving into health-related or retirement care accommodations. Women are often a surviving spouse, as they live almost a decade longer than men on average.

One recent study suggested another way to segment female consumers, some aspects of which complement the age-based life cycle profiling in Table 10.4.[14] For example, the 'pressure cooker' profile ties in well with the phase women often pass through when they are in their 30s.

1. **Fast tracker**: Economic elite who are either striving for top rank or, a smaller group, independent women who prize autonomy.
2. **Pressure cooker**: Married mothers, who often feel over-looked and stereotyped, just over half of whom say they are perpetually fighting chaos.
3. **Relationship focused**: Women with ample discretionary income and who report being happy, upbeat, and not short on time.
4. **Fulfilled empty nester**: Worried about health, focused on leisure – and largely ignored by companies.
5. **Making ends meet**: Usually not college-educated and with little money for beauty or fitness but seeking small luxuries and credit.
6. **Managing on her own**: Divorced or widowed woman trying to make connections.

What to know

Having established that a more gender balanced approach to marketing can reap huge financial rewards, a company must develop its knowledge of women customers and change its approaches accordingly. There are some obvious first questions. How significant are women in the customer base and market? Bear in mind both the current market and what it could be if the company were not so focused on men as consumers. What is women customers' worth to the business – today and in a few years? Do key people such as the leaders, managers, sales staff, and product development employees understand what

---

 ## Lenovo responds to market shift[15]

Traditionally operating in a man's world, PC companies like Lenovo are becoming increasingly sensitive to the rising significance of women customers and end users. Catherine Ladousse, Executive Director, Corporate Marketing & Communications, Lenovo Europe, North America, Japan, and Australia, says, 'We have women clients and some of them may prefer to deal with women or mixed teams. It also varies by country – for example, there are a high percentage of women in the customer base in countries in Eastern Europe and the Nordic nations.'

Isla Ramos Cháves, Director of Strategy & Business Optimization, Western Europe, says, 'Then you look at the end users and the gender split is more like 50/50.' This leads directly to a desire to recruit more women into key positions in sales, marketing, and production design. 'We know more women will be buyers in the consumer market,' says Ladousse, 'and therefore we want to increase the proportion of women in the related sales teams.' Ramos Cháves agrees that the company needs more women in sales but adds that they are needed in other consumer-related areas too. 'So, where do we need more women? Clearly, we need them in sales. But we also need them in operations – there are loads of design points where if you don't have them there you will fail at the front end. So, it sounds very ambitious, but it just has to be everywhere.'

---

women want and the kinds of branding and customer service they respond to?

Consider lost sales opportunities because of poor service or marketing to women. Lenovo, the global PC company, is in the process of examining its customer base by various categories including gender. It has no doubt that women will become more and more significant as direct corporate customers as well as

---

 'Investors laughed at my business plan'[16]

Laura Roberts, the co-founder and CEO of US chemicals company Pantheon Enterprises, found out the hard way how unresponsive investors could be when dealing with female entrepreneurs. Roberts took up the challenge of running the family firm after her father's death in 1997. She wanted to acquire the company from her mother (who had inherited it) and pursue her vision of building a company that produced chemicals that were both environmentally sound and competitively priced. 'Investors said they wouldn't invest in me because I was a school teacher and also pregnant at the time. I had hundreds of investors laugh at the business plan.' This was the era of the dotcom boom and Roberts' business idea seemed more of 'an unsexy meat and potatoes play'.

Determined to succeed, she did eventually raise the money she needed, and today the company is growing at 100% annually, with a 10% market share in some areas, Roberts says. 'So, there is plenty of potential for growth!'

---

end users and is working at increasing the proportion of women in different parts of the business, from sales to operations.

Venture capital firms also have a long way to go to recognise the value of investing in women entrepreneurs. They are likely to find women's authentic styles of leadership and approach different. One example is Laura Roberts. She found it almost impossible to get investors to take her sustainable, long term, and environmentally friendly business vision seriously.

The product and user experience: Adapting *what* you sell

You can improve your products for women consumers. It requires wanting to, and then researching what it is women (as compared with men) might prefer. As women consumers become ever more significant, marketers will have a growing opportunity to do more in-depth and relevant market research that integrates gender differences.

Find out what women want

It's not as though companies have not carried out market research. Many have huge quantities of customer information. But little of that research asked whether there were significant gender differences.

It makes a big difference who carries out the research, how it is carried out, and what are the actual questions asked. A deeper dig into these issues often reveals that women's perspectives and ways of communicating are not being recognised, so the differences – and the opportunities they offer – are not being captured.

Form of focus group research: Are focus groups run in standard, linear Q&A format in relatively neutral environments? You may get a lot more information from a more open-ended discussion among a group of women in a feminine environment that puts women at ease. Or get women who know each other to meet in groups to discuss the issue and give you feedback. At Best Buy, a senior woman brought in female customers for special feedback sessions with her senior management team. The leaders got an earful of very honest and direct customer information (see box: 'Best Buy Targets Women').

Who is asking: Are some of the market researchers women? One white goods, or home appliance, company I worked for sent researchers into women's kitchens armed with clipboards. The mostly male team followed the women around, noting their every action. I asked a group of women to write one page about their kitchens, and a torrent of emotional, nourishing metaphors about family love came pouring forth. The kitchen was central to these women's homes and hearts, but none of that had ever been captured by the men with clipboards.

Yang Mian Mian, the President of China-based white goods manufacturer Haier, used her female perspective to create products more suited to women. Access in freezers, for example, is usually designed for big-framed people. Yang recalled having to 'climb into the freezer' to get at anything. So, she designed a freezer with two parts – a top with shallow shelves

Best Buy targets women[17]

In 2005, Julie Gilbert, a VP at US electronics retailer Best Buy, launched a movement to enable the company to capture more of the women's market and the female talent pool. In the five years that followed, revenue generated by females at the stores increased by more than $4.4 billion.

Gilbert was at the time responsible for rolling out Magnolia Home Theatre stores for products aimed at the high-end male consumer. After realising that the operation was failing to sell and market to women customers well, Gilbert started the Women's Leadership Forum (WOLF), which invited women and some men from inside and outside the company to come together in small packs to discuss ways to improve the customer experience. The WOLF model that she led until leaving Best Buy in 2009 (to develop the idea further for other companies) had three key metrics:

- female generated revenue,
- retention of women staff, and
- recruitment of female Talent.

Gilbert piloted new in-store boutiques which sold electronics goods in a more experiential way, building on the connection between the products and the home experience. The stores, for example, set up living-room displays that showcased the electronics and the entertainment environment. Salespeople were also given training to interact with female customers, whom they had previously ignored. Gilbert claims that following this initiative returns and exchanges of purchases made by couples were 60% lower than those made by men.

The WOLF initiative at Best Buy had some clear business impacts:

- Revenue generated by females increased by more than $4.4 billion in less than five years of the programme.
- Female market share increased from 14.7% in the first quarter of 2006 to 17.1% in the same quarter in 2008.
- Female recruits increased by more than 37% in areas where WOLF packs existed.
- The number of women in the company grew by more than 18%.
- Female district managers increased by 300%.
- Women executives were appointed to run two out of the eight US Best Buy territories.

and a bottom with a drawer. This small change created a range that was far more appealing to women. Yang said: 'The change is small. However, it was a big success and it took everyone by surprise.'[18]

The right question: Are you asking women to compare their use of your product with that of your competitor's? That may not be the right question. Women (and most men) don't delineate product or shopping experiences by sector the way companies do. They are comparing your service and product with the supermarket where they shop, their favourite clothing store, or the hair salon they frequent. Asking what their favourite product or service is will give you more information and benchmarking data than a relative positioning to another unsatisfactory experience.

Forget benchmarking (again) – innovate!

In Markets, as in Talent management, companies spend too much time benchmarking what their competitors are doing. In the world today, very few companies have successfully adapted and responded to female consumers. This is especially true in traditionally male oriented sectors. So when IT and financial services firms seek to keep up with each other, they simply echo the poor performance of their peers. Far better to do some original research and take the relatively easy lead that is up for grabs in a wide variety of areas.

If you insist on benchmarking, take a walk out of your industry box, and look at what the very best companies in the world are doing. Bring in ideas from companies that have connected with both women and men, and analyse what they have done differently. These ideas are completely transferable, although it may require some big mindset shifts from your marketing teams.

B&Q, the home improvement store, altered its store feel to appeal more effectively to its female customers, reckoned to be as many as three of every four of its shoppers. The warehouse environment was changed in favour of lifestyle displays and in-store merchandising.[19] In fact, B&Q and many other DIY stores now feel more like IKEA home furnishings stores than like DIY depots. Benchmarking just outside of their defined industry sector helped B&Q and other enlightened companies to create hybrid stores and products that embrace and redefine the consumer experience. That reflects how women experience things, as comparable, experiential journeys, not as product-driven hunts.

 ## Redefining the game you're playing

Laurel Lindsay, Vice President of Marketing for the Toronto Blue Jays, the Canadian baseball team, helped to revive attendance at games after returning to her post from maternity leave in 2004. The team was in trouble in two ways: Its marketing position was based on the notion that the team would always win, and that wasn't happening. Lindsay aimed to market the experience and emotion of the event as a social and family activity. The alternative thinking created a new business opportunity for the Blue Jays. The author Joanne Thomas Yaccato describes the purpose of this new approach: 'Her goal was to have a visit to the ballpark placed alongside other leisure choices. In fact, she wasn't competing with other sports like basketball at all, but with the amusement park or the beach – she was competing for the consumer's time and wallet. She helped the club flip an attitudinal switch and her role then became not marketing a sport, but an experience.' With such innovations as 'Ladies Night Out' and 'Babies at the Ballpark' and a different approach to selling merchandise, Lindsay created a more balanced approach to marketing to both men and women.[20]

Don't think pink

One trick not to learn from your competitors is 'pinking' existing products to try to appeal to women. It won't work for more than a tiny segment of this huge market, if it works at all. Women are increasingly weary of the wealth of pink phones, pink computers, and pink advertising. Witness PinkStinks. co.uk, a website that recently started a British campaign to boycott children's toy stores with pink aisles for girls: 'The campaign will focus on the huge difference between the types of toys available for and marketed towards girls and boys on our high streets. Pinkstinks's argument is that while toys for boys encompass every avenue imaginable – construction, science, adventure, role play, physical, and educational – in the so-called "pink alleys" of toy stores choices for girls are much more limited – and limiting.'

These problems are not restricted to children. As the website LadyGeek.org.uk makes clear, this applies to entire sectors, like IT. 'It's clear that there are very few companies within the tech space who are effectively targeting women. Those that do fall into the clichés and stereotypes and end up pinking-up and dumbing-down their products and end up as one woman said, "Treating them like a special needs case".'[21]

The idea of gender bilingual products is to market and sell products that speak to everyone by integrating the needs and preferences of both men and women.

Polyglot IKEA is gender bilingual

Global furnishing retailer IKEA has managed to devise a shopping environment that appeals to both sexes. My colleague Jennifer Flock raved about a recent trip she made to an IKEA with her young baby son. 'It is the first time I've ever felt completely "seen" by a store in my various roles of woman, wife, mother, and design-lover. Every single step of the customer journey, from well before I left the house, seemed meticulously thought through with me in mind: The ability to check if what I wanted was in stock online before I left home, the large sign I could see from the highway, the big parking lot with parking for families close to the door, the play area for Théo, or the pushcarts if he wants to join us, the easy accessibility of products, the quick, cheap, kiddy-friendly food near the check-out counters for the inevitable meltdown. Everything has been thought of, just before I needed it.'

The service and retail experience: Adapting *how* you sell

Reconsider the whole shopping environment, online or in stores, with a gender view as well. Men and women respond differently to the environment, the messages, and the people. Men are said to prefer clearly identifiable signs in-store, for instance, whereas women want a sense of being welcomed as they walk in. Men navigate well around products that are organised by hierarchical technical specifications (good, better, best), while women want 'broader, deeper product selection that addresses women's complex lives and time poverty'.[22] They prefer products to be organised in a way that is related to the solutions they seek.

In short, most men are buying a product, most women are enjoying shopping for solutions. Companies that embrace the differences create gender bilingual experiences and communications that allow both men and women to get what they are after. Everyone in the organisation devising or delivering the shopping experience, online or off, must understand how gender affects customer preferences and expectations. Women display quite different shopping characteristics than men. These differences represent opportunities. I list some of them below.

Masculine versus feminine marketing: Men and women react differently to the messages underlying marketing and sales efforts. Men respond more favourably to marketing messages that evoke (directly or subliminally) success, strength, and performance. Women respond better to holistic messages that build around such ideals as working for the greater good, improving physical surroundings, self-enhancement, searching for new answers, and improving relationships.

Women and men buy differently: Women don't purchase things in a linear fashion as men often do. Instead, they shop in a loop-like fashion.[23] Women search for the 'perfect answer', requiring more exploration in the shopping process. They enjoy shopping, expect a theatrical experience, demand more information, believe in the power of word of mouth, and expect excellent service. They spend far more time in social relationships talking about products and services. This is a huge opportunity for amplification if they like a company's products or services, and an enormous potential liability if they do not.

Women consumers tend to approach their shopping with more attention to detail, being more open to alternative options, expecting good, informative service (relevant to their needs) – and this in a pleasant environment, where everything is easy and convenient. Women are usually juggling many responsibilities and have very little time to shop. They have very little time, period. But they are also seeking a meaningful shopping experience (Table 10.5), and they are willing to spend time to get it. (Men are more interested in simply getting the product.)

Table 10.5 Women and men buy differently

Men buy	Women shop[24]
Focused, product-centric	Holistic, experience embracing
Looking for specific products/ services, less interested in browsing	Inquisitive about products and uses, learn by browsing
Tunnel vision, no easy adoption of other options	Look at products laterally, open to alternatives
Less detailed examination	Comprehensive look at how a product is made or fits
Products/services usually take into account men's requirements	Expect product to take needs into account
Prefer to learn by doing	Want the knowledge up front
Interested in technical details regardless of what is most relevant	Want full explanations but technical detail only if relevant
Customisation and service have less impact	Spend more time, pay attention to minute details of the store, environment, people Expect customisation and service adapted to their needs
Little focus on after-service issues	High expectations of error recovery and warranty process

Apple's singular approach

Apple stores have nothing in common with the traditional electronics store. They are much more akin to a high end fashion retailer, with the hip music and trendy design of a Prada store, than to a Best Buy or a Radio Shack. Competitors are scrambling to imitate, but you can feel that they are benchmarking Apple, not sourcing inspiration from the same out-of-the-box fashion models Apple used.[25] In a recent visit to the Apple store in Chicago, the hip shop was staffed with a balanced team of male and female salespeople, both plentiful and clearly identifiable in colourful T-shirts. In the copy-cat competitor's shop down the street, the team was entirely made up of young men. The competitor grasped only a superficial understanding of Apple's innovation, not the underlying consumer understanding that led to it.

Apple's products have a fashionable, fresh feel to them, very appealing to women – and very appealing to men. The number of American women using smartphones rose to just over ten million in 2007, many of whom were attracted to the iPhone. By March 2009, a third of all iPhone owners were women, according to Nielsen Mobile. Clean design and multimedia features that appealed more to women than other brands put it ahead of its rivals.[26] Apple's R&D mantra is said to be 'beauty and simplicity', a far cry from the average consumer electronics brand. One big difference is immediately felt on purchase. As you open any new phone, you are generally met with a thick, paper User Guide. When you open your sleek new iPhone, there is no guide. Just plug the phone in, and it sets itself up. Women love technology as much as men – when it gets to be this simple and beautiful. And that is the secret of Apple and similar companies. They have become gender bilingual – women love them as much as men. And men are not excluded or 'turned off' by any overtly feminine features or feeling.

Social networking

Women enjoy the social aspect of shopping much more than men do. They prize forming relations with people, whether it is online, via a call centre, or in the store. A company should see if there is a linked networking element to its product that would appeal to the desire women have in building relationships and connections. Mobile phone brands obviously make a great deal of this theme in their advertising. Some TV shows encourage connections through book clubs, following the path pioneered by Oprah Winfrey.

A December 2009 survey found that the majority of online users on the leading social networking sites are female and that women of all age groups increasingly use social networks to find out about products and services. It showed that more than 85% of women online have a profile on a social network, up from 48% in the previous year (Table 10.6). [27]

Table 10.6 Online users of social networking sites

Social network[28]	% female users
Bebo	68
MySpace	64
Gaia Online	61
Ning	59
Twitter	57
Facebook	57
Flickr	55

The web

The research on online social networks suggests that women use the Internet differently from men, to do different things, search for different terms, and access sites via different sources. Companies need to track Internet usage and purchases by gender and find out if they are making enough of the importance of online shopping to women.

Many consumer goods companies have not developed an ideal website interface with customers nor have many of them backed it up with good, prompt, and intelligent service. There is huge potential in getting this right. Up-to-the-minute web designers are recognising gender differences in web usage and building gender bilingual websites. They need to take into account that time-pressed women want websites they can navigate around easily and quickly, with the appropriate information and support when they need it.

Call centres

Women expect different things when being contacted by telephone as well, and the traditional call centre approach does not meet their needs, requiring telemarketers or service personnel to limit the time spent with each customer. Women need more time to consider their options and answers, which in turn gives companies more opportunity to discover what products it can best offer.

 Selling insurance bilingually

In 2008, Royal Sun Alliance brand introduced More Th>n Women Drivers' Insurance – an auto insurance package targeted at women. It focuses on direct marketing and the service has benefits like the availability of toys in all breakdown vans for children. The company negotiated discounts on women's magazines and other products, handbag and shopping insurance, and more.

Direct marketing campaigns were followed up by call centre chats with customers. As in most call centres, the staff worked to framework scripts and had a set time to keep to regardless of different conversational styles and needs.

Then with external support from UK marketing expert Collette Dunkley, the company altered its training of call centre staff because of the issue of gender. Letting call centre's staff spend more time with its clients and spend that time in a more gender bilingual style paid off quickly: In the first week, More Th>n sales to women increased by 43% – and sales to men rose by 10%.[29]

Challenge the old ways

Lacking sensitivity can lead to embarrassing and damaging sales and service techniques. Avoid losing female customers by checking your systems:

- **Review the approach to service**: What is in the company's training that would pertain to gender? If there is nothing about this, introduce a module for managers and front-line staff. Women appreciate fast, efficient, and proactive service whether that is by phone, online, or in a store. They may be busy, but they expect a helpful, can-do staff to give them a fully detailed picture of the product or service.

- **Don't rush buyers**: Women want to take time to explore their options once they have set time aside for shopping, so they don't want to be rushed by a salesperson. Service staff should be attentive and patient, and follow up with information and helpful advice. Women don't want to be drowned in technical detail or financial information that is unconnected to their personal situation. In the financial services industry, for example, they don't want to be blinded by numbers. Barclays Wealth retrained its relationship managers to approach female clients differently. Women generally want time to discuss their concerns and worries. With a more fine-tuned awareness of the gender differences, the bank's salespeople improved their relations with female customers. In feedback, customers said the advisers were more patient and did not rush through conversations peppered with lots of references to the numbers. They said that quality of service and reliability was much more important to them.[30]

- **Word of mouth**: Women pass on recommendations about good service more frequently than men. Equally, they will warn their friends and acquaintances of any bad service. So, the need to perfect service towards women is even greater than with men.

- **Negotiating techniques**: As there are cultural differences in negotiations, there are also gender differences. (And some cultures have negotiation styles that are more feminine or masculine than others.) Include gender bilingual negotiation information in training for salespeople (Table 10.7).

- **Gender balance**: Consider the gender balance in the management and front-line staff. It seems obvious, but how many sales teams are all male (or almost) in sectors where women are the majority of the consumers or influencing spending? Conversely, women may appreciate some gender balance where sales teams are presently all female. Don't automatically assume that men sell best to men, and women to women. Test it, and make sure you have some balance on hand. Consider hiring goals to improve sales teams' gender balance.

Table 10.7 Gender differences in negotiation[31]

Masculine	Feminine
The main issues to deal with are substantive	Quality of relationship is most important
Expect to do a deal and then move on	See it as part of ongoing relationship
Seek specific information	Learn through dialogue – sharing concerns and ideas
Being aggressive is expected	Being aggressive is perceived negatively

Companies that have increased the involvement of women in leadership positions often notice that those women bring a new sensitivity to the product and the way in which it will appeal to the consumers and end users. Klaus Holse Andersen, Corporate Vice President of Microsoft and the Area Vice President of the Western Europe region, found this to be the case when he hired more women into Country Manager positions. In Western Europe, Microsoft has four women Country Managers out of a total of 12, unusual for IT, which is commonly dominated by men at the top.

Andersen, fully committed to promoting women to senior business roles, believes that they bring something valuable to the table that links directly to the company's impact in the marketplace. He has appointed female country managers in Portugal, Spain, Austria, and Norway. He has seen that a more balanced dialogue among the country leadership teams over the details of products and specific markets has improved the quality of the conversation. More specifically, he notes, women bring a new sensitivity to market issues. 'We typically get women who are more attuned than the men to some of the consumer issues. The men tend to be more attuned to the technical audiences. You get a good balance, therefore, between those who push on technical issues more and those who push on consumer ones.'

Claudia Goya, the new Country Manager for Portugal, brought new sensitivities to meeting the needs of consumers and developing the best products for them. 'When she thinks about how to go to market,' says Andersen, 'she thinks much more about branding and how a product will be perceived by the consumer.' She also thinks about how to mass market products. 'This is something we want to get better at,' he says, 'so bringing in a talent like this into the company has been very helpful in general.'

Advertising and communications: Adapting *what* you say

In the 2000 movie *What Women Want*, Mel Gibson plays a high-powered, macho ad man in New York who can suddenly hear what women are thinking after being electrocuted by a hairdryer. I recommend a non-violent approach. Advertising creatives need to consider carefully what women really want and how best to connect with them. Brands such as Apple, Dove, Nike, Haier, and IKEA are doing that very successfully. Whether or not businesses are in consumer goods, it makes sense to benchmark communications approaches against some of these companies. Check the messages and motives as well as the visuals and vocabulary that are being used. Do they appeal to women as well as to men? Do they overly feminise or masculinise the brand?

 What you say[32]

Masculine achievement impulse	*Feminine utopian impulse*
What are the strengths we currently have that would facilitate improving the gender balance?	Inspire, encourage, and support women as they try to create utopia

---

Minding the message: Marketers Jane Cunningham and Philippa Roberts argue that women follow a 'utopian impulse', while men respond more to an 'achievement impulse'.[33] They write that while 'men are driven by the Achievement Impulse and by self-interest, hierarchy, power, and competition, women, by contrast, are driven by the need to create a safe environment in which they, their offspring, and other people upon whom they depend, feel safe, secure, and happy'.

 Does British Airways care about me?

Blogging on Fast Company Online in October 2009, Kate Sweetman, the US leadership coach and writer, described an advertisement by British Airways aimed at the frequent flier business market. It was selling a service in which customers could earn miles for 'complimentary companion tickets' for their family or friends. At the centre of the ad was a male stick figure with arrows coming out pointing to different people the customer could treat to a flight, such as mother, best friend or boss (who was also male). 'I wish you could see the image currently on BA's frequent flier site,' blogged Sweetman, 'and see how well you think the image captured the interests and lifestyle of at least 50% of the business flying public (in other words, women).'

'What's going on here? And, how could this have happened at my beloved BA? I have always really enjoyed flying with them. Finally, don't they like me? Surely I am not the only potential British Airways business passenger who is not a married man?'[34]

Part of the reason for a poor advertising approach towards women is in the ratio of male to female creative directors. In the UK it is 80 : 20, with most chief creative directors in the UK being male. Yet, women usually prefer the work of female creatives while men usually prefer the output of men.[35]

Most advertising is very masculine oriented, appealing to the desire for power, hierarchy, speed, and so on. Women are not immune to these impulses, but consider whether other approaches will win over women more effectively.

Ethics/values

Every company should consider some of the psychological drivers that women consumers are said to have. For example, can it develop an ethical approach such as Fair Trade goods that would appeal to the altruistic impulse? Is there something about the design of its product that represents order and harmony, which might appeal to those women who desire an ordered, cared-for environment?

Companies are finding that women respond more than men to a range of 'green' issues, and companies can connect by building on environmentally responsible credentials. Paul Ray, in a research project on American 'cultural creatives', found that two-thirds of US environmentalists were women.[36] This is a potent, utopian platform for many companies.

Mini cars, from BMW, are very popular with women. A typical print advertisement from the company is a narrow column next to an ad for an environmental charity. The text suggests that the Mini doesn't want to hog the page, nor the road. This is an example of a company that is aligning its messaging to the utopian preferences of its market.

 ## GM and the FBI (female buyer influence initiative)[37]

Between 2003 and 2006, Collette Dunkley, then Executive Communications Director at General Motors, knew she had to challenge the status quo when she read a report forecasting that new car sales growth in Western Europe would be driven by an increase in female drivers from 2005 to 2020. In other words, market growth would be almost entirely driven by women. But further research revealed that 86% of women hated the car buying experience and everything related to it. Dunkley persuaded her CEO and Chairman, Bill Parfitt, of the need to improve GM's sales and marketing experience for women.

The company created FBI, the Female Buyer Influence initiative, a long term management change programme overseen by Dunkley. Project groups were set up to look at various strands of the business. Auto dealers were brought on board since they dealt directly with customers. 'This was a big task,' says Dunkley. 'After presenting the market opportunity and research to them I told them we really needed their help. We were delighted by a unanimously positive response. This was driven by the combination of both the business case and Bill's great relationship with them.'

To adapt the retail experience, the dealers' sales and service staff needed to be trained on how to deal with women, men, and couples. They agreed to this and Dunkley helped train staff from all dealers in the network. The dealers also agreed to implement small but important changes such as different reading material aimed at women in waiting areas, and branded toiletries and refreshments.

Dunkley says, while her company found that women instead were increasingly interested in the environmental impact and utility of their vehicles, 'The traditional technical and product approach and the focus on car performance, which appealed to men, did not resonate with most women at all.' So a programme Dunkley ran looked at how to present cars within the context of women's lives. Display cars were loaded with Christmas presents or child seats. Promotional messages and images were adapted, as were the media used to communicate with women and input was sought from a group of women into the early design of cars, with particular interest in the typically mundane interior materials used.

The goal was to increase the number of women who would consider a GM model as their next car (a standard measure of customer interest in the industry). This clearly is linked to views of the company, the brand, and the products. With the new information about how to appeal to women customers, the group piloted the project at three dealerships. After two years, the retailers had achieved 'significant results' in the number of women prepared to look at buying a GM.

Honesty and authenticity can also draw in women consumers, as Unilever discovered in its Dove beauty products campaign, in which it photographed 'real' women.

 ## How Dove made the business case for its new approach to marketing[38]

In 2003, the Dove brand was in danger of stagnation, with declining markets and stores like Wal-Mart delisting its products. Ad agency Ogilvy & Mather developed a campaign based on the notion of 'real beauty', recognising that women consumers wanted a brand that celebrated the way 'real' women looked, instead of that of a 20-year-old pencil-thin model. The agency described how it won the case for the change with the Board. 'Most of the stakeholders were men, not likely to intuitively recognise the power of this strategy. So in the first place we aimed to appeal to their rational side by highlighting the significantly higher rate of return at 6:1 expected from "visionary companies" compared with "comparison companies".' However, what really hit home for the business leaders who had daughters was when they considered their girls' attitudes to their appearance and beauty. 'Following this highly personalised "micro" version of the communications strategy, making it human, personal, relevant, and engaging – the board were convinced.'

Put gender at the heart of the strategy

Companies may explicitly user gender in their advertising, but how conscious are they of the interplay of gender differences between men and women in the way they are likely to respond to different campaigns? Part of the educative process is for all the teams involved, in the company's marketing and branding departments and in the external agencies that serve them, to bring gender much more consciously into the discussions, the creative work, and the evaluation of their success or otherwise.

The first and usually best way to do that is to review the gender ratios in the internal and external groups that handle the creative and planning work for advertising and communications. A good gender balance will increase the input and effectiveness in testing and responding to particular campaigns.

The market that matters

For many companies, reaching the female consumer market will be the key goal in the gender initiative. The reward of getting better at designing products for women in different markets, and selling and servicing them, is clearly huge. Not only are women increasingly wealthy in the developed world, they are also becoming relatively more well off in developing nations, the future engine of the global economy. The business case is clear. The challenge is putting energy and time into reviewing matters from a gender perspective and potentially transforming the organisation's approach as a result.

Checklist

☐ *Do you have all the customer data you need to assess the gender split among customers in different product ranges?*

☐ *What are the customer satisfaction scores of your male and female customers? Do they differ?*

☐ *Have you developed customer segments for women in different markets and geographies?*

☐ *What are the principal shopping impulses of your male and female customers? Do they differ?*

☐ *What is the gender balance in your sales teams? How satisfied are male and female customers with the service they get before and after sales?*

☐ *Are your product development teams aware of the different needs of men and women customers?*

☐ *Is your advertising agency fully aware of the gender issue, and does it apply that thinking to its campaigns?*

Part IV

SUSTAIN

How do we measure
progress and maintain
momentum?

Chapter 11

COMMUNICATING

'Keep linking the reason why you wanted gender balance in the first place. ... If you don't do that, the initiative can easily get derailed.'

Feike Sijbesma, Chairman of the Board, DSM

Authenticity, consistency, and repetition are the key communication rules on gender. While the first priority is to walk the talk, knowing how to *talk* the talk is equally important. Here, the gender bilingualism metaphor is particularly relevant. Organisational leaders need to learn to speak the language of men and women, impacting both genders intentionally. It soon becomes obvious whether or not managers truly understand the gender differences in the workplace and can consequently communicate adeptly to both sexes. This ability will increasingly be a part of 21st century leadership competencies.

What is true for individuals is also true at an organisational level. Does everything the organisation says externally and internally speak to both men and women? Are the positions taken, the terms used, and the perspectives put forward gender bilingual? The image of the company will be particularly shaped by external communications. To become a leader in communicating in this way, companies will want to reach out beyond their traditional channels of communication.

As in all the other areas described in this book, communication efforts must not over-focus on 'women'. The objective should be to position gender as a business issue central to leadership, managing Talent, and reaching customers. In fact, the principal objective of all communications is to reposition the topic from one that is branded a 'women's issue' to one that leads managers to take responsibility for becoming gender bilingual, and then to implement gender balance across their teams and businesses.

This is not, of course, all about talk. Communications must be a support of actions aligned with a set of corporate values. Many companies have already improved their communications about gender, without backing up the message with significant change in internal realities or beliefs. Eventually, such dissembling will out, diminishing those companies' credibility, and in more than just gender balance. As Bob Elton, former CEO of BC Hydro suggests: 'Do something concrete. Decide *now*, don't start by talking about it. Get the women in senior positions.'

This chapter gives an overview of when and what to say, once you have done something worth saying.

Leadership: The vision, the message, the words

Leaders need to explain tirelessly and repeatedly *why* gender balance will benefit the business. The business case is the basis for all of the initial communication internally.

Feike Sijbesma, head of Royal DSM, the Netherlands-originated life and materials sciences company, underlines this point. He personally pushes his company's initiative through to his managers and other employees, and makes sure they always know the reason behind it (see 'Stressing the *Why*', Chapter 4).

For the subject to be a business priority, gender balance will have to be communicated (repeatedly) at all key strategy business meetings. Ideally, communication on this topic will come from the CEO. All leaders should be repeating the messages across geographies, business units, and divisions. A one-page summary of the corporate business case for the company and industry – built on the key business-focused messages outlined in Chapter 4 – is essential as the basis for global communications.

Mastering 21st century language

Business leaders must be careful about the vocabulary they use on this issue. Be bilingual by avoiding overtly masculine business metaphors (of which there are many) like references to war, military operations, or sports. As this is a subconscious bias, most leaders need coaching even to become aware that they are doing it.

Updating language and metaphors is more than just trading explicitly masculine terms for more female-friendly forms. It is becoming conscious of language patterns and their 20th century roots, allowing leaders to modernise the values and assumptions that dictate their language. Motivating 21st century knowledge workers requires new management and communication styles. When a company makes these more explicitly inclusive of women it automatically makes the company more progressive and inclusive of a wide range of differences and styles.

The shift is an important one: It takes companies from a 20th century focus on winners and losers to references based on partners and teams. As companies can modernise only if their leaders support and engineer the change, it is crucial to think about the words used by the CEO and other top leaders on this topic. Self-awareness is critical here, and it takes curiosity and a willingness to listen. Smart CEOs get coached on how to do this well (or at least they seek feedback from their senior women on how they come across). Just as managers discover on their first international posting that they are very much products of their home cultures and countries, so many male managers understand how 'masculine' they are only when they actually experience women dominated groups or meetings. Getting this consciousness is crucial for managers who aim to adapt their communications style and use a more inclusive vocabulary.

Expanding the conversation

Women bring 'all of themselves' to work every day. This is something that corporate cultures have long frowned on: They want work to infringe on life but fight letting life intrude into work. Many managers disdain the 'emotion' that women's communication styles bring to the table. Yet the leadership literature is rife with the need for more modest, motivating, and 'coaching' styles that engage people into giving the best of their authentic selves. Women can help achieve this.

'What do men talk about among themselves?' asks Elton. 'Mostly they talk about their families and their futures. But men don't bring those conversations to work. Women do.' His engineering-dominated teams created a 'culture of strong, silent types. They don't talk a lot'. This can lead to a dangerous reluctance to address problems. 'Accidents can come from having the wrong conversations. Now that there are more women in our teams, there are also more varied conversations. We spend more time talking about behaviours, such as why people won't ask for help. We need both male and female inputs.'[1] Table 11.1 compares old 'masculine' language and new gender bilingual language.

Table 11.1 Old 'masculine' language and new gender bilingual language

Old 'masculine' language	New gender bilingual language
Exclusion	Inclusion
Superstars, success, individual heroes	Collective prosperity
Hunger for power	Thirst for new solutions
Competition	Collaboration
Opposition, fight, hardship	Supportiveness, learning, growth
Winners and losers	Winners and winners

Multiplicity of stakeholders

There are many opportunities, internally and externally, for leaders to communicate on a topic of growing interest to many different audiences. Internal channels include such usual forms as company newsletters, magazines, and online intranets as well as meetings with staff.

Externally, business leaders have a growing number of opportunities to speak on gender. There is, of course, a wide range of events related to women in leadership and women's careers. It is equally important to speak about gender at general business and management conferences and summits, where the issue can be clearly positioned as a business issue.

The World Economic Forum's summit in Davos in 2009 included a Global Gender Parity workshop. HEC, one of Europe's leading business schools, runs an annual panel discussion for CEOs to talk about gender balance as a business issue. In 2009, CEOs from Sodexo, Cisco, and Bain & Co spoke at this event.

Stakeholders are increasingly on the look-out for companies that are committed to gender balance. This includes investors, governance bodies, and many professional women's organisations.

An example of the financial community's growing interest is the Gender Investment Index developed by KLD Research & Analytics and Pax World for the International Finance Corporation. IFC, which is a member of the World Bank Group, is sponsoring the index series as part of its global Gender Entrepreneurship Markets programme, which seeks to better tap the potential of women in emerging markets. The five indices – a benchmark, three regional indices, and global top 100 best performers in gender empowerment – cover large and mid-cap companies that recruit, retain, and promote women, beginning with rankings of companies in the FTSE All-World Developed Index. Julie Gorte, Senior Vice President for Sustainable Investing at Pax World, said, 'Our review of literature indicates that

Leaders make gender balance a priority

In 2009, the leaders of three major international businesses discussed their commitment to gender balance as a business imperative at a round table discussion on gender bilingualism at the HEC School of Management, one of Europe's top business schools, as part of its Vision of Leadership Week. The discussion was moderated by me, and the panel included Michel Landel, CEO of Sodexo; Laurent Blanchard, Vice-President, Cisco Europe, and Director General, Cisco France; and Olivier Marchal, Regional Managing Director of Bain, Europe, Middle East, and Africa.

During the session, I asked for a vote from the several hundred MBA students (mostly young men) on the strategic importance of gender, on a scale of one (highly strategic) to three (business irrelevant). Most of the room voted two. The CEOs disagreed. 'I would have said that a few years back,' said Landel. 'Now I consider it a one. There *is* a business case for gender balance. It is a central strategic issue.' Marchal said, 'It is not a fairness issue, but a strategic business issue and it is evolving rapidly.' Describing the need for versatile, collaborative leaders, Blanchard said: 'My key driver is to improve performance. And to do so, we need to have more women.'[2]

Companies must have this same conversation internally, with leaders following the three panelists' model in communicating convincingly how strategic an issue gender is.

with very few exceptions a positive correlation, and in some cases a positive causality, can be found to exist between gender empowerment and financial performance.' She added, 'What we found to be especially interesting in our research was the positive correlation between gender diversity in Boards of Directors and senior management and the quality of earnings reported by companies.'[3]

Several companies have started funds that offer investors the opportunity to profit from such outperformance by companies that have communicated successful gender balance. For example, Zurich-based Naissance Capital started a Women's Leadership Fund at the end of 2009, which it expected to attract $200 million in just a few months, largely from 'ideologically inclined wealthy individuals'. Naissance will base its investment decisions on gender balance within a company's senior management structure. One of its managers, Daniel Tudor, said at the time of the launch, 'We thought if these companies are genuinely outperforming then it would be good to offer investors something. This is not a bra-burning exercise, this is business. But if the Fund does well, then people will realise that gender balance is a good thing. The two go hand-in-hand.'[4]

In the US, Pax World Investments has created the Pax World Women's Equity Fund. Its objective is to 'seek long-term growth of capital', and in selecting investments, the Fund seeks companies that 'promote gender equity and women's advancement through internal policies and programs, transparency regarding the effectiveness of those policies and programs, and accountability among employees to assure implementation and observance of the same.'[5] A new French vehicle, the

Women's Equity Fund, does the same. The growth of all these funds is testimony to the research that has shown a correlation between gender balance and performance.

Who hears what

Businesses with well designed gender initiatives need to leverage the programme with a strategic communications accompaniment. Table 11.2 lists internal and external audiences. But it is never good to talk before you can walk. Sceptics, both external and internal, abound, ready to spot unwarranted claims. Since most gender data needs to be kept confidential, there is often only one obvious place to spot progress (or lack thereof): the top. If the senior executive team is still all male or there is but a single, token woman, what credibility will the company have on gender?

Table 11.2 Internal and external audiences

Internal audiences	External audiences
Executives	Suppliers
High potential leaders	Partners
Senior managers	Media
All managers	Investors, shareholders
Employees	Community

The core metric is the balance of men and women on a company's Executive Committee, something I track every year in my WOMENOMICS 101 survey (see Chapter 2). For instance, I published an article providing the gender balance ratio of eight global companies lauded by *Le Figaro Madame* magazine in France as progressive on the gender balance issue. Only one of them (Mondial Assistance) had more than a single woman at the top level. Other French companies with a better gender balance at the top did not make the list because, despite their successes, they do not elicit a lot of attention on the issue.

Tempo and timing

Each phase of a gender initiative requires carefully designed communications (Fig. 11.1). The goal is not to maximise communication, but to ensure that your communications support the cultural changes and management mindset shifts required. Here is how to roll out communications across the different phases of the gender initiative.

In the Audit Phase, avoid general communication. Keep the team gathering the quantitative and qualitative data small. Because this is all in preparation for the presentation to top management for discussion, it is important *not* to communicate until you have figured out what the existing situation is and where you want to go. The key communication elements

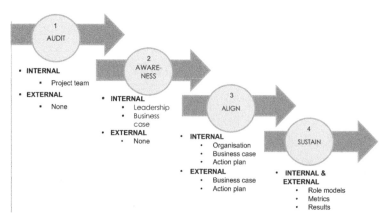

Fig. 11.1 Tempo and timing

here will be the development of the business case and the presentation to the topmost leadership.

During the Awareness Phase, the company needs to communicate the issue to those executives who will participate in the Awareness Sessions. Usually, the CEO sends the message in his or her Awareness Session invitation to senior executives, with a collection of key messages and recommendations from the workshops as follow-up. Again, no other communication is necessary. Too much communication now can raise expectations before executives have had a chance to understand the issue and finalise their action plans. Premature communication has often torpedoed gender initiatives. Get the whole leadership team aligned behind the *why* and the *how* of gender balance before making formal communications internally. The leadership teams can then become effective spokespeople and role models.

Then, in the Alignment Phase, communicate the initiative and the action plan to the wider organisation. Include explanations of the business case, illustrations of best practice around the group, demonstrations of shifts in practices and processes, and toolkits for how managers can implement progress. External communication can begin at this time as well. But beware. Schneider Electric embarked on a gender balance programme which included Awareness Sessions for all of its top managers and the introduction of an e-learning module to train all managers. But Mai Lan Nguyen, the HR manager responsible for the initiative, still waited before pushing communications externally (see Chapter 7).

Finally, maintain active communication and track progress throughout the Sustain Phase. This can include profiles of divisions or country units that have gender balanced and the business benefits that they gained, as well as case studies of balancing tactics that work, and those that don't. This should be accompanied by the expansion and development of external communications and PR on the issue, demonstrating to external audiences what is being done to improve the gender balance and why.

 ## Internal drive for change

In PepsiCo's SAMEA region (South-East Asia, the Middle East, and Africa), the percentage of women in executive roles quadrupled from 5% in 2004 to 20% in 2008. Ümran Beba, who was one of the GMs in the SAMEA region before becoming President, Asia Pacific Region, made sure that the issues were communicated internally to maintain momentum. She says, 'We have 21,000 employees [in the SAMEA region]. So, every three months we made presentations on the importance of these policies and we developed them in pilot projects, after which many people felt more comfortable about the changes. The pilots showed them that there was not going to be a negative impact on the work. If you show the facts, the managers are very reasonable. They will support it.'[6]

Inside: Internal communications

Companies need to communicate internally before they go outside. To start with, the top management will want to communicate the business case and the implementation phases to all managers and employees in order to engineer an effective change programme.

From the top: CEO-led

The CEO needs to be the principal spokesperson on gender initiatives: His or her commitment will bring the most support and engagement from the employees. At the same time, the executive team must be unanimous on these messages. As the message cascades down, the various managers and employees will take their cue from the executive in charge of their unit or

---

 'If I let the pressure off 30 seconds, it's over'

Influenced by his time managing Sodexo's US business, CEO Michel Landel was determined to introduce a new gender programme to the services solutions company. And he found he needed every ounce of his commitment and drive on the topic to maintain momentum and break through scepticism from managers and employees.

'My colleagues smiled at the beginning, thinking I was importing political correctness from the US. But we have worked at educating and demonstrating that we live in a world with two genders. And I have not let it go. We started with the Executive Committee, where we carried out both training and personal objectives on gender. Then all the managers that report to the members of the Executive Committee were trained as well. But still today, if I let the pressure off 30 seconds, it's over.'[7]

---

division. Therefore, it is important that all the executives adopt and express the principal message. The CEO needs to monitor this carefully.

Business-focused branding

Getting the branding and positioning of the gender initiative right is absolutely critical to success. It ensures that the business benefits the company expects are clearly spelled out, and are at the heart of all communications on gender. Explain the customer trends and shifting demographics if these are relevant. Use data and facts from the sector and country to make the case explicit.

Internally, think carefully about whether you want to communicate about gender as a single issue, or integrate it with other key business initiatives or changes. Integrating gender with such broad and important themes as modernising leadership, globalisation, and international understanding may work more powerfully as a message.

The best way to drive home the fact that the initiative is a business one is to put men in charge of the communications. Giving the programme a male voice will subconsciously challenge old mindsets and bring about a new awareness. Schlumberger, the oil and gas company, sent a clear message when it put a senior male manager, Jim Andrews, in charge of its gender balance programme in 2007.[8] At industrial gas company Air Liquide, the person in charge of the issue is Augustin de Roubin, Vice President, HR: Making him responsible sent a deliberate message to all employees that the programme was seen as a business issue, concerning both men and women.

The messages at this stage can be brief and to the point. They can be nothing more than a one-page briefing sheet, and a PowerPoint presentation, setting out the key messages at each phase of the initiative.

Don't get lost in diversity

Think about context. Everyone must recognise that gender is related to the bigger picture of the company's future and organisational performance. Make sure gender does not get lost in the diversity puzzle.

Non-American companies' diversity efforts usually focus on two aspects: gender and culture. But US companies tend to adopt a very broad definition of 'diversity': In addition to gender, programmes generally embrace a broad remit, including multiple cultures, religions, and ethnic groups, as well as forms of disability, plus the gay, lesbian, bisexual, and transgender communities. Either form complicates quick headway on gender balance, diffusing the focus necessary for this crucial business issue. In addition, diversity means different things at different local and national levels. For instance, race and ethnicity do not mean the same thing in Malaysia, India, South Africa, and the US – or even in Alaska and Alabama. They often require much more culturally relevant approaches.

That's why I recommend two options on communicating gender initiatives:

- **21st century leadership innovation**: Ideally, a company should put the issue of gender balance under the umbrella of other change initiatives that are designed to adapt corporate mindsets and management styles to other Markets and Talent trends. In this context, becoming gender bilingual is part of the modern manager's basic toolkit and a strategic lever to business performance.

- **Globalised world**: Gender balance can be twinned effectively with cultural diversity at companies trying to include more different nationalities on their management and leadership teams to better reflect the global markets they operate in. Amusingly, companies often see the two efforts as either/or choices. Remember: Half of every culture is female. In no area is the saying 'two birds with one stone' more fitting. Especially since in many of the major emerging markets, especially Russia, China, and India, women are a formidable and highly educated force.

Use language that emphasises the underlying objectives behind the gender initiative; the choices here are endless, but possibilities include gender balance, 21st century leadership or management innovation, customer focus, consumer experience. All such terms embrace the men who are more likely to be the ones responsible for carrying out the change. People do need to understand that the aim of the programme is to reach a balance between men and women at all levels of the company and in elements that reach markets and deal with customers.

Make clear that balance is not necessarily 50–50 across the board. Balance means the business-relevant level of balance for each part of the business. That should be closer to 50–50 than to 90–10, but in its communications the company should focus on the issue of improving performance through balance. It will, of course, be some time before most men accept that gender balance applies as much to them as it does to women. As companies pull more women into higher positions in the near future, men will become more familiar with real gender balance and witness the benefits it brings. Until then, it may be up to the convinced leaders to make the case.

Outside: External communications

The gender balance process yields vast publicity benefits. A successful initiative is good for a company's all-round reputation as a progressive, forward-looking organisation attractive to both sexes. Specifically, publicising success in gender balance promotes the company's employer brand to prospective female executives, and interests investors and the financial press who note gender balance's link to outperformance.

When to start

The company should start thinking about its external communications strategy from the moment it starts the programme. Record all the information and data gathered in the Audit Phase and discuss with the communications team what should be publicised when the time is right. Think about how the company wants to be seen. What are the markers worth celebrating? Which leaders to put forward for comment? Which media to engage with? How to respond to any criticism of the starting gender balance and of the process?

Working with the media

Decide which audiences to reach and with what information. From this, divide the plan into different forms of media, such as radio, TV, print, and the internet, and develop a core list of editors, journalists, and producers to contact. Just informing them of the initiative might be enough at the start. But to be more pro-active, think about setting up introduction meetings with key members of the media to discuss the issue informally.

For initial publicity, look to such obvious places as publications and programmes that specialise in diversity and women in the workforce. See if the company deserves a place on the many lists that rank the best employers for women or in terms of diversity. If the company is confident it has reached the right level of excellence, control the message by making its adaptation known rather than waiting for the media to catch on.

In general, the media do not perceive gender balance as a core business issue, driving sustainable success. It is reported as a women's issue – one of fairness and equality at work – and so media are interested in new data that show pay gaps between men and women or the lack of advancement of women in senior positions. The media have also realised that there is a market for women readers, listeners, viewers, and browsers. Publications from the *Financial Times* to *Forbes* and *Fortune* produce regular lists of the top women in the business world to respond to the female business reader.

However, few media outlets expect the CEO or top executives of a company to go on record discussing the gender balance initiative as a major business driver. One need only look at the many interviews with male CEOs in which the issue of gender balance is rarely, if ever, discussed. It comes up only when the interviewee is a woman business leader – and she is usually and understandably not interested in discussing the issue. She wants to be taken seriously as a business leader and not treated like a 'minority' concerned only with the so-called 'women's issue'.

But the media's approach provides an opportunity for companies that wish to publicise the issue. The CEO of a major company publicly discussing gender balance as a business issue – now, that is newsworthy! And it would put the issue squarely on the mainstream business agenda in the media and help to educate people beyond. If the company is willing to follow this path and if the CEO is passionately leading the issue as well as good at talking to the media, encourage interviews and panel discussions on the topic. As well, look into media training for the managers involved in implementation and focus on a particular media form in the training. For example, for TV or radio, instruct the managers to give succinct and articulate answers to questions on an issue new to most of them.

Look at bringing gender balance into presentations to the investor community. Bear in mind that this is a relatively new area, and the investor community will be impressed only by hard data and well considered points. I do not recommend that a company scramble for convincing metrics to put forward. As in all other areas, it is best to be open and transparent. As the company improves its balance, investors will come to see the issue as an increasingly important predictor of the company's future success.

Sustaining the impact

The media have a short attention span and look for new stars all the time. So beware the boredom effect. If the evidence is compelling, the company will keep cropping up at the top of lists and be referred to as a leader in the field. If the data are variable and sometimes weak, the media may stay interested for the wrong reasons. Be ready for negative comment before it surfaces. Ensure that the key people in Communications are monitoring the gender balance numbers, especially among senior executives, and that they are ready to explain any dips in the ratio.

Consider other ways to sustain a corporate image as a 21st century organisation which supports men and women equally. Look into funding research into key issues such as organisational change, work flexibility, or leadership development, perhaps via a business school programme or a magazine feature. The resulting publicity will keep the company's name associated with adaptation in the eyes of stakeholders from investors to employees to customers.

Communication is a critical component of success in the gender initiative; it must be driven from the top and then rolled out to the whole organisation and beyond. It is the force that will maintain the momentum and help push change and sustain it once it has been established.

Checklist

☐ *Have you identified and prepared messages for each key stake-holder group?*

☐ *Have you planned the various stages in communicating gender balance?*

☐ *Have you identified pockets of excellence inside the company to publicise internally and, later, externally?*

☐ *Are you clear about the messages you will take outside?*

☐ *Have you listed the best spokespeople for the issue from the top management?*

Chapter 12

MEASURING

'The first thing we did when this project began was to frame a number of indicators. The purpose was to provide a focus for the initiative while ensuring that a momentum was built up and sustained.'

Augustin de Roubin, VP, HR, Air Liquide

Every good manager knows how important it is to track and measure the progress of a change programme. It is the best way to monitor results and assess whether the approach is working. It also helps in maintaining momentum. This is no different in regard to gender. In fact, it is a crucial component of long term success.

In 2004, Gerald Lema, Corporate VP and President, Asia Pacific, Baxter International, set a six-year goal of increasing the percentage of women in what the company termed 'critical' management and executive positions throughout his regional businesses from 31% to 50%. With the aid of a team dedicated to this effort, the goal was reached in 2008, two years ahead of schedule. Throughout the process Lema insisted on being sent the key gender balance metrics on a weekly basis, so he could monitor progress.[1]

Reports

Regular reporting of measurable criteria is critical to maintaining pressure and keeping the visibility of the gender initiative high on the agenda. *Who* is reporting on *what* will define where the focus and accountability of the programme lies – both in terms of functional responsibility and level of reporting responsibility.

Many companies ask the HR department to track the numbers. This may be appropriate if the major driver of the initiative is related to Talent management. But if the organisation wants the initiative to be perceived as a strategic business issue for which all managers are responsible, make reporting an individual, team, and divisional priority. Have each manager report back on individual progress on developing a gender balance of men and women in his or her teams and key functions or units. The report should not address the promotion of women solely. Because the ideal is a balance, across all areas, functions, and geographies, that is what should be measured. Include in every single metric the statistics for both women and men, and the (im)balance between them.

A company focused on the equally important issue of gender balance in relation to reaching customers will need to identify key marketing, sales, and customer metrics that reveal the level of progress being made.

As well as which unit, department, or function should measure the issue, decide who exactly will be accountable. This is crucial as it is the managers who will drive decisions on such things as the approaches to Markets and Talent management, and therefore, they need to be made accountable for the gender balancing results. In most cases, the best first approach is to have the most senior people reporting and tracking the data on gender. The higher the seniority, the more priority and importance the initiative will get. Ideally, the Executive Committee members will be reporting back on their own data and the progress being made in their areas of responsibility.

What to measure

What the company asks for in the reports will focus the minds and efforts of everyone, so make sure that the criteria being measured are the right ones for the business concerned.

While most organisations want to track many indicators, I recommend focusing on just a handful as *key* priorities and measures of progress. Too much data can dilute the focus. What are the key, measurable objectives of the initiative? This should be related back to the key metrics that were analysed in the Audit Phase, as those will be the starting point numbers from which to evaluate progress.

Focus on simple numbers that accurately represent progress. Prioritise which of the issues to focus on, such as the proportion of women and men being identified in high potential leadership pools. The company must decide which set of measures best reflects the goals of its gender initiative. But there are some common approaches that provide an idea of how this might look.

Internal – Talent

- **High-potentials**: Many organisations focus on righting the gender balance in their most senior groups and their high potential pools. The latter obviously represent the future Talent base of the company's leaders and as such provide the most sustainable way for many companies to reach the goal of gender balance. Where this pool is not balanced, the organisation has to depend on external hires to redress the balance. So, one measure could relate to top management: monitoring the gender balance at the most senior levels of the head office, different markets, and different functions.

- **Leadership development programmes**: The leadership development programmes within companies are the source of future top leaders and often the most immediate way a company can start to move toward balance. Many companies choose to set a target percentage of women they want to see in their top 250 or so leaders. This can focus executives and managers on ways to increase the representation of women.

- **Recruitment**: Track the gender balance among new recruits at all levels.

- **Retention**: Focus on the numbers relating to the proportion of Talent being retained, since many companies find that the higher the grade level, the more women have left. See if women and men are being retained in equal measure at senior levels and, if not, why not.

- **Employer branding**: Look at ways to measure the company's attractiveness as an employer to graduates and more senior hires. Measure the gender balance in the hiring figures and use group feedback and other methods to establish the level of interest prospective employees have in working for the company.

External – Markets

- **Customer satisfaction levels**: Compare the satisfaction of male and female customers, purchasing decision makers, and end users. Divide by gender across different product lines and carefully delineate among user experiences, retail experiences, online experiences, and so on. Also look at customer satisfaction levels linked to male and female account managers to track any differences.
- **Female market share**: Measure the growth in sales revenues to women and men and/or the growth in revenues by male and female account managers.
- **Product usage**: One obvious measure is the gender balance of consumers by product, market, and division. This can provide useful information when tracked over time.
- **Channel usage**: Check the gender balance related to different purchasing and delivery channels, including online and offline channels.
- **Brand image**: Monitor the perception of the company and brand image by men and women, and check for differences.
- **Client-facing staff**: Track the gender balance of client-facing functions, such as salespeople, account managers, and call centre personnel.

Indicators

Having decided which measures to track, set the schedule for reporting and review.

Change is the point of the gender initiative, so look for evolution. The Audit Phase will have pointed up areas needing redress and also a sense of past advances and retreats on balance. Watch for new patterns under the programme.

Where to look depends on the company's priorities in balance.

 Air Liquide

It is sometimes quite clear from the start which indicators to measure and track. In 2006, for example, French-based global industrial gas supplier Air Liquide selected a number of key Talent-related indicators that it has monitored ever since, says Augustin de Roubin, Vice-President of HR. They include the following:

- Number of women in management.
- Number and percentage of women in operational and functional roles among the company's top 250 managers.
- Percentage of high potential women identified.
- Number of women Country Managers.
- Percentage of women managers and engineers hired.

'The first thing we did when this project began was to frame a number of indicators. The purpose was to provide a focus for

---

the initiative while ensuring that a momentum was built up and sustained,' recalls de Roubin.[2]

Today, the company can see how well it is progressing using the same indicators. In September 2009, Benoît Potier, Chairman and CEO, discussed Air Liquide's progress on gender balance with senior businesswomen at an event run by Grandes Ecoles au Féminin.[3] He was able to show that the percentage of women hired had risen slightly from 18% in 2006 to 22% in 2008. Using a 'master list' of high-potentials the company had also managed to increase the number of women identified as having leadership potential from 28% in 2006 to 34% in 2008. De Roubin says Air Liquide has increased the number of women Country Managers from 12 in 2006 to 35. 'The idea of having a woman in this position is no longer an issue for people – it is the norm. This is one of the key aims of the programme: to change mindsets.'

Table 12.1 Balance at Air Liquide (2008)

Category	No. of women	Total no.	% women
Board	2	12	17
Executive Committee	1	10	10
Top 250	36	250	14.4
Identified high potential leaders	155	450	34
Management	3000	10,000	30
All employees	10,000	44,000	23
Country Managers	11	100	11
Graduates hired (engineers and managers)	717	2514	29

Talent

For a company concerned about its top Talent pipeline, data on top management might include the percentage of men and women on the board, the Executive Committee, and the top executives below that (at least down to the second level below the Executive Committee). It might also measure gender statistics in support or staff roles versus operational or line roles. Some companies might also want to compare 360 degree feedback scores aggregated and segmented by gender.

 Baxter International's Talent-building metrics

Baxter Asia Pacific built clear metrics to drive its 'Building Talent Edge' initiative, which won a Catalyst Award in 2009. Baxter's goal in 2005 was to achieve gender balance in the leadership and critical positions cadre by 2010. This was driven along two dimensions: recruitment of new Talent and internal recruitment, development, and communication. The region comprised 14 countries with very different cultural approaches to women in management. In Japan, for example, only 13% of the managers were women in 2006; in China, the figure was 45%.

These simple and effective metrics were delivered on a weekly, monthly, quarterly, and annual basis to the senior leaders, including the President, Gerald Lema. They included:

- percentage of senior leadership positions held by women.

- percentage of positions in different management bands held by women.
- percentage of new recruits (director and critical positions) who were women.
- percentage of staff promoted within who were women.

Table 12.2 Metrics at Baxter International

Metrics at Baxter International (Asia Pacific)	% women in 2006	% women in 2007	% women in 2008
Asia Pacific Leadership Team	25	...	37
Management Band 2 + (director and above, including those termed 'critical')	28	...	48
New hires (director level and above including 'critical' positions)	...	36	45
New promotions (director level and above including 'critical' positions)	...	30	41

Source: Data from Catalyst.

Table 12.3 Metrics at Baxter International in China and Japan

Country	% women on Executive Team		% women directors and managers	
	2006	2008	2006	2008
China	44	85	45	62
Japan	17	33	13	16

Source: Data from Catalyst.

Professor Herminia Ibarra of INSEAD business school carried out this kind of research based on a 360 degree evaluation of 2816 executives – one in five of them women – from 149 countries who were taking executive education courses. Women outperformed men in this exercise on seven dimensions: energising, designing and aligning, rewarding and feedback, team building, outside orientation, tenacity, and emotional intelligence. The only dimension where women were perceived by some to have performed less well was 'envisioning'.[4]

To track indicators for the leadership pipeline, display the gender balance in succession planning lists and those *actually* promoted over the past few years. Some companies need to devote more attention to the lower rungs of the ladder to build the pipeline. At French-based nuclear company Areva, the goal is to have at least 20% of women at senior management levels. The company also tracks the percentage of female engineering graduates it hires. It said recently that women engineering graduates represent 35% of the company's hires against a national average of 17%.[5]

Others are more concerned about balancing the pipeline. Global services company Sodexo has made significant strides in overall gender balance, but is now focused on, and monitoring, the dispersal of its Talent. CEO Michel Landel is clear on the importance of this indicator: 'Our biggest challenge is to move women into operational management roles. We are working hard on this particular topic, and are keeping a strict review of what kind of experience our new recruits receive. Of our 250 top executives, 18% are women and our objective is to increase this to 22% by 2012. The targets are not (yet) linked to incentive compensation, but I may introduce that soon.'[6]

Markets

There is a wide range of possible indicators related to Markets, organised around internal Talent and external customer-related factors. Internally, a company could track the gender balance of its salespeople, account managers, and client contacts. Or of its product managers, consumer researchers, R&D personnel, and brand managers. Externally, it should gather valuable intelligence about customer perceptions and market trends. The relevant indicators would be the gender mix for some of the following: product, market, and division, the brand loyalty, satisfaction levels in the customer experience, satisfaction with sales staff and after-sales staff, and word of mouth recommendations.

Reporting on the reports

With the data demanded arriving at a regular pace, the company can develop clear, visual reporting that lets it quickly check its status at any given time, and compare it across businesses, countries, and functions. This keeps the pressure on managers and employees and creates internal competition to make progress. A simple, colour-coded global management scoreboard on gender can work wonders in this regard. Define three levels of gender balance vis à vis the company's targets:

- **Green**: Goals achieved, satisfactory balance (i.e. at least 30% or 40% of both genders).

- **Yellow**: Needs further improvement but has achieved acceptable minimums (i.e. at least 20% or 30% of both genders).
- **Red**: signals unsatisfactory gender balance levels (i.e. less than 20% or 30% of one gender).

Comparing these results across divisions, businesses, and products will keep minds focused and usually yield interesting contrasts that can themselves lead to many lessons. The company can spread best practices from the 'green zone' experiences and examples internally.

Quotas, targets or objectives?

There has been a lot of ink (including some in Chapter 7) spilled over whether or not companies should impose some form of mathematical objective setting to their gender initiatives. Some managers are instinctively opposed to setting quotas or targets, others believe it is imperative. But whatever form it takes, the most critical factor to success or failure will be the degree of determination and drive with which the overall objective of gender balance is pursued. With a high level of determination, companies will tend to drive the programme through, finding their own way of maintaining momentum.

That said, quotas are usually an admission of poor leadership – a last resort (usually imposed from outside) to push behaviours that are not yet understood or accepted. This book and the phases it describes offer an alternative approach. One of the benefits of gender balance is new, more progressive approaches to leadership, employee motivation, and customer relationships.

'Conscious decision to find a better gender balance'

Feike Sijbesma, Chairman of the Managing Board of Dutch-originated life and materials sciences company Royal DSM, is clear about the gender balance levers he needs to focus on.

'By looking at the inflow (promotions and hires) and the outflow (leavers), managers have an opportunity to make change. For example, they might be able to retain someone who would otherwise leave.' He finds that this is a calmer (and more acceptable) approach than telling managers to rebalance their teams (and so compelling them to fire people because of a less optimal gender or nationality balance on their teams). 'It is less threatening to them than saying, "Look, the composition of your team is wrong." Every time you have an internal promotion or an external hire you have a decision point – you can do something. You can look longer for a different nationality or for somebody female.'

In this way, Sijbesma managed to improve the balance on his Supervisory Board by hiring two women as directors: one for the overall company board and one for the subsidiary board in the Netherlands. 'I deliberately looked longer for good and excellent women. I could have filled the posts much more easily by sticking to male directors. But in order to achieve a better balance, I spent a little bit longer looking for women. And I want the leaders at DSM to take that same conscious decision to find a better gender balance more often.'[7]

So dropping old labels is a helpful part of the process. Instead, leaders can set a vision for balance, explain why it's better for business, and then educate and empower individuals – both men and women – to make it happen. Gender bilingualism is a basic building block to 21st century success. Good leadership in this area should trump the need for quotas.

However, government-mandated quotas in some regions like Europe are becoming a reality. This is already the case in Norway, Spain and France, and is under discussion in a number of other countries. If companies do not manage to make their own progress on gender balance, they will find that this will very likely result in external rules being established. This should serve as an added incentive to manage the change internally first.

Better, if you can, to educate people, as DSM's Feike Sijbesma does, than to regulate to compel them to change whether they want to or not.

After setting up the indicators and measures, the next and final challenge is to build the reward structures to drive and motivate the managers and employees to make this area a key priority for them over the long-term. This is the subject of the next chapter.

Checklist

☐ *Have you decided who is accountable for the entire gender initiative and for tracking and reporting on progress?*

☐ *Have you devised the internal and external measures that matter most to you, keeping them as simple and relevant as possible?*

☐ *Have you checked that the main measures and indicators cover Markets and Talent, tied to your main goals, so that they will drive progress and maintain momentum?*

Chapter 13

REWARDING

'In some ways, we don't want to make this seem exceptional – it should be viewed as basic good practice at all times.'

Isla Ramos Cháves, Director of Strategy & Business Optimization, Western Europe, Lenovo

Celebrate success

It is important to recognise and celebrate successful gender balancing initiatives – and the leaders who drive them. This has a powerful effect on the motivation of managers and employees to succeed in this area in the long-term. If they see it as a performance criterion, and a key factor of successful 21st century leaders and companies, they will be stepping over themselves to achieve a good balance. One way to drive this point home is to make sure that managers and employees understand that this is one of the aspects of being a good leader.

More successful than you think

Many leaders look elsewhere for best practice and sometimes forget to look inside their own organisations, where there are usually pockets of good practice. These are certainly worth finding and celebrating, as such successes will be highly relevant and appropriate for other parts of the organisation and are more likely to resonate with people than external examples.

A good start is to identify the managers in the company (male and female) who have successfully developed gender balanced teams – at any level, in any country. Interview them, tell their stories, and get them to explain the context. Why did they promote balance? Was it unintentional, or a conscious effort to change things? How did they implement change and what did they and the business get out of it? Some of this will best be supported by comments from the individuals involved. Has the quality of decision making improved? Have there been new complementary skills brought into the mix? What has been the impact on revenues and on customer satisfaction?

Emilio Umeoka, President of Microsoft in the Asia Pacific Region (APAC), practises this approach. He expects his People Management team to 'create heroes, people doing well in this area, from which everyone else can learn lessons', adding that he will maintain focus on the issue until it becomes 'natural'[1].

Share the success stories widely across the organization, while giving the people directly involved some form of recognition, reward, or award. Leaders should make it clear that this kind of performance will be spotted and recognised. Once managers realise that such behaviour is highlighted as a valuable leadership skill, critical to their future advancement, many will be falling over themselves to do well on this issue.

Damien O'Brien, CEO of executive search firm Egon Zehnder International, refers to the company's London office as an example of excellence in this area. By providing greater flexibility to its senior women, the office has achieved an almost 50/50 gender balance among its consultants (see 'A Gender Balanced Head-Hunter', Chapter 9). 'When I look around,' he says, 'I can see our London office where almost 50% of our consultants are female and I can see that [flexibility] is increasingly happening. We are supporting our consultants, both women and men, when they need to take time out for critical family issues for a period of time.' He adds that the 'payback' from the senior staff who have been given this kind of understanding is 'very significant'. This pocket of excellence provides O'Brien with a perfect illustration to use in discussion with other members of the firm around the world.[2]

Isla Ramos Cháves, Director of Strategy & Business Optimization, Western Europe, at PC company Lenovo agrees that best practice should be celebrated but seeks to avoid any hint that greater balance is exceptional. Like many of the leaders I have interviewed, she wants gender balance to become the norm. 'In some ways, we don't want to make this seem exceptional – it should be viewed as basic good practice at all times. But I would see the celebrating as the basic sharing of good practice, so if a manager has achieved balance, he or she can explain how he or she did it.'[3]

To pay or not to pay

Some companies tie gender balance achievements to compensation. While incentive compensation has been much criticised during the economic crisis of the late 2000s, it can still, in certain cultures, serve to emphasise the priority given to different issues, and whether gender balance is included in the bonus mix sends out a clear signal of its relative weighting.

But in most organisations incentive compensation is not seen to be the most effective motivation for change on longer term topics of this kind.

For instance, Ramos Cháves does not like to see bonuses attached to balance at Lenovo. 'The minute you make it bonus-related it becomes something that is on top of your everyday duties. It is important to share the best practice but you must be careful to avoid creating a feeling that this is an add-on to their normal business. They must understand why the company sees this as a competitive advantage.'[4]

Because of the broad, cultural nature of the gender shift, it is often enough to make it very clear that fostering balance will be an important criterion in determining the organisation's future leadership and executives' success within the company. This is why the issues of role models play such a strong part. And why it becomes equally important that not delivering on gender must have consequences.

Walk the talk – manage failure

Recognising success needs to be accompanied by recognising the lack of it too. Executives and managers should not be afraid to point out the failures, where important lessons can be learned. Also, they should make sure they follow through on their rhetoric with action, recognising and advancing the people who promote gender balance – and doing the opposite for those who don't. Leaders should find out why some of their managers have not done well on gender balance, which is after all now a dimension of their performance, and offer suggestions and support for improvement. This will set the right tone in the organisation and reinforce the notion that anyone who wants to be considered a good leader or employee must take the gender initiative seriously.

Role models

Role models are a key part of the change management process on gender. They help clarify and explain desirable behaviours, confirm compelling communications, and demonstrate that progressive leaders will 'get' gender bilingualism.

The role of the CEO

The CEO is the most important role model on gender. His or her visible and consistent leadership on this topic sets the tone for the whole organisation. Communication by the CEO needs to be consistent and constant, particularly in the early phases of the initiative.

Many people will look at the CEO's own team (the Executive Committee) to check commitment to this issue. It is hard to be a convincing role model if there is no gender balance at this level. At the very least, people need to believe that the company is truly committed to change and that there is a clear programme to redress the balance on the Executive Committee and other key areas.

The role of managers

Once the gender balance programme has been implemented, it is time to multiply the role models. Companies can communicate stories about the men and women who succeeded in bringing about balance in their own teams.

It is particularly important to feature men in this role, and get them to explain why they did it, and what business benefits they reaped. Most companies focus all their communications on this issue on successful women as role models. It is just as important to focus on the men who are actively developing and promoting those women as well as on the managers who are ensuring that their teams are gender balanced with men as well as women. That is what needs to be made visible, and encouraged as part of progressive leadership culture in any organisation.

Employees

Gender balance can be as impactful at employee level as it is at management level. Across the organisation, including factories and secretarial pools, it reduces stress[5] as well as staff turnover and absenteeism[6]. Some companies have reported to me that gender diversity improved labour relations and even reduced alcoholism in the workforce. One way to drive change and get across the message well is to undo the gender stereotypes that dictate roles and jobs. Gender balance is equally as important among secretaries and assistants and on the factory floor as in the C-suite.

In some regions of the world this is already happening and can have a positive effect on the whole company. For example, Lenovo, the PC company, saw an opportunity to start afresh when it established a service and support centre in Bratislava in the Czech Republic in 2006. 'We made sure,' recalls Catherine Ladousse, Executive Director, Corporate Marketing & Communications, Lenovo Europe, North America, Japan & Australia, 'that we hired a balance [of men and women] when setting this up, and have since achieved a ratio of 50/50.' The challenge now for the company is to increase the proportion of women in management. 'We are very focused on Bratislava and want to make sure women there have the same opportunity to be promoted as the men. Nobody can say that we cannot promote women in the same number because the base is low, when we all know that it is 50/50.'[7]

Women

Without focusing entirely on the women, it is useful to heighten the visibility of women and work to raise the volume of their voices and ideas. In most cases, they are still the minority in positions of seniority and other women need to see role models to inspire them and drive their enthusiasm for the change.

Renault's all female engineering team

Odile Desforges, the first woman to make it to the Executive Committee of the male dominated French automaker Renault, initiated an interesting experiment to showcase the value of women engineers. Desforges had worked her own way up through the ranks in Purchasing and Development, where she got to understand the intricacies of making and selling cars. In 2009, she became Executive Vice President for Engineering & Quality.

'I wanted to find a different way of looking at some problems and their solutions, perhaps, something that was more pragmatic.' So, she experimented with setting up an all women team of engineers under the leadership of a male manager. The result was encouraging. 'The team was extremely efficient, it went straight to the point, there was no time-wasting, and everything was well prepared.' She saw how the manager reacted to his female team. 'He told me later he was very impressed by the speed at which they proposed very clear and pragmatic ideas to simplify the company.'

This is a good example of how executives and managers can approach things in a new way and challenge the status quo. It clearly opened up one manager's eyes to the potential of women engineers.[8]

Also, it helps all managers to see women managers who are successful in the organisation, as they become models for them when they are devising the criteria for their next hire or in developing high potential employees. This is a point made by Gerald Lema, Corporate Vice President and President, Asia Pacific, of Baxter International. He says that as there are more and more successful women in top management positions, other managers will have more female role models as reference. 'A manager will be able to tell a recruitment agency to look for someone similar to a particular woman or several women who have been hired and are performing well in the organisation.'[9]

Featuring successful women role models in internal and external communications can also have a very strong impact on the next generation in the pipeline and give credibility to the assurance that they can 'make it' too.

Choose wisely

But it is important to make sure that the role models featured are actually inspiring to others and fit more closely to the ideal woman leader of the 21st century. In other words, a good female role model is a woman who has been able to thrive in her career and reach the top heights without having to conform completely to the masculine culture of the past century. She won't necessarily have had to choose not to have a family or any life outside work. Instead, she will be comfortable balancing work and life and do well in both spheres.

Putting the spotlight on women leaders who look and sound like men can be counterproductive. This is especially true if many of these women have no family, much less children. One client of mine was pleased to have added a couple of women to his Executive Committee in Europe. It was not enough in his eyes, though the global Executive Committee in the US had none.

But the two women who sat on his team both had husbands who did not work and took care of the family issues, just as the men on his team had wives who stayed at home. While this is a fair sign of equality, it also signals to all the younger women *and men* in the organisation that they are unlikely to make it to the top in the company unless they have a spouse willing to take over family duties. In an era of dual career couples, this may hugely limit the pool of totally available Talent, or simply self-select out many managers (especially women) whose spouses are attached to their own careers.

Instead, feature people who have managed to combine their professional lives with rich personal lives. Let them talk about both spheres. Ask them to give advice and ideas about career management, about balance, and about raising children while pursuing a career. Younger women are hungry for guidance and mentoring on such issues. Men care about these issues too, and the best leaders are conscious of the need for balance. Get them to address the issues too.

One way these women can succeed is by harnessing technology. At Lenovo, Ramos Cháves and Ladousse both work remotely from wherever they want so that they can balance work and life, and they manage other men and women who can be equally flexible. They focus on the objectives and drive things forward with passion and the human touch. Doing it any other way would be unthinkable to them. Further, they are convinced it is the only way to manage in a sector that moves forward at breakneck speed.

Best practice

It is always helpful to capture the lessons of success. When celebrating success and recognising role models, be sure to find out what these leaders did, how they actually implemented their ideas, and what recommendations they have for others.

 Key success factors

- It's a business issue, not a women's issue.
- Requiring strategic and sustained initiative like any other change management programme.
- Led by credible leaders.
- Evaluated with measurable success criteria and milestones.

Benchmarking best practice

Now that the company has found and spotlighted internal successes, use their experiences to set a relevant and company-specific benchmark for best practice that is disseminated at management meetings and key leadership conferences. Have other parts of the company seek detailed analytics and 'how-to' from these successful managers, units, or functions. Promoting the leaders of these areas to larger roles can expand their capabilities, which probably are just as considerable in other change management areas.

Learn from outside too

It is worth knowing what other companies are doing, but mostly to get a fact-based evaluation of what they have actually achieved. Too many companies have a tick-the-box approach to gender. They do a lot of things (with a preference for organising or sponsoring high visibility women's conferences that increasingly connect with clients), without necessarily following through on measurable deliverables – for their customers or their employees. Look beyond their often time-consuming and costly activities, which usually are aimed at some award or official label, to see if they have achieved real improvement.

Take, for example, the ratio of men and women in the Executive Committee of some of the companies that received awards in 2009 from US research organisation Catalyst for their achievements in the area of gender balance. While Baxter International (which won an award because of its initiative in Asia) has four women and seven men on its top global executive team, engineering and construction company CH2M Hill, another recipient, has an Operations Council manned (literally) by five men, just like winner KPMG's Global Board.

Beware of benchmarking only against companies in the same sector or country. Few industries or countries are models of best practice. If you must benchmark, benchmark against the best companies in the world on gender, and see what they are doing.

Rewarding and recognising managers who implement gender balance reinforces the message that the company is serious about the issue. It positions the topic among the other priorities that managers are being asked to focus on, and communicates that it is part of the desired leadership behaviours the company seeks to develop. This keeps the momentum strong, the focus clear, and the company on track to deliver the benefits of improved gender balance.

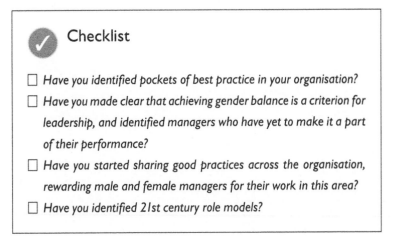

Checklist

☐ *Have you identified pockets of best practice in your organisation?*

☐ *Have you made clear that achieving gender balance is a criterion for leadership, and identified managers who have yet to make it a part of their performance?*

☐ *Have you started sharing good practices across the organisation, rewarding male and female managers for their work in this area?*

☐ *Have you identified 21st century role models?*

CONCLUSION

Many thinkers see the first decade of the 21st century as the time when power shifted to the East. China's economy is predicted to surpass that of the US by 2030.[1] But commentators are still downplaying another great historical shift: the rise of women as a global economic force.

The signs of change are all around us. The major tectonic plates of the global economy are being reshaped by women. The labour force in several countries is going majority female for the first time in modern history, and there is a decline in fertility globally, in both rich and poor countries, for the first time ever. Women are the majority of the Talent pool emerging from universities around the world. While most of the world points to wage disparities in favour of men, we can spy the tip of a new trend in New York City, where educated young women out-earn educated young men.[2] At least 3 in 4 of the jobs lost in the late-2000s recession in the US had been held by men, mostly in manufacturing,[3] while a similar share of the jobs created in the EU since 2000 were filled by women, mostly in services.[4]

Women are the biggest economic revolution of our time. The tides of history are unstoppable and irreversible. It is no longer time to debate why this has happened or why it matters. The urgency is to adapt to the mammoth change – and the opportunities it opens up. Too many business leaders ignore the change, inside and outside their organisations, much as they cling to their old management models despite the modern, globalised and technology-enabled economy.

The key to economic and commercial progress lies in businesses tearing down the remaining barriers to the full utilisation of female Talent, enabling them to create balanced teams of men and women in all parts of their businesses and at all levels. Developing gender balanced teams is the one critical way they can break the old management mould, generating diverse perspectives and skills to drive greater innovation and meet the demands of customers and end-users.

However, businesses also have to approach the issue of gender balance in the right way. They must extract it from the Diversity & Inclusion and HR departments, where it is watered down amidst other 'minority' groups, and place it where it belongs: in the boardrooms and Executive Committees. They need to stop calling it a women's initiative and instead root it in their central strategic change programmes. They must recognise it as an essential component of success in the modern economy.

Clearly, gender balance requires new ideas, new approaches, and courageous, enlightened leadership. In my experience, top teams (still mostly made up of men) are very good at analysing the opportunities, the challenges, and the solutions related to gender balance. More than most women suspect. They should be encouraged to do so, without too much need for copy-cat references to unconvincing efforts by others. Best practice is yet to be designed on a global scale. The leaders in this book have innovated in their teams, countries, and regions.

I hope that this book has pointed business leaders, both male and female, in the right direction, toward huge business benefits. Few companies have achieved global gender balance... yet. Those that do will reap competitive advantage for the century ahead. Are you ready?

NOTES

Introduction

1 Maitland, A, 'Fathers & daughters,' *Management Today,* November 2009.

2 *The Economist*, 'Female Power,' January 2, 2010.

3 Silverstein, M J and Sayre, K, 'The Female Economy,' *Harvard Business Review,* September 2009.

4 Interview with the author, December 2009.

5 Interview with the author, November 2009.

6 www.20-first.com, 'Tapping into Female Talent in India,' November 9, 2009.

7 www.20-first.com

Chapter 1

1 Interview with the author, November 2009.

2 Cunningham, J and Roberts, P (2006) *Inside Her Pretty Little Head*. Cyan, London.

3 Parmar, B (2009) 'Women as Consumers of Technologies,' www.20-first.com. Parmar based her facts on research she conducted with Forrester in 2007 as well as articles in the UK press.

4 Gender bilingualism is a term I invented to describe a specific management competency: that of having an in-depth understanding

of the differences between men and women, both as Talent and as customers, in the 21st century economy required to deliver high performance, sustainable prosperity for global business.

5 McCracken, D, 'Winning the Talent War for Women,' *Harvard Business Review*, September 2000.

6 FT.com, September 2009.

7 Hewlett, S A, Sherbin, L and Sumberg, K, 'How Gen Y & Boomers Will Reshape Your Agenda,' *Harvard Business Review*, July–August 2009.

8 Silverstein, M J and Sayre, K, 'The Female Economy,' *Harvard Business Review*, September 2009.

Chapter 2

1 McKinsey & Co (2007) *Women Matter: Gender diversity, a corporate performance*; McKinsey & Co (2008) *Women Matter 2: Female leadership, a corporate performance driver*.

2 *The New York Times*, 'The Place of Women on the Court,' July 7, 2009.

3 *The Observer*, 'Observer Survey Reveals Gender Barrier Stopping Women Reaching the Top,' August 23, 2009.

4 *The Wall Street Journal*, 'No Such Thing as Work-Life Balance,' July 14, 2009.

5 Hewlett, S A (2002) *Creating a Life: Professional Women and the Quest for Children*. Miramax, New York.

6 GE corporate website, December 2009.

7 Annis, B, Barbara Annis & Associates, 2008.

8 Author's interview with Siân Herbert-Jones, CFO, Sodexo, and Rohini Anand, Senior VP and Global Chief Diversity Officer, Sodexo, October 2009.

9   Interview for www.20-first.com, 2009. The interview took place before Piyush Gupta was appointed CEO of Singapore-based bank DBS Holdings Group in November 2009.

10 *The Observer*, op. cit.

11 Bain & Co (2008) *Gender Math Unlock Key to Achieving Diversity in Executive Ranks*.

12 Interview with the author, Women's Forum, Deauville, October 2009.

13 IPSOS, Grandes Ecoles au Féminin (2009) 'Les pratiques destinées à favoriser la mixité des équipes dirigeantes,' www.grandesecole-saufeminin.net

14 Wittenberg-Cox, A and Maitland, A (2008) *Why Women Mean Business*. John Wiley, Chichester.

15 www.catalyst.org

16 *The Observer*, op. cit.

17 www.som.cranfield.ac.uk

18 www.nafe.com

19 *Daily Telegraph*, 'Call for More Women in the Boardroom,' October 19, 2008.

20 Sir John Parker also became non-executive Chairman of Anglo American plc in August 2009.

21 This information was drawn from the relevant corporate websites in December 2009.

Chapter 3

1   Interview with the author, December 2009.

2   Interview with the author, November 2009.

3   Exxon Mobil corporate website, viewed in December 2009.

4   BP corporate website, viewed in December 2009.

5   Higher Education Statistics Agency, 2009.

6 *The Observer*, 'Observer Survey Reveals Gender Barrier Stopping Women Reaching the Top,' August 23, 2009.

7 http://womensleadershipfund.com/

8 Silverstein, M J and Sayre, K, 'The Female Economy,' *Harvard Business Review,* September 2009.

Chapter 4

1 Interview with the author, November 2009.

2 Interview with the author, November 2009.

3 This is drawn from a talk given by Bob Elton at the Women on Board Forum on Transforming Corporate Cultures held in Vancouver on October 22, 2009, when Elton was still CEO of BC Hydro.

4 'Message from BC Hydro Chair,' November 9, 2009, www.bchydro.com

5 Wittenberg-Cox, A and Maitland, A (2008) *Why Women Mean Business*. Wiley, Chichester.

6 Catalyst (2007) *The Bottom Line: Corporate Performance and Women's Representation on Boards*.

7 McKinsey & Co (2007) *Women Matter: Gender diversity, a corporate performance driver*; McKinsey & Co (2008) *Women Matter 2: Female leadership, a corporate performance driver*.

8 Interview on www.20-first.com, 2009.

9 Silverstein, M J and Sayre, K, 'The Female Economy,' *Harvard Business Review,* September 2009.

10 Interview on www.20-first.com, 2009.

11 Goldman Sachs (2009) *The Power of the Purse: Gender Equality and Middle-Class Spending*.

12 Wittenberg-Cox and Maitland, op. cit.

13 Interview for www.20-first.com, 2009.

14 BBC online, 'Men "out-performed" at University,' June 7, 2009.

15 OECD (2008) 'The Reversal of Gender Inequalities in Higher Education: An On-going Trend,' in *Higher Education to 2030 – Volume 1 – Demography*.

16 McKinsey, *Women Matter 2*, op. cit.

17 London Business School (2007) *Innovative Potential: Men and Women in Teams*, Centre for Women in Business.

18 Catalyst , op. cit.

19 McKinsey, *Women Matter*, op. cit.

20 McKinsey established the relative success of several hundred companies against nine criteria: leadership, direction, accountability, coordination and control, innovation, external orientation, capability, motivation, and work and environmental values.

21 McKinsey, *Women Matter 2*, op. cit.

22 Adler, R and Conlin, R, 'Profit, Thy Name is ... Woman?' Miller-McCune.com, March 2009.

23 *Financial Times*, 'Soapbox: why women managers shine,' March 2, 2008. For more information on the latest research on the link between women and profits, go to the business website 20-first. com (section: why/better bottom line).

24 Adams, R and Ferreira, D (2008) 'Women in the Boardroom and Their Impact on Governance and Performance,' SSRN, October.

25 Dezsö, C L and Ross, D G (2008) ' "Girl Power": Female Participation in Top Management and Firm Quality'. Available at SSRN. July

26 *The Economic Times*, 'Women promoters beat big daddies,' March 8, 2009.

27 *Daily Telegraph* (letters page), October 19, 2008.

28 Interview with the author, October 2009.

29 Interview with the author, November 2009.

30 McKinsey, *Women Matter,* op. cit.

31 Cunningham, J and Roberts, P (2006) *Inside Her Pretty Little Head*. Cyan, London.

32 *The New York Times*, 'Women Now a Majority in American Workplaces,' February 5, 2010.

Chapter 5

1 Prime, J and Moss-Racusin, C A (2009) *Engaging Men in Gender Initiatives: What Change Agents Need to Know*. Catalyst.

2 Interview with the author, October 2009.

3 SHE figures 2009, Europa (portal site of EU), November 25, 2009.

4 Rachel Campbell was promoted at the end of 2009 to become the global head of people, performance, and culture (PPC) and a member of KPMG's global executive team.

5 Interview for www.20-first.com, 2008.

6 Rockwood, K, ' "Forget Shrink It and Pink It": the Femme Den Unleashed,' *Fast Company*, October 1, 2009.

7 Ibid.

8 Ibid.

9 This is drawn from a talk given by Bob Elton at the Women on Board Forum on Transforming Corporate Cultures held in Vancouver on October 22, 2009, when Elton was still CEO of BC Hydro.

10 *The Economist*, November 21, 2009.

11 Wittenberg-Cox, A and Maitland, A (2008) *Why Women Mean Business*. Wiley, Chichester.

12 *Middle East Online*, 'Tunisia – the land of female university students,' November 28, 2008.

13 Linder-Ganz, R, 'Government firms lacking over 30% directors,' Haaretz.com, September 7, 2009.

14 Catalyst (2009) *Women in Management – Global Comparison*.

15 *Today's Zaman*, '22.8 percent of large corporations' management women,' December 30, 2009. The report quoted the Turkish Confederation of Employers Unions' Female Managers Survey.

16 Alepin, L, 'Women make strides in Turkey,' www.womenentrepreneur.com, July 23, 2009.

17 Cárdenas de Santamaría, C (2008) 'Why Are Colombian Women Executives So Special?' www.20-first.com

18 Catalyst, op. cit.

19 Catalyst (2009) *Women in Emerging Markets*.

Chapter 6

1 Drucker, P, 'The Next Workforce,' *The Economist*, November 1, 2001.

2 Interview with the author, 2009.

3 Information provided by Giovanni Ciserani, President Western Europe MDO, Procter & Gamble, by e-mail, December 2009.

4 Hamel, G [with Breen, B] (2007) *The Future of Management*. Harvard Business Press, Boston.

5 Tannen, D (1998) *Talking from 9 to 5: Women and Men at Work*. Virago, London.

6 Interview with the author, November 2009.

7 Interview for www.20-first.com, 2009.

8 Milne, R, 'View from the Top,' FT.com, September 25, 2009.

9 Lashinsky, A, 'Oracle's enforcer – Safra Catz,' *Fortune*, September 10, 2009.

10 Barsh, J and Cranston, S (2009) *When Women Lead: The Undiscovered Link Between Joy and Remarkable Performance*. Crown Business, New York.

11 Interview for www.20-first.com, 2009.

Chapter 7

1 Interview with the author at the Women's Forum, Deauville, October 2009.

2 Interview with the author, November 2009.

3 Interview with the author, November 2009.

4 Interview with the author at the Women's Forum, Deauville, October 2009.

5 Panel discussion with the author, EuroFinance Conference, Frankfurt, November 19, 2009

6 Sweetman, K, 'It Takes a Tough Man to Get the Right Corporate Board,' *Fast Company* blog, July 1, 2009.

7 Catalyst (2009) *Women in Management – Global Comparison*.

8 Interview with the author, November 2009.

9 Interview with the author, November 2009.

10 Prime, J and Moss-Racusin, C A (2009) *Engaging Men In Gender Initiatives: What Change Agents Need To Know.* Catalyst.

11 Cohn, A 'Women and Negotiation: Why and How Men Should Come to the Table,' Lighthouse Consulting blog (www.lighthouseteams.com/ideasatwork), December 6, 2009.

Chapter 8

1 McCracken, D M, 'Winning the War for Talent – Sometimes It Takes a Revolution,' *Harvard Business Review,* November-December 2000.

2 Ibid.

3 Speech at Cass Business School, 'Why Women Mean Business,' November 28, 2009.

4 Interview, November 2009.

5   Silverstein, M J and Sayre, K, 'The Female Economy,' *Harvard Business Review,* September 2009.

6   Cunningham, J and Roberts, P (2006) *Inside Her Pretty Little Head* (Cyan); Thomas Yaccato, J and McSweeney, S (2008) *The Gender Intelligent Reader* (Wiley).

7   Coronary heart disease in women (2005), BMJ, Volume 331.

8   King, I, 'Women ready to break into boardroom,' *The Times,* November 18, 2009.

Chapter 9

1   Interview with the author at the Women's Forum, Deauville, October 2009.

2   Interview for 20-first.com, 2008.

3   Presentation by Julie Gilbert at Cass Business School, September 28, 2009.

4   Cunningham, R and Roberts, P (2006) *Inside Her Pretty Little Head*. Cyan, London.

5   Interview published on www.20-first.com, 2009.

6   Interview with the author, November 2009.

7   Interview with the author, November 2009.

8   Interview with the author, November 2009.

9   Interview with the author, November 2009.

10 Interview at the Women's Forum, Deauville, October 2009.

11 Equal Opportunities Commission (2007) *Working outside the box: changing work to meet the future*.

12 Interview with the author at the Women's Forum, Deauville, October 2009.

13 Equal Opportunities Commission, op. cit.

14 http://www.grandesecolesaufeminin.fr/dejeuner_b_potier.html

15 Hamel, G [with Breen, B] (2007) *The Future of Management*. Harvard Business Press, Boston.

16 Interviews with the author, October 2009.

17 Interview for www.20-first.com, 2009.

18 McKinsey & Co (2008) *Women Matter: Female leadership, a corporate performance driver*.

19 Interview for www.20-first.com, 2009.

20 76 companies out of the total 303 were excluded because in some cases it could not be verified who was on the Executive Committee. All percentages referred to in this document are based on the number of companies retained in the survey (227 out of 303).

21 Hamel, op. cit.

22 Interview with the author at the Women's Forum, Deauville, October 2009.

23 Interview with the author at the Women's Forum, Deauville, October 2009.

24 Milne, R, 'View from the Top,' FT.com, November 6, 2009.

25 Interview for 20-first.com, 2008.

Chapter 10

1 Goldman Sachs (2009) *The Power of the Purse: Gender Equality and Middle-Class Spending*.

2 Silverstein, M J and Sayre, K, 'The Female Economy,' *Harvard Business Review,* September 2009.

3 Foroohar, R and Greenberg, S, 'The Real Emerging Market,' *Newsweek*, September 21, 2009.

4 Silverstein and Sayre, op. cit.

5 Goldman Sachs, op. cit.

6 Interview for www.20-first.com, 2008.

7 Interview at the Women's Forum, Deauville, October 2009.

8   Stanfield's news release (2002) 'The Men's Underwear Market'.

9   McKechnie, D, Grant, J, Korepina, V and Sadykova, N, 'Women: segmenting the home fitness equipment market,' *Journal of Consumer Marketing*, Issue 1, 2007.

10   Silverstein, M J and Sayre, K (2009) *Women Want More* (Harper Business); Silverstein, M J and Sayre, K (2009) 'The Female Economy,'op. cit.; Yaccato, J T and McSweeney, S (2008) *The Gender Intelligent Retailer – Discover the Connection Between Women Consumers and Business Growth* (Wiley); and Goldman Sachs, op. cit.

11   Goldman Sachs, op. cit.

12   Yaccato and McSweeney, op. cit.

13   Gail Sheehy, speaking at the Chautauqua Institution, August 2009, www.ciweb.org

14   Silverstein and Sayre, 'The Female Economy,' op. cit.

15   Interview on behalf of the author at the Women's Forum, Deauville, October 2009.

16   Interview at the Women's Forum, Deauville, October 2009.

17   Professor Bettina Buechel, Developing WOLF, IMD Case Study, 2009. (IMD-3-2098); Heifetz, R, Grashow, A and Linsky, M, 'Leadership in a (Permanent) Crisis,' *Harvard Business Review,* July-August 2009.

18   Silverstein and Sayre, *Women Want More*, op. cit.

19   Dunkley, C, 'Differences between the sexes: it's all in the brain,' *Market Leader,* Quarter 3, 2009.

20   Yaccato and McSweeney, op. cit.

21   'Why Jeremy Clarkson may just be the answer,' ladygeek.org.uk, November 17, 2009.

22   Yaccato and McSweeney, op. cit.

23   Cunningham, R and Roberts, P (2006) *Inside Her Pretty Little Head*. Cyan, London.

24 Yaccato and McSweeney, op. cit.

25 Ibid.

26 Holson, L, 'Smartphones Now Ringing for Women,' *The New York Times*, June 10, 2008.

27 Maul, K, 'Women's participation in social networks on the rise,' *PR Week*, December 14, 2009.

28 www.informationisbeautiful.net

29 Interview with the author, November 2009.

30 Ibid.

31 Yaccato and McSweeney, op. cit.

32 Cunningham and Roberts, op. cit.

33 Ibid.

34 Sweetman, K, 'British Airways Travel Promotion: A Leadership Failure,' *Fast Company* Online, October 26, 2009.

35 Dunkley, op. cit.

36 Ray, P H and Ruth Anderson, S (2000) *The Cultural Creatives: How 50 Million People Are Changing the World*. Harmony Books, New York.

37 Interview with the author, December 2009.

38 AGF Ogilvy Awards Case Study (2009) 'Dove's Big Ideal – From Real Curves to Growth Curves'.

Chapter 11

1 This is drawn from a talk given by Bob Elton at the Women on Board Forum on Transforming Corporate Cultures held in Vancouver on October 22, 2009, when Elton was CEO of BC Hydro.

2 20-first.com, 'Why Is It an Interesting Debate to Have?' 2009.

3 Socialfunds.com, 'Goal of new index series is to advance gender equality,' March 11, 2009.

4   20-first.com, 'Women's Leadership Fund Aims to Profit from Women-Friendly Firms,' 2009. The author is a member of the advisory panel of Naissance Capital's Women's Fund.

5   www.paxworld.com/funds/pax-world-mutual-funds/womens-equity-fund/

6   Interview for www.20-first.com, 2009.

7   Interview for www.20-first.com, 2008.

8   Case study, 20-first toolkit website, 2009.

Chapter 12

1   Interview for www.20-first.com, 2009.

2   Interview with the author, September 2009.

3   http://www.grandesecolesaufeminin.fr/dejeuner_b_potier.html

4   Ibarra, H and Obodaru, O, 'Women and the Vision Thing,' *Harvard Business Review*, January 2009.

5   Areva news release, November 2009.

6   Interview for www.20-first.com, 2009.

7   Interview with the author, November 2009.

Chapter 13

1   Interview with the author, September 2009.

2   Interview with the author, November 2009.

3   Interview with the author, Women's Forum, Deauville, October 2009.

4   Ibid.

5   Australian Attorney-General's Department (2008) *Workplace Diversity: Strength in Diversity.*

6 European Commission Directorate-General for Employment, Social Affairs and Equal Opportunities (2005) *The Business Case for Diversity: Good Practices in the Workplace.*

7 Interview with the author, Women's Forum, Deauville, October 2009.

8 Interview with the author, Women's Forum, Deauville, October 2009.

9 Interview, www.20-first.com, 2009.

Conclusion

1 Ferguson, N, 'The decade the world tilted East,' *Financial Times*, December 27, 2009.

2 Roberts, S, 'For Young Earners in Big City, a Gap in Women's Favor,' *The New York Times*, August 3, 2007.

3 Boushey, H, 'Equal work without equal pay,' *The Guardian* (Comment is free), September 7, 2009.

4 European Commission Directorate-General for Communication (2009) *Europe for Women*.

BIBLIOGRAPHY

This bibliography is segmented into the following themes: Leadership, Talent, Markets and General.

Leadership

Adams, R and Ferreira, D (2008) *Women in the Boardroom and Their Impact on Governance and Performance*. SSRN, October.

Adler, R and Conlin, R (2009) 'Profit, Thy Name is...Woman?' *Miller-McCune.com*, March.

Alepin, L (2009) 'Women make strides in Turkey,' 23 July, www.womenentrepreneur.com , July 23.

Barsh, J and Cranston, S (2009) *When Women Lead – The Undiscovered Link between Joy and Remarkable Performance*. Crown Business, New York.

Baxter, J (2009) *The Language of Female Leadership*. Palgrave Macmillan, New York.

Cárdenas de Santamaría, C (2008) 'Why Are Colombian Women Executives So Special?' www.20-first.com.

Catalyst (2009) *Women in Management – Global Comparison*.

Catalyst (2009) *Women in Emerging Markets*.

Daily Telegraph (2008) 'Call for More Women in the Boardroom,' October 19.

Godin, S (2008) *Tribes*. Portfolio, New York.

Gurian, M, with Annis, B (2008) *Leadership and the Sexes: Using Gender Science to Create Success in Business.* Jossey-Bass, Chichester.

King, I (2009) 'Women ready to break into boardroom,' *The Times,* November 18.

Kropp, R (2009) 'Goal Of New Index Series Is To Advance Gender Equality,' March 11, www.socialfunds.com, March 11.

Kunin, M M (2008) *Pearls, Politics, and Power: How Women Can Win and Lead.* Chelsea Green Publishing, White River Junction.

Hewlett, S A (2007) *Off-Ramps and On-Ramps: Keeping Talented Women on the Road to Success.* Harvard Business Press, Boston.

Ibarra, H and Obadaru, O (2009) 'Women and the Vision Thing,' February, *Harvard Business Review, February.*

Lashinsky, A (2009) 'Oracle's enforcer – Safra Catz,' *Fortune,* September 10.

Le Figaro Madame (2009)'Les Femmes Bousculent L'Hégémonie Masculine,' November 7.

Le Figaro Madame, (2009) 'Quinze patrons s'engagent pour la parité,' November 7.

Linder-Ganz, R (2009) 'Government firms lacking over 30% directors,' Haaretz.com, September 7.

McKechnie, D, Grant, J, Korepina, V, and Sadykova, N (2007) 'Women: segmenting the home fitness equipment market,' *Journal of Consumer Marketing,* Issue 1.

McKinsey & Co (2007) *Women Matter: Gender Diversity, a Corporate Performance Driver.*

McKinsey & Co (2008) *Women Matter 2: Female Leadership, a Competitive Edge for the Future.*

Ruderman, M N and Ohlott, P J (2002) *Standing at the Crossroads: Next Steps for High-Achieving Women.* Jossey-Bass, Chichester.

Stead, V and Elliott, C (2009) *Women's Leadership*. Palgrave Macmillan, New York.

Sweetman, K (2009) 'It Takes a Tough Man to Get the Right Corporate Board,' July 1, *Fast Company* blog.

Tarr-Whelan, L (2009) *Women Lead the Way*. Berrett-Koehler Publishers, San Francisco.

Thomson, P and Graham, J (2005) *A Woman's Place is in the Boardroom*. Palgrave Macmillan, Basingstoke.

Thomson, P and Graham, J (2008) *A Woman's Place is in the Boardroom – The Roadmap*. Palgrave Macmillan, Basingstoke.

Talent

Babcock, L and Laschever, S (2003) *Women Don't Ask: Negotiation and the Gender Divide*. Princeton University Press, Princeton.

Baron-Cohen, S (2003) *The Essential Difference*. Allen Lane, London.

BBC (2009) 'Men "out-performed" at University,' June 7, www.bbc.co.uk, June 7.

Deszo, C and Gaddis Ross, D (2008). *Girl Power: Female Participation in Top Management and Firm Quality*. SSRN.

The Economist (2006) 'Womenomics,' April 12.

Fels, A (2005) *Necessary Dreams: Ambition in Women's Changing Lives*. Anchor, US.

Financial Times (2008) 'Soapbox: why women managers shine,' March 2.

Flett, C (2007) *What Men Don't Tell Women about Business: Opening Up the Heavily Guarded Alpha Male Playbook*. Wiley, Hoboken.

Frankel, L (2004) *Nice Girls Don't Get the Corner Office*. Warner Business Books, New York.

Gurian, M (2004) *What Could He Be Thinking? How a Man's Mind Really Works.* St. Martin's Griffin, New York.

Hewlett, S A (2002) *Creating A Life: Professional Women and the Quest for Children.* Hyperion, New York.

Hewlett, S A, Sherbin, L and Sumberg, K (2009) 'How Gen Y and Boomers Will Reshape Your Agenda,' *Harvard Business Review*, July–August.

Hirschman, L R (2007) *Get to Work: A Manifesto for Women of the World.* Viking, New York.

IPSOS Public Affairs, Grandes Ecoles au Féminin, (2009) 'Les pratiques destinées à favoriser la mixité des équipes dirigeantes,' September 30, www.grandesecolesaufeminin.net.

Kimmel, M (2007) *The Gendered Society.* Oxford University Press, New York.

McCracken, D M (2000) 'Winning the Talent War for Women: Sometimes It Takes a Revolution,' *Harvard Business Review*, November–December.

Middle East Online (2008) 'Tunisia – the land of female university students,' November 28.

Moss Kanter, R (1977) *Men and Women of the Corporation.* Basic-Books, New York.

The Observer (2009) 'Observer Survey Reveals Gender Barrier Stopping Women Reaching the Top,' August 23.

OECD (2008) 'The Reversal of Gender Inequalities in Higher Education: An On-going Trend' in *Higher Education to 2030 – Volume 1 – Demography*.

Parmer, B (2009) 'Women as Consumers of Technologies,' www.20-first.com.

Peters, T (2005) *Talent: develop it, sell it, be it.* Dorling Kindersley, New York.

Pinker, S (2008) *The Sexual Paradox: Troubled Boys, Gifted Girls, and the Real Difference Between the Sexes.* Atlantic Books, New York.

Potier, B (2009) 'Les Petits Dejeuners GEF: Rencontre avec Benoît Potier,' September 7, www.grandesecolesaufeminin.fr.

Prime, J and Moss-Racusin, C A (2009) 'Engaging Men In Gender Initiatives: What Change Agents Need To Know,' Catalyst.

Sax, L (2005) *Why Gender Matters.* Doubleday, New York.

Tannen, D (2001) *Talking 9 to 5: Women and Men at Work.* Harper Paperbacks, New York.

Quirk, J (2006) *Sperm are from Men, Eggs are from Women.* Running Press, New York.

The Wall Street Journal (2009) 'No Such Thing as Work-Life Balance,' July 14.

Markets

ARF Ogilvy Awards (2009) 'Dove's Big Ideal – from Real Curves to Growth Curves,' www.warc.com, Silver winner.

Barletta, M (2006) *Marketing to Women: How to Increase Your Share of the World's Largest Market Segment.* Dearborn, New York.

Barletta, M (2007) *PrimeTime Women – How to Win the Hearts and Minds and Business of Boomer Big Spenders.* Kaplan Publishing, New York.

Brizendine, L (2006) *The Female Brain.* Broadway, New York.

Buechel, B (2009) *Developing WOLF,* IMD Case Study, (IMD-3-2098).

Chan Kim, W and Mauborgne, R (2005) *Blue Ocean Strategy: How to Create Uncontested Market Space and Make Competition Irrelevant.* Harvard Business Press, Boston.

Cunningham, J and Roberts, P (2006) *Inside Her Pretty Little Head: A new theory of female motivation and what it means for marketing*. Cyan, London.

Dunkley, C (2009) 'Differences between the sexes: It's all in the brain,' *Market Leader*, Quarter 3, June.

Ellwood, I and Shekar, S (2008) *Wonder Woman: Marketing Secrets for the Trillion Dollar Customer*. Palgrave Macmillan, New York.

Foroohar, R and Greenberg, S H (2009) 'The Real Emerging Market,' *Newsweek*, September 21.

Goldman Sachs (2009) *The Power of the Purse: Gender Equality and Middle-Class Spending*.

Heifetz, R Grashow, A and Linsky, M (2009) 'Leadership in a (Permanent) Crisis,' *Harvard Business Review*, July–August.

Holson, L (2008) 'Smartphones Now Ringing for Women,' *The New York Times*, June 10.

Johnson, L and Learned, A (2004) 'Don't Think Pink: What Really Makes Women Buy and How to Increase Your Share of This Crucial Market,' *Amacom*.

Maul, K (2009) 'Women's participation in social networks on the rise,' *PR Week*, December 14.

Popcorn, F (2000) *EVEolution: The Eight Rules of Marketing to Women*. Hyperion, New York.

Rockwood, K (2009) ' "Forget Shrink It and Pink It": the Femme Den Unleashed,' *Fast Company,* October 1.

Silverstein, M J and Sayre, K (2009) 'The Female Economy,' *Harvard Business Review*, September.

Silverstein, M J and Sayre, K (2009) *Women Want More – How to Capture Your Share of the World's Largest, Fastest-Growing Market*. HarperCollins, New York.

Tungate, M (2008) *Branded Male, Marketing to Men*. Kogan Page, London.

Thomas Yaccato, J and McSweeney, S (2008) *The Gender Intelligent Retailer: Discover the Connection Between Women Consumers and Business Growth*. Wiley, Mississauga.

Thomas Yaccato, J (2003) *The 80% Minority: Reaching the Real World of Women Consumers*. Viking, New York.

Warner, F (2006) *The Power of the Purse*. Pearson Prentice Hall, Upper Saddle River.

General

Australian Attorney-General's Department (2008), *Workplace Diversity: Strength in Diversity*.

Bain & Co (2008) 'Gender math unlock key to achieving diversity in executive ranks,' Bain news release, October 17, www.bain.nl.

Catalyst (2004) *The Bottom Line: Connecting Corporate Performance and Gender Diversity*.

Catalyst (2007) *The Bottom Line: Corporate Performance and Women's Representation on Boards*.

Churchyard, C (2009) 'Gender balance drives success at Cisco,' *People Management*, November 9.

Daly, K (2007) 'Gender Inequality, Growth and Global Ageing,' Goldman Sachs *Global Economics Paper No 154*, April.

Drucker, P F (2007) *Managing in the Next Society*. Butterworth-Heinemann, Oxford.

Drucker, P F (2001) 'The Next Workforce,' *The Economist*, November 1.

The Economist (2010) 'We Did It!' January 2.

Equal Opportunities Commission (2007) *Working outside the box: changing work to meet the future*.

European Commission Directorate-General for Employment, Social Affairs and Equal Opportunities (2005) *The Business Case for Diversity: Good Practices in the Workplace.*

Foroohar, R and Greenberg, S (2009) 'The Real Emerging Market,' *Newsweek*, September 21.

Hamel, G [with Breen, B] (2007) *The Future of Management*. Harvard Business School Press, Boston.

Heffernan, M (2007) *How She Does It, Redefining power and the nature of success for the 21st century*. Penguin, New York.

Heffernan, M (2004) *The Naked Truth*. Jossey-Bass, San Francisco.

Kelan, E (2009) *Performing Gender at Work*. Palgrave Macmillan, New York.

The New York Times, (2009) 'The Place of Women on the Court,' July 7.

OECD (2004) *Babies and Bosses.*

Ray, P H and Ruth Anderson, S (2000) *The Cultural Creatives: How 50 Million People Are Changing the World*. Harmony Books, New York.

Wittenberg-Cox, A and Maitland, A (2008) *Why Women Mean Business*. Wiley, Chichester.

INDEX

ALSO AVAILABLE

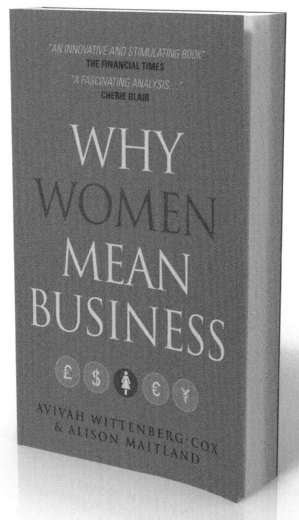

Find out more @ www.WhyWomenMeanBusiness.com

978-0-470-74950-0 | 392 pages | Paperback

Printed and bound by CPI Group (UK) Ltd, Croydon, CR0 4YY
27/09/2021

03084447-0001